SCOTTISH

FAIRY AND FOLK TALES

So they turned Alexander Jones out, because he was so stupid and said
nothing.—Page 106.   *Frontis.—Scottish Fairy Tales.*

SCOTTISH

FAIRY AND FOLK TALES

SELECTED AND EDITED

WITH AN INTRODUCTION

By SIR GEORGE DOUGLAS, Bart

FULLY ILLUSTRATED

NEW ORLEANS

ARABI MANOR

(A REBEL SATORI IMPRINT)

Printed in the United States by
Arabi Manor, A Rebel Satori Imprint

Originally published in 1900 by
A. L. Burt Company
New York

ISBN: 978-1-60864-187-1 (hc)
978-1-60864-240-3 (pb)

CONTENTS.

4　　　　　　　　　CONTENTS.

CONTENTS. 5

INTRODUCTION.

It is only within comparatively recent years that the homely stories in the mouths of the country-people have been constituted a branch of learning, and have had applied to them, as such, the methods and the terminology of science. No doubt a very noteworthy gain to knowledge has resulted from this treatment,—a curious department of research has been opened up, and light has been cast upon various outside things of greater importance than the subject of study itself. But, side by side with this gain to knowledge, is there not, involved in the method of treatment indicated, a loss to the stories themselves? Classified, tabulated, scientifically named, they are no longer the wild free product of Nature that we knew and loved:—they are become, so to speak, a collection of butterflies in a case, an album of pressed wild flowers. No doubt they are still very interesting, and highly instructive; but their poetry, their brightness, the fragrance which clung about them in their native air, their native soil, is in large measure gone! Well then,—with all due recognition of the value of the labours of the scientific folk-lorist, the comparative mythologist, whose work I would not

7

for one moment be understood to undervalue,—is there not room, even at the present day, to study these stories from another point of view, and that the simplest and most obvious one—the point of view, I mean, of the *story-teller* pure and simple? One would hope that the time had not yet come when the old tales, considered on their own merits, have entirely ceased to charm; and it is an undeniable fact that there are still persons among us who would regard it as a real and personal loss could they be made to believe that the ideal hero of their childhood, as he falls heroically, in a bloody battle, wounded to the death, is in reality a myth, or an allegory to embody the setting of the sun; and who would even feel themselves aggrieved could they be brought to realise that the bugbear of their baby years—their own particular bugbear—is common also to the aborigines of Polynesia. So great is the power of early association. Well then, my proposal is to consider the Tales of the Scottish Peasantry simply from the literary, critical, or story-teller's point of view,— from the point of view, that is, of persons who actually tell them, to whom they are actually told.

I suppose that most nations, whilst their life has remained primitive, have practised the art of storytelling; and certainly the Scotch were no exceptions to the rule. Campbell of Isla, who wrote about thirty years ago, records that in his day the practice of story-telling still lingered in the remote Western Islands of Barra; where, in the long winter nights, the people would gather in crowds to listen to those

whom they considered good exponents of the art. At
an earlier date,—but still, at that time, within living
memory,—the custom survived at Poolewe in Ross-
shire where the young people were used to assemble
at night to hear the old ones recite the tales which
they had learned from their fore-fathers. Here, and
at earlier dates in other parts of the country also,
the demand for stories would further be supplied by
travelling pedlars, or by gaberlunzie men, or pauper
wandering musicians and entertainers, or by the
itinerant shoemaker or tailor—" Whip-the-Cat " as
he was nicknamed,—both of which last were accustomed to travel through thinly-populated country districts, in the pursuit of their calling, and to put up
for the night at farm-houses,—where, whilst plying
their needles, they would entertain the company with
stories.

The arrival of one of these story-tellers in a village was an important event. As soon as it became
known, there would be a rush to the house where he
was lodged, and every available seat—on bench, table, bed, beam, or the floor—would quickly be ap-
propriated. And then, for hours together—just like
some first-rate actor on a stage—the story-teller
would hold his audience spell-bound. During his
recitals, the emotions of the reciter were occasionally
very strongly excited, as were also those of his listeners,—who at one time would be on the verge of
tears, at another would give way to loud laughter.
There were many of these listeners, by the way, who
believed firmly in all the extravagances narrated.

And such rustic scenes as these, as I hope presently to show, have by no means been without their marked effect upon Scottish literature.

In his tour through the Islands, Campbell of Isla —my authority for these particulars—visited one of the old story-tellers in his home. The man was far advanced in years, and he lived in a rude hut on the shore at South Uist. Campbell describes the scene in detail. The hut consisted of one room only. The fireplace was the floor, and the chimney a hole above it,—so that the air was dense with peat-smoke, whilst the rafters were hung with streamers and festoons of soot. The old man himself had the manner of a practised narrator,—he would chuckle at certain places in his story, and, like an Ancient Mariner or like one of the Weird Sisters, would lay a withered finger on the listener's knee when he came to the terrifying parts. A little boy in a kilt stood at his knee, gazing in his wrinkled face, and devouring every word. Whilst the story lasted, three wayfarers dropped in, listened for a while, and then proceeded on their way. The daylight streamed down the chimney, lighting up a tract in the blue mist of the peat-smoke and falling on the white hair and brown wrinkled face of the old man, as he sat on a low stool by the fire, and on the rest of the dwelling, with its furniture of boxes and box-beds, dresser, dishes, gear of all sorts,—until at last it faded away, through shades of deepening brown, to the black darkness of the smoked roof and the corner where the peat was stored.

To turn now from the story-teller to the stories.

Perhaps the most characteristic of the Highland tales are those—somewhat tedious they are, it must be confessed, with all their repetitions of dialogues, all their reproductions of what is practically one situation—which deal with heroes and giants. The shortest kind of popular tale, on the other hand, is that which is concerned with the dumb animals,—by no means dumb, of course, in the stories. The Highlands, too, are particularly rich in these tales; and it is easy to understand how the country-people generally—living so near to nature as they do—may come to have an insight into, and an appreciation of, the character of the brute animals; together with a sympathy with them in their tussle for existence, which is not attainable by those who lead a more artificial life. Some of the apologues and traits of animal life in which this knowledge and appreciative sympathy have been embodied are decidedly naive and quaint. Nor do they lack a pungent human application.

The class of stories next to be considered displays a higher degree of fancy. And it must not be imagined that this quality of fancy is anything less than a characteristic attribute of the minds of many of the Scotch peasantry. It displays itself in its simplest form perhaps in their nomenclature—in the names which they have given either to natural objects, or to places which are characterised by some striking natural feature. In the Highlands, the Gaelic place-names are often very elaborate indeed; but to turn now to the Lowlands. A waterfall in the

Selkirkshire hills, where the water, after pouring
dark over a declivity, dashes down in white foam
among rocks, is known as The Grey Mare's Tail;
twin hills in Roxburghshire, which have beautifully
rounded matched summits, have been christened
Maiden's Paps. Then, the cirrus, or curl-cloud, is
in rustic speech, " goat's hair "; the phenomenon of
the Northern Lights, among the fishermen of Shetland, is the " Merry Dancers "; the Pleiades are the
" Twinklers "; the constellation of Orion, with its
star *iota* pendant as if from a girdle, is the " King's
Ellwand," or yard-measure; the noxious froth which
adheres to the stalks of rank vegetation at mid-sum-
mer is the " Witches' spittle." There is a root of
poetry, I think, in this aptitude for giving names;
and, as a matter of fact, in the Lowlands of Scotland, rustic poets and rhymesters are far from uncommon. Nor are the peasantry, in their name-giv-
ing, wanting in literary allusiveness—allusiveness,
that is, to the only book which has ever obtained
universal currency among them. For example,
among the fishermen of the East Coast, the black
mark below the gills of a haddock is " Peter's
Thumb "; whilst a coarse plant commonly found in
corn-fields, which has its leaves strangely clouded and
stained as if with droppings, and is called, I believe,
by the botanists, *Polygonum persicaria,* is locally
known on the Borders as " The Flower which grew
at the Foot of the Cross."

Perhaps the deepest thinkers among a people who
have their philosophers as well as their dreamers,

are to be found among the hill shepherds. And it is chiefly through the instrumentality of one of these hill shepherds that we can now, in fancy, enter that realm of fancy, the world of Fairyland. James Hogg, the Ettrick Shepherd, was one of those common men, *plus* genius, who every now and then in the history of literature give to a whole world of floating thought, fancy, tradition, a permanent substantial form. No man in literature is his master in the wierd tale. No man, but Shakespeake—not even excepting Drayton—has written so well of the fairies.

Hogg was born in the Arcadia of Scotland, Ettrick Forest, where, as Scott tells us, the belief in fairies lingered longer than elsewhere—about the year 1770. When he was a young man, the spirit of emulation was stirred in his breast by the example of the poet Burns. And so, as he wandered through the pastoral solitudes, keeping his sheep, he carried an ink-horn slung from his neck, and taught himself to write,—and so committed his first poem to paper. And as he thus wandered and mused, he is said to have fallen asleep one day, upon a green hill-side, to dream the dream of Kilmeny, and to bear her image in his heart for ever after.

The story of Kilmeny is that of a girl of poetic nature, a lover of solitude, who, wandering alone at twilight, disappears in a wild glen among the hills. She is sought for by her friends—at first hopefully, at last despairingly. No trace of her is found. Years pass, and the mystery remains unsolved; but

at the close of the seventh year, in the same twilight
hour in which she had vanished, Kilmeny returns to
her home. She has been rapt away by fairies, with
whom the intervening years have been spent. But in
the midst of Fairyland, her heart still yearns tenderly to her home; and when seven years have expired,
and the fairies have no longer power to detain her
against her will, she chooses to leave the life of pleasure which she leads among them, to return to the
common earth. Such is an outline of the story; but
the story is the least part of the poem. Its charm
lies in its exquisitely flowing and melodious verse,
in its suggestion of the twilight world, and of a world
of shadows—" a land where all things are forgotten "
—in its wistful tenderness,—in a word, in the unique
and perfect aptness of the style to the subject. So
magical, indeed, are the fairy touches throughout
the writings of the Ettrick Shepherd, that one might
almost be tempted to dream that the experience with
which tradition credits Thomas the Rhymer had been
shared by this rhymer of a later day.

As in England, tales of fairies caught sight of on
the country green, at twilight or by moonlight, of
services rendered by mortals to fairies and gratefully
and gracefully repaid, find a place among the fables
of the Scottish peasantry. But it is by no means in
such airy, gracious, and harmless if not beneficent,
creations as this that the genius of the Scottish nation
finds its fancy's most congenial food. That genius
is upon the whole essentially a sombre one—relieved,
indeed, by a rough humour—but tending most to an

affinity with gloom. The hostility of Nature, its permanence as contrasted with the transient character of man, its victoriousness in the never-ending battle waged against it by man,— a battle in which he fights for life, in which he gains a few trifling and temporary advantages, but in which he must recognise from the first that he fights against impossible odds : these are facts which a barren soil and a bleak and stormy climate have thrust forcibly upon the Scottish popular imagination, and which have impressed themselves deeply upon it. The shepherd battling for his life, and for the lives of his flock, against the force and darkness of driving snow, is a far more characteristic Scottish figure than that of James Hogg asleep on the hill-side, dreaming of Fairyland.

This gloomy view of Nature has tinged the superstitious beliefs, and through them the stories of the Scottish peasantry. And upon the back of this gloomy view of Nature has come a sense, stronger perhaps than is felt by any other nation, of fate and doom, of the mystery of life and death, of the cruelty of the inevitable, the pain of separation, the darkness which enshrouds the whole. In this sense the Scotch are a nation of pessimists. They have found their religious vocation in Calvinism, the gloomiest and most terrible of creeds; and the spirit which embraced Calvinism like a bride informs their mythology and their fireside tales. Their tendency to devilworship—to the propitiation of evil spirits—is illustrated by the hideous usage of the Good-man's Croft

—a plot of ground near a village which was left un-
tilled, set apart for, and dedicated to, the **Powers of
Evil**, in the hope that their malignity might be ap-
peased by the sacrifice, and that so they might be
induced to spare the crops on the surrounding fields.
Of the state of superstitious dread in which some
Scotchmen passed their lives, Mrs. Grant, of **Laggan**,
gives a further curious illustration when she tells us
that, in the Highlands of her day, to boast, or to con-
gratulate a friend, was to rashly court retribution;
whilst to praise a babe upon the nurse's arm was to
incur suspicion of wishing to bring down ill upon its
head.

Holding such beliefs as these, it is not to be wondered at if, in their stories, the Scotch are the passed-
masters of the weird. Their very nursery tales—
many of them—would appear to have been conceived
with a view to educating, for some strange purpose or
other, the passions of horror and sorrow in the child
to whom they are told. Such rhymes, for instance,
as " The Tempted Lady," " The Fause Knight and
the Wee Boy," " The Strange Visitor," are uncanny
to a degree. In the two former, the Evil One himself appears, in specious guise. The Strange Visitor is Death. The nursery ballad of " The Croodin'
Doo "—a term of affection applied to a child—is as
full of combined piteousness and sinister suggestion of underhand wickedness as any little tragedy of
its length could well be. The suggestion is that of a
man's childless, lawful wife bearing a bitter grudge
against another woman who has borne him a child.

The babe returns from a day's outing, and is questioned by his slighted mother as to where he has been, and what he has done. But he is tired, and cries out to be put to bed. The jealous woman, however, persists in her interrogatory, and asks him what he has had for dinner. He replies that he has dined off " a little four-footed fish." (The eft, or newt, is, like the toad, in the common superstition, venomous.) " And what was done with the bones of this singular fish ? " asks the woman. They were given to the lapdog. And what did the dog do? After eating them, he " shot out his feet and died." There, with admirable art, the ballad ends. Its effect is immensely heightened by a burden, or refrain, in which, at the close of every verse, the child, with wearisome iteration, and with child-like importunity, cries out to his mother to " make his bed soon." This little song of child-life is queer fare to set before a child.

Stoddart, the tourist, long ago pointed out the contrast between the fairies of the English popular mythology and those of the Scotch; and certainly the delicate, joyous, tricksy, race of moonlight revellers whom we meet in the pages of Shakespeare are scarcely to be recognised as belonging to the same family with the soulless, man-stealing, creations of the Scottish peasant's fancy. The effect exercised upon popular superstition by the ruling passion of Calvinistic religion is one of the most striking things in Scottish folklore. For example, the belief in fairies did not cease to exist. It does not seem even to

2

have been universally discountenanced by the
Church; for we find mention of cases in which Ministers of the Gospel combine with their parishioners
to take measures for the restitution of infants which
the fairies had changed at nurse, or for the recovery
of women who had been spirited away. And, indeed,
two of the most curious pieces of composition known
to me are, a pamphlet on the Second Sight, written
by a Minister of Tiree, and an article on the Fairies,
written by a Minister of Aberfoyle,—both in the
Seventeenth Century. Both writers were obviously
firm believers in the superstitions upon which they
wrote; and in both cases the gross ignorance and
darkness of the writer's mind is only equalled by the
authoritative weight and pedantry of his style. The
Solemn League and Covenant had left its mark even
upon the fairies, as the touching little story of " The
Fairy and the Bible-reader " shows.

The fairies, and that rough, grotesque, humour-
some, but good-natured figure, the Brownie, occupy,
however, but a small space in the popular mythology
in comparison with such shapes of awe, of terror, or
of ill-omen, as the ghosts, " more real than living
man," which the Highland Ezekiel saw borne past
him on the wind, in Morven of the gloomy skies; or
as the witch, the wraith, the " warning," the water-
kelpie, the man or woman who has the " second
sight," the evil or lost spirit.

The characteristic rough humour of the Scottish
peasant, as it affects the creations of the fancy, em-
bodies itself almost exclusively in the Brownie. This

was a half-human creature, of uncouth appearance.

> " His matted head on his breat did rest ;
> A lang blue beard wan'er'd down like a vest ;—
> But the glare o' his e'e hath nae bard exprest."

During the day he would lurk in out-of-the-way corners of some old house which he had chosen to inhabit; and in the night-time would make himself useful to the family to which he had attached himself. But the conditions of his service were the most disinterested ever drawn up, and on the slightest attempt being made to reward him for his labours he would disappear for ever. The Brown Man of the Moors is another of these twilight, or half-seen, creations; but he is not of a domestic character. Wanderers upon lonely moors might, on rare occasions, catch a glimpse of him squatting in a hollow—a short, thick, powerful figure; earth-coloured, or of the tint of the surrounding ling. "Shellycoat" dwelt in the waters. He was accustomed to appear decked out with the spoils of the sea—his coat being hung with shells, which clattered as he moved; and his delight was in mischief,—such as, for instance, like the Spunkie, or Will-o'-the-Wisp, in leading travellers astray. "Nuckelavee," the Sea-Devil of the Orkney Islanders, a more formidable figure, seemed to be shaped like a man above and like a horse blow; and his peculiar horror lay in the fact that, being skinless, his raw, red flesh was exposed to view. Then there was the River Horse, a supernatural being supposed to

feed, in the shape of a horse, on the shores of Loch
Lochy, and when disturbed to plunge into its waters.
The River Bull emerged from the lake to visit the
cow-pastures; and there were cow-herds who pretended that they could distinguish the calves of which
he was the sire. Most of these creatures of the fancy
are peculiar to the Scotch; and one cannot help fond-
ly speculating as to the poetic use which Shakespeare
would have made of them, had they happened to be
among the associations of his childhood. But a more
subtle water-spirit than any of those yet mentioned
was the Kelpy, whose appearances were generally
timed either to give warning of death by drowning,
or to lure men to a watery grave. The Kelpy story
of *The Doomed Rider,* to be found in the present collection, admirably illustrates the sentiment of fatal-
ism inherent in the Scottish peasant's mind. In illustration of the kindred feeling of the " malevolence
of Nature," inherent there also, the poet Alexander
Smith has aptly quoted the following popular rhyme
—a dialogue in which two rivers are supposed to be
the speakers:—

> "Said Tweed to Till,
>   What gars ye rin sae still?
>   Said Till to Tweed,
>   Though ye rin wi' speed,
>   And I rin slaw,
>   For every ane that ye droon
>   I droon twa!"

Here it appears that the elements are our enemies,
and war against us to the death.

But, beyond a doubt, the most valuable element in

the peasant tales, considered from the poetic stand-
point, is not the fanciful or the imaginative element,
but the human. This is, in some cases, brought out
in extraordinary strength by the juxtaposition of the
supernatural. Space allows me to cite but a single
instance. By far the strangest, the most startling,
and to us the most incomprehensible, of all the Scottish superstitions is the belief in the periodical return
of the dead to their former homes—not as night-walk-
ing ghosts, encountered only by solitary persons in
the dark—but as social beings, come back to join the
family circle, and share in its festivities,—in short,
in the old phrase, come back " to dine and dance with
the living." How anything so incredible should ever
have come to be believed, we may well be at a loss to
understand. Yet believed it seems to have been.
There are two of the old ballads which are concerned
with the belief, and they are two of the most beautiful which have come down to us.

The fragment entitled *The Wife of Usher's Well*
sets forth how a thriving country-woman made pro-
vision for her three sons by sending them to sea. But
they have not been long away from her, when she
hears that they have perished in a storm. Then, in
the madness of her grief, she puts up a blasphemous
prayer to heaven,—praying that the conflict of wind
and wave may never cease until her sons come home
to her, in their likeness as she knew them of old.
Her prayer is heard, and answered.

> " It fell about the Martinmas,
> When nights are lang and mirk,

> The carline wife's three sons cam' hame,
> And their hats were o' the birk.[1]

> " It neither grew in syke nor glen,
>   Nor yet in ony sheuch ;
> But, at the gates of Paradise,
>   That birk grew fair eneuch ! "

Rising to a height of simple, unconscious, tragic irony, which is little less than sublime, the ballad goes on to detail the domestic preparations made by the mother to *fête* the home-coming of her sons. In a fever of happiness over the restoration of her lost ones, she issues her orders to her maids. The fatted calf is slain, and so on; and a brief hour of joy goes by. Then, as it grows late, the young men betake themselves to rest. The mother has prepared their bed with her own hands. But the dawn draws near —the period of their sojourn is almost up. The cock crows; and they recognise the signal for their departure.

> " Up then crew the red, red, cock,
>   And up and crew the grey :
> The eldest to the youngest said,
>   ' 'Tis time we were away ! "

> " The cock he hadna craw'd but ance,
>   Nor clapt his wings at a',
> When the youngest to the eldest said,
> ' Brother, we must awa.

---

[1] That is, the birch. A "syke" is a marshy bottom, with a small stream in it. A "sheuch" is a sort of swamp. The small natural birch-tree, common in a hill-country, is often found on such ground.

    " ' The cock doth craw, the day doth daw,
        The channerin' worm doth chide ;
    Gin we be miss'd out o' our place,
        A sair pain we maun bide.

    " ' Then, fare-ye-weel, my mither dear
        Fareweel to barn and byre !
    And fare-ye-weel, the bonny lass
        That kin'les my mither's fire ! ' "

In this instance, the superstition of the return of the
dead to their homes, to visit their friends, is compli-
cated with the idea of punishment for a rash utter-
ance, or impious prayer. But in the other ballad
which deals with the same theme—*The Clerk's Twa
Sons o' Owsenford*—the fundamental idea appears
in its simplest form. In other respects the two stories
resemble each other; except that, in the second case,
the young men, two in number, are represented as
paying the penalty of death—like the cavaliers of
the *Tour de Nesle*—" for a little of dear-boucht
love," and that their home-coming is timed at Christmas.

These two tales are probably the wildest in the
whole range of Scottish popular story; but, wild as
they are, they contain, I think, a distinct and deep
human significance. It will be observed that, in
either case, the home-coming of the dead is placed at
a season of relaxation and festivity—at martinmas,
namely, in the one case, and at Christmas in the
other. At such seasons as these, the thoughts of the
working-people, set free for a space from their daily
occupations, are at liberty to wander; whilst it is a
fact that the annual recurrence of such red-letter

days, or land-marks in time, with their familiar ac-
companiment of ceremonies and usages, bring bygone
years before the mind with a peculiar clearness—or,
at least, brings them before the minds of people who
lead simple, monotonous, lives, with few events to
vary them. Nothing is commoner at such seasons
than to hear people refer to the friends whom they
have lost since that time last year, dwelling, as they
do so, upon the characters, ways, and particular acts
of the departed. Well, from this peculiar vividness
of mental realisation, it is, for a bold and poetic imagination, but a single step to conjure up the actual
bodily presence of the lost ones. Hence may have
arisen these wild stories; and hence, no doubt, arose
the fancy—a beautiful and touching one, I think,—
that at Christmas the dead return to their homes to
dine and dance with the living.

The few specimens at which we have now glanced
must suffice to illustrate for us the more striking
characteristics of the Scottish peasant-tales generally,
—these characteristics being, as I take it: first, an
ever lively and inventive fancy. Secondly, a powerful imagination. The Scottish peasant story-teller is,
like Homer, εὐφαντασίωτος—" qui sibi res, voces,
actus, secundum verum, optime fingit," as Quintilian
hath it;—we should say, perhaps, that he had " poetic vision "; but the phrase does not cover quite the
same ground. And this powerful imagination is apt
to be gloomily affected, and at times distempered, by
the natural features of the country, the conditions of
life there, and the broodings of the national mind.

Thirdly, a love of humanity, coupled with a keen sense of the hardness of its lot, manifesting itself in a poignant pathos. Of course, in a country of mixed races, like Scotland, the general characteristics of the tales vary widely in different parts of the country. The Celt of the West Highlands, for instance, has a *penchant* for giants, and a perfect callousness of the feelings—at which it is impossible not to marvel —where the lives and sufferings of the said giants and of their belongings are concerned. In one word, the giant of the West Highland tales is always " fair game "—you cannot, by any contrivance, take a mean advantage of him. Again, the trolls, trows, " hill-folk," or " grey neighbours," of the Norsemen of the Shetland Islands have a character of their own, distinct from that of the fairies of the rest of Scotland, and harmonising perfectly with the colourless landscape of their native melancholy shores. In general terms, it may perhaps be said that the Highland tales display the more inexhaustibly luxuriant invention, whilst those of the Lowlands have the advantage of a more clearly defined outline, and enjoy a monopoly in depth of human significance.

To glance now at the literary bearing of these tales. In this respect, the oral traditions of the Scottish peasantry have enjoyed particular advantages, from the fact that the rich mine which they afford has been industriously and admirably worked by modern Scottish writers. Perhaps the most marked features of Scottish poetry have been, in the earlier times, its national, and in later times its popular, character. Well, in modern times at least, both of these charac-

teristics have been shared by Scottish prose. **This**
may not indeed be true, or at least not without large
reservations, of the writings of Smollett; but, from
Smollett's day onward, the Scottish prose *belles-let-*
tres have been essentially a " growth of the soil."
And the Scotchmen who have laboured the field of
popular tradition have been far from working it upon
the lines of such writers as, for instance, Musæus,
Tieck, and La Motte Fouqué,—making the popular
tale a mere foundation upon which to rear their own
structures of philosophy or fancy, and often trans-
forming it almost, if not quite, beyond recognition.
Neither have they worked in the spirit of such a
writer as Théophile Gautier, who, though he would
sometimes use the popular tale as material to work
on, had, in this regard, nothing national about him,—
being before all things a " stylist "—an artist, pure
and simple, indifferent, isolated from ties of country,
from ties of kindred, almost from ties of humanity.
The Scottish writers, on the other hand, are, in the
first case, *objective;* and, in the second, highly *na-*
tional.

First and foremost among these writers ranks, of
course, Sir Walter Scott. Neglected as, in comparison with his other books, his *Border Minstrelsy* has
been, the fact remains that he produced no more
highly characteristic work; whilst of that great literature of fiction of which he afterwards became the
author, the best and most vital parts may, I think,
truly be said to " have their roots in the hearts of the
people." And the further he departs from that

source of his inspiration, the less valuable his work becomes. Though not born in the peasant class himself, Sir Walter knew the Scottish peasantry, in his own way, as few man have known them, and he lived on terms of friendly intimacy with his valued Tom Purdies and Swanstons, and of close literary confidence with such men as William Laidlaw and Joseph Train.

The two writers who rank next in the group alluded to were, however, peasants born. James Hogg has already been spoken of. Allan Cunningham, born in 1784, was a son of the land-steward on the estate on which Robert Burns occupied a farm,—a circumstance which, no doubt, had its effect in stimulating the poetic impulse that was in him. On growing up, he adopted the trade of a mason. An antiquarian, Cromek by name, was at that time engaged in forming a collection of " Remains of Galloway and Nithsdale Song," on the model of Percy's *Reliques;* and he applied to young Cunningham to collect old poems for him. " Honest Allan," as his friend Thomas Carlyle styled him, was not successful in his quest; but, nothing daunted, he set to work to compose songs and ballads which, if they could not in the nature of things possess the quality of age, should at least be as good as old, or better if possible. These he transmitted to his employer, without explanation. Cromek's love for antiquity would appear to have been a pure passion, inasmuch as he seems to have loved it for the sake of any κῦδος or profit, which was to be derived from the attachment, and for no other reason. He was delighted with his young correspondent's contributions to the "Remains of Galloway and Nithsdale Song;" and Cunningham's literary career was thus begun. His *Traditional Tales of the English and Scottish Peasantry* are perhaps the best of the many books which he wrote; and are especially distinguished by the sweetness of his style, and by the picturesque traits of old-fashioned country-life and the exquisite touches of fresh nature-painting in which they abound.

After Cunningham comes Campbell of Isla, born in 1822. He was of gentle birth, but understood, and sympathised with the peasantry. A proficient in the Gaelic language, he went about on foot among the people of the West Highlands and Islands—like a sort of Romany Rye, or like Catskin, the Wandering Young Gentleman of the *Garland*—and got them to tell him stories, which he accurately noted down. In his writings, therefore, we get the stories as nearly as possible in the exact words in which they were told. He died about six or seven years ago.

Then there is Dougal Graham, the chap-book writer, who has been called the "Scottish Rabelais." He began life as a chapman, and came in course of time to be *skellat* bell-man of Glasgow. His *magnum opus* is a metrical narrative of the Jacobite Rising of '45, in which he himself took part; and to him are also attributed the invention of Turnimspike, and John Cheap, and the history of the Witty Exploits of George Buchanan, the King's Jester.

Then, after Graham, come Robert Chambers—

whose fame as a publisher has somewhat obscured his well-earned fame as a writer; Hugh Miller, the geologist; and, among men of merely local reputation, James Telfer, of Saughtree, and many others.

Literature takes the life of tradition, and then embalms the dead body. What stories, then, have taken the place, as genuine peasant-tales, though belonging to a period of decadence, of the old stories which introduce the supernatural and have ceased to be believed? Well, there are a variety, which do not tax the power of credulity quite too far. Stories of old local battles, for instance, and of how some neighbouring stream, or river, ran discoloured with blood for three whole days after the fighting. Stories of buried treasures:—there is the English knight whom Jock of Heavyside slew, and who lies buried, in his silver armour, not far from Agricola's Camp at Pennymuir. Then there is a neighbouring treasure which lies, wrapt in a bullock's hide, buried in a hill. It is said, circumstantially enough, to have been concealed by two brothers, in time of war; but is described, with judicious vagueness, as lying exactly midway between two places, only one of which is known. A third treasure is more particularly localised. The field in which it lies buried is well known; but if any man set spade in that field to dig for it, the sky, we are told, will ere long grow dark, and a muttering of thunder will be heard, and a flash of lightning seen. (This story certainly does trench perilously near to superstition.) Then, again, there are other treasures, with which—even if one did hap-

pen to light upon one of them—it would not be safe
to meddle. They are supposed to have been buried
in a time of the plague—perhaps as sacrifices to ap-
pease some Unknown Power—and the infection of
the pestilence is supposed to have been buried with
them; so that, were they to be unearthed, the plague
would probably break out again. On the sea-coast,
sunken treasure-ships take the place of buried treasures. Then there are the stories of mysterious caverns, into which people enter, but from which they do
not come out. There is one cave of this kind into
which a huntsman and a pack of hounds are said to
have pursued a hunted fox; but from which neither
fox, hounds, huntsman, nor horse, were ever known
to emerge again. Then there is another cave into
which a piper penetrated, playing upon his pipes.
He never came out either. His music was listened
to for a long time by persons at the mouth of the
cavern. At first it was loud and cheerful, then it
grew fainter and fainter, more plaintive and more
plaintive, until at last it died away in the bowels of
the earth. Then, there are kindred stories of subterranean passages of great length—sometimes said
to have been fashioned by the monks—uniting ancient castles or religious establishments. Then, there
are modern varieties of the hero-tale,—stories of
fights, and of adventures by flood and field—a favourite one is that of a prodigious leap taken by the
hero in escaping from pursuit. There are, also,
stories of remarkable local characters—the desperate
ones being preferred. There is, for instance, the

sceptical country-gentleman, who, having led a merry
life and scoffed at the Minister, preserved at least the
virtue of consistency by leaving directions in his will
that he was to be buried, in a vaulted chamber, seated
at a table, with a church-warden pipe in his mouth,
and a bottle and a glass before him. Or else there is
that other reprobate, who, when lands were gone and
money spent, resolved to put an end to his life. So
he blindfolded a favourite mare, mounted her, and
rode towards the cliff-heads. There he put her to the
gallop, and prepared for a leap into space. But, just
as she reached the brink, by some instinct the blind
mare swerved and turned. He set her at the frightful
leap again, and again she refused; and, after a third
failure, he is said to have seen the error of his ways,
and to have ridden home, and from that day to have
led a reformed life. Then, lastly, there is the mur-
der-tale—the narrative of some desperate deed. It
must not be hastily classed with the literature of the
" penny dreadful " and the " shilling shocker " order;
for, whatever may be the shortcomings of Arcady,
vulgarity at least is not one of them, and the peasant-
tales never sink to so low a level as that. Blood may
be spilt in them—and spilt freely it often is; but
there are always present redeeming touches of fancy,
of poetry, of character-painting, of the picturesque,
to raise the terrible histories from the rank of the
" sensation novel " to that of the poetic tragedy.

What, in conclusion, is there in these rude " old-
wives' tales " to justify their withdrawal from the
limbo of forgotten things? They have a place,

though it be a humble one, in the history of the workings of the human mind. They are the manifestation, in its simplest form, of the literary, or poetic, impulse; and nothing that has been thus generated, and that has stood the test of time as these tales have done, can ever, I believe, be unworthy of our study. To take an instance from another art. Anthropologists tell us that, ages and ages ago, there was a savage, dwelling in a cave, in a bleak northern country, among mountains which were covered with pine-trees. He was agile, able-bodied, and ingenious; and he faced the mighty beasts of the forest in his hunting, to obtain food for his wife and children. We know next to nothing about him; but we do know that, one day, it somehow occurred to him to make a drawing on the wall of his cave of something which he had seen and had no doubt admired. So he etched a little picture of a reindeer, copying faithfully the outline of the body, and the branchings of the antlers. This, reader, is the man whom we speak of as Paleolithic Man. His performance had the innate permanence, from a human point of view, of all true art. It remains, and it continues to interest, to this day; for it is the outcome of the first faint stirrings in the human breast of two passions: the Love of Beauty, and the Thirst for Fame. "One touch of nature makes the whole world kin." The lapse of countless centuries does not prevent our entering into the feelings of that simple artist; and what he felt, in his day and hour, is felt, in their degree, by the tellers of the Tales of the Scottish Peasantry. Art is not only a thing of bound volumes and of exhibitions; and the Scottish peasant has shown perhaps as keen a sense of it—of the story-teller's art, at least—as his mental development and the conditions of his existence would admit.[1]

GEORGE DOUGLAS.

[1] The substance of this Introduction was delivered as a Lecture at the Royal Institution, January 29th, 1892.

Donald, Dougald and Duncan starting out to seek their fortune.—Page 35.
Scottish Fairy Tales.

THE THREE GREEN MEN OF GLEN NEVIS.

PART I.

"WELL, it is not the least use talking about it; there is not more than one loaf of bread in the house or one bawbee in the stocking," said the widow of Rannoch to her three sons, Donald, Dougald, and Duncan. "So go, each of you, and seek a fortune; and if a fortune you get, don't forget your old mother, for she's tried to do her best by you for many a long day."

And Donald, Dougald, and Duncan all agreed that she spoke the truth, and that the best thing they could do for her now was to go at once, returning as soon as good fortune would let them.

So the widow of Rannoch divided the loaf into

four portions and gave a bit to each, putting it in their wallets, and keeping one bit for herself. Then she gave them her blessing, and off they started.

Now, they set their faces towards the west, where lay the great ocean. Perchance they would get a passage there in a ship to the south, where the bright gold lay for the gathering, and that would be much better than making for the east, where every one was as poor as themselves, they knew already, only too well.

Over the moor they trudged, and Donald sang a song to cheer Dougald and Duncan; and, when he was tired, Dougald told a story to while away the time for Donald and Duncan. When his story came to an end, Duncan was just going to show them some other kind of diversion, when he stopped, seized both of his brothers by the arms, and, pushing them before him into a peat-hole, bade them for their life's sake hide among the high hags at its side, and not utter a syllable, or make the slightest sound. " For," said he, " I see the witch of Ben e Bhreac coming in the distance towards us."

And, sure enough, there she was, coursing over the moor in a direct line with them, waving her magic staff. As she strode over the pools, the water splashed upwards in brown foam before her; as she clambered over the peat-hags, the divots and turves flew away on every side; as she swept along the dry path, the dust in clouds whirled behind her like an attendant spirit.

So she passed by them, without a thought of human creatures being so near to her; for, you may be sure, they lay very close and still, and did not move till the last trace of her vanished behind the slopes of the Black Mountains.

" Now is our chance," said Duncan, the youngest, to his two brothers. " The old bird has gone on a journey; let us harry her nest."

" Oh! but that would be stealing!" said Donald.

" Stealing?" said Duncan; " stealing the stolen. How do you know we won't find some of our own goods there? At any rate, if they are not ours, they are not hers, whoever it is they belong to." So, as Duncan was the clever one of the family, and never was contradicted, although the youngest, there was no more to be said about the matter, and off they started for Ben e Bhreac.

It did not take them long to arrive at the summit where the witch's home was, and where her well can be seen to this day, for they were anxious to get through the business as soon as possible before the good lady should return, and they were brave lads and had stout hearts for a stiff brae, and fear gave them an extra toe to each foot, as the saying is.

Up at the bothie they found all quiet, and they judged the witch had gone for a long journey, for the door was fast locked, and no smoke was to be seen coming out of the chimney.

Yet, in a very short time they made an entrance, by taking off the divots from the roof, and getting in that way; but they were disappointed at seeing very little of value inside. Certainly the witch, if she had any valuables, did not keep them in that house.

"Now, we must have a good look round outside," said Duncan; "but before we do so, just let me prepare for the accident of her sudden return. I know a trick that will checkmate the hag even if she does. Only you do as I say, and all will be well."

As usual the other two agreed, for they never ventured to contradict Duncan, as I told you before, but believed in his genius implicitly.

"Donald, you go up and keep a good lookout, up the stack to the north-east, and give an alarm if you see anybody coming. Dougald, you turn your face towards the south-west and do the same." So they went out, and did as they were told.

Now, the hag's bothie was built over a well, and the way to it was through the floor of the bothie by means of a trap-door set on iron hinges; seeing which, Duncan loosened the hinges with his dirk, till he felt sure a little added weight would send trap and all into the water below. Then he put the hag's chair on the top of the trap, tying a stout cord to the leg of it, and one end of this he flung over the iron girdle standing in the corner. Next, pulling the table up towards the chair, he furnished the board with a large aschet and a couple of knives, just as if a feast had been laid by her imps against the return of their mistress. Then he collected a dozen large stones, and set them up by the wall, to be handy if occasion required.

Well, scarcely had he finished all these arrangements, when a cry from Dougald gave the alarm that the hag was returning full speed from the direction of the Black Mountains; and, looking in that direction, the three brothers saw her, sure enough, coursing over the waste in a direct line with her home, waving her magic staff.   As she strode past the pools, the water splashed upwards in brown foam before her; as she clambered over the peat-hags, the divots and turves flew away on every side; as she swept along the dry paths, the dust in clouds whirled behind her like an attendant spirit.

"Quick!" said Duncan.   "Get in through the hole in the roof; sit down both of you on the big aschet on the board; garnish your heads with kale, shut your eyes, and don't move or say a word, and all will be well."

So Donald and Dougald did as he told them. They crept in through the hole in the roof, and got up on the table, and, sitting down on the big aschet, they decorated their heads with kale and shut their eyes. And Duncan hid behind the large girdle in the corner, holding the cord light in his hand.

Thus they waited in silence for what was going to happen.

They had not to wait long, for the witch was soon at the door, which sprang open at the touch of her staff, and disclosed the horrid hag entering with upturned and snorting nose, for she had smelt food a long way off, and could not make out whence came the scent.

"Ha, ha!" she muttered in delight.   "By my troth, my imps have provided a fair feast for me in my absence.   'Tis capital!" and she flung her magic crutch into the corner, took up the knife and fork, and sat down on the chair at the end of the table, ready to enjoy her gruesome supper.

But the supper was not for her this time. Just as she was in the act of sitting down, Duncan pulled the cord with a mighty tug, and the chair flew away from under the witch, so that she came down with a mighty crash on the trap-door, which, giving way, suddenly precipitated her backwards into the bubbling water below!

"Now for it!" said Duncan; and the brothers, leaping down from the table, seized the large stones that Duncan had placed in readiness along the wall, and flung them down with all their force on to the top of the old hag below. When these were all done, they turned the table over the hole, and heaped on it everything they could lay their hands on. Nothing that they could lift and move came amiss. Then they sat themselves exhausted on the top of the pile to rest and wipe their faces, for it had been a desperate hard job.

"No, you don't," said Duncan, leaping down as he saw the magic staff creeping and crawling like a snake towards the door. But the crutch was too sharp for him, and wriggled under the door, and, gliding off, was soon lost among the heather and fern that surrounded the summit of Ben e Bhreac.

Now, there had been no sound or disturbance from the well for some time, so they concluded that the old hag was safely settled once and for all this time, and Duncan gave it as his opinion that they might now go and have a leisurely look round about the place to see if there was anything worth carrying off.

So Donald searched about the summit to the north, Dougald to the south, and Duncan to the east. There was no use at all in going towards the west, for a precipice went straight down on that side, and it would have been waste of time to have done so.

To the north, where Donald went, was what one might call the garden, if such a collection of weeds might be given that name. There Donald went up and down, up and down, yet nothing of the slightest value to himself or any one else did he see, and he felt disgusted at taking all this trouble for nothing.

Well, he was just going to give up the search in despair, when he espied a very handsome flower growing beside a rock at the further end, and thought he would go and have a look at it before telling his brothers of his unprofitable search. And the plant was a really pretty one. It had a splendid yellow flower like a great gowan growing on the top of a stout stalk which sprang from a bunch of large green leaves below. He certainly never had seen the like before, and he stood there admiring it very much.

" I wonder what sort of plant this can be ? " said Donald.

" Oh, I'm a Thunder-plant," said the flower.

" A what ? " said Donald.

" A Thunder-plant," said the flower again.

" Indeed; and what sort of kind can that be ? " said Donald.

"Just smell me, and you will soon **see**," **said the** flower.

Well, Donald was curious to know **what sort of** plant a Thunder-flower could be, so he leaned **down** and gave a truly good sniff in the very **centre of the** petals.

HE LEANED DOWN.

BANG! There was a startling report, **and the** echoes of it rolled and rolled round the **mountains,** and Donald fell flat on his back with **astonishment** and alarm.

"Well, we live and learn something **new every day,** certainly," said Donald as he got up rubbing **his legs** and elbows. "I'm not sure but that you would be **a** good companion in a pinch, if you could always do that when you were asked."

" I don't object to going with you as a companion," said the flower. " Dig me up carefully, and put me in your wallet. I may be of some use to you on the way."

So Donald dug the Thunder-plant up carefully with his knife and put it in his wallet. " At any rate I shall not go home empty. A plant is better than nothing," quoth he ; " though of what use a Thunder-plant may be to me I assuredly do not know at present."

" Time will show that," said the Thunder-plant.

" Ay will it," said Donald.

In the meantime Dougald, the second brother, had gone to seek for treasure on the south side of the bothy. Here at first he sought most carefully, but could discover nothing of even the smallest value, and, like Donald, getting tired of seeking, he was almost giving up the hunt in despair, when he heard, or thought he heard, a strange, weird chuckle, like laughter, proceed from behind a heap of rank grass in the shade of the wall. Examining more closely, he discovered the cause of the noise in a queer-looking gray hen, seated amongst the rubbish. She had a bright red comb and a yellow beak, and from her eyes came such a strange look, unusual in an ordinary fowl, as she fixed them upon the stranger, that Dougald at once understood the bird was something decidedly out of the common.

" Dear me," said Dougald, " what sort of fowl are you ? "

" A Thunder-fowl," said the bird.

" What ? " said Dougald.

" I believe I answered loud enough," remarked the bird; " *A Thunder-fowl.*"

" Oh, I beg your pardon ! " said Dougald; " you did so, but my good mother has kept poultry for many a long year at home, and I have never seen the sort before, and that astonished me."

" Put the coop over my head, and leave me in the dark for a short space. Then take it off suddenly, and you will soon find out all about it," said she.

Well, Dougald did not like to refuse so civil-spoken a request, especially as it was owing to his curiosity the bird suggested the proceeding.

So he put the coop over her head, and counted maybe twenty, and then lifted the coop off again.

To say that he was astonished at the terrific crow the fowl emitted is not an adequate expression: he was startled out of his wits. No thunder could produce so mighty a report, or echoes more loud among the mountains, than the sound which came up under his nose when once more the light shone upon the red hackles of the Thunder-fowl, and Dougald fell flat on his back with astonishment and alarm.

" What do you think of that ? " said the fowl.

" You don't belie your name," said Dougald, getting up and rubbing his legs and elbows. " Don't do that again without giving me warning. Still, you would not be a bad companion at a pinch, if you could trumpet like that whenever you were asked."

" Well, take me with you as a comrade," said the fowl. " It's cold enough and lonely enough living up here, anyway."

" I can carry you in my wallet, if you don't mind," said Dougald.

" Capital," said the fowl; " only, don't cover my head, or you may be startled when you least expect it."

" WHAT DO YOU THINK OF THAT ? " SAID THE FOWL.

So Dougald put the Thunder-fowl in his wallet, and her head looked out through a hole in the top, and, quite pleased with his discovery, he went to seek his brothers.

Now, as for Duncan, the youngest brother, he went as was arranged to the east side of the mountain, to see what he could find in the way of a treasure, and, like the others, it was not long before he got dead tired of searching. There was nothing to be seen but an enclosure of stones in which were a few

unpleasant nettles growing, and a pile of sticks set up
on end in the corner for fuel.   He kicked up some of
the nettles, to see if anything was hidden among them,
and stamped on the ground in all directions, to hear
if it sounded hollow underneath, but nothing did he
gain by either performance, and, getting cross, for he
did not care to be defeated in anything he undertook,
as a last resource before giving it up as a bad job, he
poked a long stake into the heap of sticks and rattled
it up and down in a very vicious manner.

Certes, but he was astonished, when from under the
fagots arose a pink, fresh-coloured pig, with beady
eyes and a snout as black as ebony.

" You must find it a bit cold living upon this hill-
top with so miserable a shelter as these sticks," said
Duncan.

" I'm not a common-bred pig," said the brute.

" Would it be rude to ask what breed you are ? "
said Duncan.

" Not at all," replied the pig.   " I'm a Thunder-
pig, at your service."

" What sort of breed is that ? " said Duncan.

" If you want to know, just kiss me once between
the eyes; it will save a lot of explanation."

Now, Duncan was not accustomed to kiss swine
between the eyes, or anywhere else, for the matter of
that, but he thought he had better not decline, as it
was his fault that the pig had been disturbed, and one
never knows what may be got by being civil to anything, man or beast, and the pig looked clean as pigs
go.

So he kissed the pig between the eyes.

The next moment Duncan felt himself flat on the ground, for such a grunt came from the porker that he fell over backwards from alarm and astonishment at the terrific explosion.   And the mountain-tops so long resounded with the report, that you would think the echoes were never going to cease talking about it to one another.

HE KISSED THE PIG.

" It's lucky you don't produce lightning as well," said Duncan, getting up with a wry face and bruised elbows.   " I would rather have you for a friend than a foe any day."

" I am quite willing to be the first," said the pig. " For myself, I don't mind if I go with you as a companion ; I am rather sick of the life up here."

" I, too, shall be glad of your company, and that's
a bargain," said Duncan; "and now, let me introduce you to my brothers whom I see coming towards
us."

So the three brothers met and told their discoveries,
and introduced each to the other his new companion;
then, having nothing more to do at the summit, they
descended to the glen below.

Even to this day there is more thunder round Ben
e Bhreac than any of the mountains in the neighbourhood, and when storms are at their loudest round its
crags, "Hark," say the good wives of Rannoch;
"'tis the witch of Ben e Bhreac working with her
thunder servants." And the mountain is avoided
to this day.

So, towards the west these three brothers, with
their new friends, travelled all that afternoon; and
just as they arrived at the head of Glen Nevis, the
sun set. So they rested for the night under the
shadow of Bennein Beg, since not for all the world
would they have ventured to pass through that glen
after nightfall for fear of the three green men who
inhabited it, and who were reported savage and fierce
to all travellers.

PART II.

It was very early the next morning that the three
brothers arose, for Dougald had put the Thunder-fowl
under his plaid when they went to sleep, quite forgetting what would happen if he took it off suddenly

in the morning sunshine. This very thing really occurred quite unexpectedly at sunrise, for the wind blowing up the valley flung a corner of the plaid aside, and a beam of light glancing on the red comb of the bird made that creature crow as only it of feathered creatures could crow.

The mountains rattled with the report, and the three brothers awoke with a jump. The folk dwelling in the neighbourhood put their heads out of their

THE FOLK PUT THEIR HEADS OUT OF THEIR WINDOWS.

bothy windows, and said to one another, " Ha, thunder in a clear sky; strange! " and a good many things, both man and beast, awoke that morning earlier than their usual.

But our heroes knew better by this time what it was; and so they arose, and slung their wallets over their backs, and, with the Thunder-pig trotting beside Duncan, they proceeded on their way.

4

But not far had they travelled before the bothy of the first green man met their view rising beside the pathway. A queer building it looked—circular, flat-topped, and without windows; for Trolls and such like can bear but little light. Nothing, in fact, broke the plain appearance of the building but a small, low door, formed of three slabs of stone, one at each side, and one for the lintel, and that not even high enough for the evil creature to creep through without stooping.

" Now," said Duncan to Donald, " you go and try your luck with the first green man, while Dougald and I wait here. When you give us a call, or require assistance, we shall be at hand.

Donald did not dispute the matter with Duncan, for, though the youngest, he was the cleverest. But I told you that before.

So, taking up his wallet, which contained the Thunder-plant, he went to the bothy of the green man and gave a good rap at the door.

" There is nobody at home," said the Troll within; " go away."

" But it is just that nobody I want to see," said Donald, and he gave the door a kick and crept in.

There he saw an ugly Troll, squatting by a turf fire, and that Troll had green eyes and a green plaid mantle cast over his shoulders, and green hair twisted in plaits hung down behind.

" That's a very vulgar trick to play in another man's house," said the Troll; " what is your business ? "

"I am come about a situation," said Donald; "perhaps you may want a servant."—Page 51.

Scottish Fairy Tales.

" Oh! I am come about a situation: perhaps you may want a servant," said Donald.

" No, no, go away," said the Troll; " I have enough to do to find room for myself."

" But just listen," said Donald; " I am a first-rate gardener, and could put your kale-patch in order in a jiffy. It is desperate untidy, and I am sure it wants tidying badly."

" Oh! very well, then, go and dig your fill in the garden," said the Troll, with more urbanity than Donald expected; " go along and dig, go along and delve." The fact was, the Troll was much upset in his mind that morning, and he felt too sick to go on arguing, having heard thunder (which, you know, is fatal to Trolls), and he wanted to get rid of the intruder at any price. He also considered that, as soon as Donald was the other side of the door, he would be able to bolt it within, and if Donald got in again after that, well then, the Troll would be much surprised indeed.

As soon as Donald got outside the door, he looked round carefully and quickly, and, when he was sure the Troll was not looking, he swiftly planted the Thunder-plant in the centre of the kale-patch between the bothy and the road.

In an instant the Thunder-plant raised its stalk and spread its leaves around, while the blossom at the top unfurled itself like a gigantic gowan.

" Oh, do come out, do come out, dear master, and see the lovely flower that has grown in your kale-patch!" said Donald.

" Not if I know it," thought the Troll, and he sat silent. But Donald continuing to call out the same thing, the Troll thought he might just as well have a look and see what really was going on. So he peeped through a crack in the side of the door.

And astonished he was at the size and beauty of the plant. He could not make out for the life of him how the plant got there; he had not seen it before. Then he thought this must be inquired into, for Trolls, of all creatures, are the most curious, and, knowing nothing, want to understand everything.

So the Troll forgot all about the thunderstorm, and opened the door, putting his ugly head through the aperture.

" What's the use of that plant ? " said the Troll.

" Oh ! it has the most lovely smell you ever smelt in the world for one thing," said Donald. " Come out and smell it."

" Smell it yourself," said the Troll.

" I have already done so," said Donald, " and was —oh, so astonished ! " Which was anything but a story on his part, you will readily admit.

" Bring the plant here," said the Troll; " for I won't come out for you or any plant."

" Oh, then," said Donald, " I shall carry it down the glen somewhere else, if you don't think it worth coming out even to smell it."

Now to think anything of his was being carried off made the Troll very angry; also he was seized with a desire to smell the plant, so he persuaded himself there was no danger in going out just this little way.   Throwing open the door, he crawled out, waddled up to the Thunder-plant, and took a good long sniff with his ugly snout.

Bang! and you know what happened then.

But the Troll, thinking that the thunder was bursting under his very nose, as in truth it was, fled helter-skelter back to his bothy so swiftly, that, forgetting to bob his head on entering the low doorway, he dashed his brains out on the lintel and fell dead on the threshold, and that was the end of him.

Then Donald cried out to his brothers, and they came running up, and these three together ransacked the bothy, finding, as they expected, gems and jewels, silver and gold, hidden in the four corners, besides a lump of fiery-coloured crystal above price, stowed away below the hearthstone.

" Now, Donald, do you stay here," said Duncan. " Keep what you have fairly earned, while I and Dougald go a bit further on and try our luck with the other two green men of the glen."

So Donald stopped behind and waved a farewell to his two brothers as they went down the valley under the shade of Ben Nevis.

And it was not long before they saw a round tower like the first, built in the middle of the glen close to the roadside.

" That's the bothy of the second green man," said Duncan.   " Go you, Dougald, and try your luck.   I will wait for you here with the Thunder-pig till I hear you call out."

So off Dougald went with the Thunder-fowl looking out of his wallet.

" Is any one within ? " said Dougald, rapping with his stick at the little, low door.

" No," said a harsh voice, which he knew was the Troll's; " go about your business."

" A word with you first," said Dougald.

" That word will be your last, then," said the Troll, " if you don't move on."

" Flatly, I won't move on," said Dougald ; " I must and will speak to you ! "

" In the name of all that's ugly, tell your business, then ! " said the Troll, opening the door and showing his hideous green face to Dougald.

" Well," said Dougald, " I am a master cook, and cook broth out of nothing; and I am on the lookout for a situation."

Now the Troll considered for a moment. He had not had a good meal for a day or two, owing to the thundery weather, especially to the violent reports heard both yesterday and that very morning, and being unable to go out and procure food, and feeling really very hungry, the thought of broth made his chops water. " Besides," said he, "what need have I to be afraid of this intruder ? If he fails in his cooking me the broth, it won't take long to destroy him and stew him into broth instead."

So he said aloud, " Broth, indeed ! Well, cook it and serve it; but if you fail, and it proves not savoury to my taste, cook or no cook, off goes your head in a trice," and he scraped and scrubbed a long dirk on the threshold to sharpen it and to give point to his words.

" Oh ! you'll find it savoury enough to last for a long time," said Dougald. " Give me that kale-pot with the cover on it that I see lying behind the door."

So the Troll gave him the kale-pot with the cover

PUT THE FOWL INTO IT INSTEAD.

on, and Dougald carried it outside, as if to fill it with water at the burn. But when he was below the bank, out of sight of the Troll, he deftly put the Thunder-fowl into it instead, and shut down the lid.

Then he brought the pot back again to the bothy, and placed it on the ground before the Troll.

" Now take yon spoon up," said Dougald; "wait

till I count twenty, then lift up the lid and see what sore of broth I can cook. Take my word for it, my friend, you will never want to taste any other after that."

" Oon, da, tre, cahir," counted Dougald, and scarcely had he got to the word " fichead " when the impatient Troll flung aside the lid, and, plunging the iron spoon into the pot, stirred up the Thunder-fowl that was sitting quietly at the bottom.

And the light from the chimney above smote suddenly on the red comb of the Thunder-fowl, and she gave such a crow that the walls of the bothy shook as if it were stricken with a thunderbolt.

Then up leaped the Troll, and fled shrieking with dismay towards the door, for he thought the fire had come through the roof; but so full of terror was he, that he quite forgot to bob his head, and so, dashing out his brains on the lintel, he lay dead and still on the threshold, and that was the end of him.

Then Dougald called out to his brother Duncan, who was keeping watch as he had promised, a short way up the road, and Duncan and the Thunder-pig came up to his call as quick as they could.

Indeed, it was not long before they had unearthed the Troll's treasure—gems and jewels, silver and gold, hidden in the four corners of the bothy, and a large slab of golden topaz, worth a king's ransom, stowed away under the hearthstone.

" Now," said Duncan, " you stop here and look after your possessions, while I go to the end of the glen with the Thunder-pig. Wait for me here till I

return—I hope with treasure,—then we will pick up
Donald and go home together."

So Dougald remained in possession of the second

DUNCAN AND THE THUNDER-PIG CAME AS QUICKLY AS
THEY COULD.

green man's bothy, and Duncan and the Thunder-
pig went on alone down the glen towards the sea.

Just as he had expected, on emerging from the
glen, he saw, on the right-hand side of the road, a

bothy exactly like the last, enclosed within a dyke of loose stones. There was no sign of life about it, and it looked so particularly forbidding, that Duncan determined to have a good look round, and inspect the place from every side, before he knocked at the door.

Getting over the dyke he crept quietly round the back of the bothy, and there, on a level with his head, he saw a window, just big enough to crawl in or out of, filled with wattles twisted up and across like bars.

" This will be of some use, I feel sure," said Duncan; and he then asked the Thunder-pig to be so good as to lie down under the window and to wait till he called.

Oh! the Thunder-pig was quite agreeable to do so.

Having settled that, Duncan went to the little door in front, and knocked and knocked, but no sign or answer came from within. But he felt sure the green man must be at home, for Trolls never steal abroad in the daytime, but love the dark gloaming and night alone.

" This Troll must be either deaf or very uncivil," said Duncan; and so saying, he took a short run and gave the door such a fierce kick that he sent it crashing inwards, bolts and fastenings flying into the middle of the chamber.

" How dare you intrude in my bothy, you good-for-nothing scamp, you ? " said the Troll; for, of course, as soon as he saw there was no further use of concealment, the ill-omened creature emerged from behind a heap of turf in the corner.

"How dare you kick my furniture about in that way? Where are your manners? I tell you, if your parents ever taught you any, they taught you them upside down."

"Oh!" said Duncan, putting on an air of complete composure, "I heard you were a bit lonely, and so I came in to call on you in a friendly sort of way in passing."

"Who told you I was lonely? I'm not lonely, d'ye hear?" screamed the Troll: "I'm not lonely! and I don't care if she never comes back again?"

"Oho!" thought Duncan. "She never comes back again? There's a she in it. I'm on the scent of something." So he said as a shot: "Oh! then she has not come back yet. That's very curious?"

"Hush! hush!" said the Troll, putting out both his hands as if to hide some horrible vision. "I see you know all about it. No, she has not come back; but I am desperately afraid she will. Look what she did this morning," said he, pointing to the broken furniture and crockery that strewed the floor.

For you must know the Troll had that day had a fierce and fearful quarrel with his spouse, which ended in his turning her out into the road, and she had marched off fuming, and threatening to return in a very short time with her brother, a more powerful Troll, and so be avenged.

"That accounts for the hubbub I heard a short while ago up the glen," said Duncan. "I have no doubt at all she is coming back very shortly."

"Oh! now, don't you say that; it is too horrible! What shall I do? what do you advise me to do?" said the Troll; for by this time he was thoroughly frightened. "You don't know what a nasty, spiteful, revengeful thing my wife is."

"Well," said Duncan, laughing to himself at how the simple Troll let out his secret. "I'll tell you what to do in the first place. I would put the house a bit in order and remove all signs of the quarrel. You do this room up, and I will make that little chamber yonder tidy, for I am a good hand as a house servant, and then, don't you see, when your wife comes back to pay you out for this morning's work, you can easily say she must have dreamt it all."

"Capital!" said the Troll, much relieved; "you shall have a nice reward if I succeed in this." But the evil thing only wanted an opportunity to give him a smack on the head as soon as he had the chance, you may rely on it.

So Duncan went to the recess in the wall where the little window was, and where he saw the Troll-wife's bed lying in an untidy heap on the ground, and while the old Troll was busily engaged in redding up the large chamber, he whistled softly to the Thunder-pig outside. It came to the window, and lifting it in through the wattles, he made it lie down in the bedclothes.

Then he fixed the Troll's nightcap on the Thunder-pig's head, tying it under the chin, and having pulled a plaid up as far as its neck, he tucked it in all round, so that nothing was seen but a pink face under a nightcap. He then bade the Thunder-pig lie still, and not move till he got the word.

" Oh my! " cried Duncan, coming into the middle chamber; " here's a fine thing happened! There's something strange asleep in the bed; it must surely be your wife come back unknown to you."

" Good life! " said the Troll, sitting down with a plump on the hard floor; " you don't say so? "

HE TUCKED IT IN.

" But I do say so," said Duncan.

" Whatever am I to do? " said the Troll. " Come, you won't mind putting on my clothes and pretending to be me for a bit while I hide. Yes, do; I'll make it worth your while, and she will be that terrible when she wakes; oh, I think I shall have a fit! "

" Nonsense! " said Duncan. " I'll tell you a much better plan; it's the very chance for you. Just you creep in quietly and wake her with a good sound kiss between her eyes. Take my word for it, you won't hear any more on the subject."

" Think so? " said the Troll. " I'm not so sure; she's so revengeful."

" Think so? " said Duncan. " I say so; I'll stake my life on it if it don't succeed, or if you have another row with your wife after you have done so. I'll tell you what, I promise to marry her myself." And Duncan laughed to himself to think what a real, honest truth he was speaking.

" Done with you! " said the Troll, as he crept carefully on tiptoe to the recess over there. Sure enough, he saw something pink, with closed eyes, snoring in his wife's bed. So without more ado or further investigation, for now he was alarmed to think his wife might wake up before he gave her the peace-making caress, he bent over the sleeping figure and gave it a good sound kiss between the eyes.

" Wake up, my lass, wake up! " said the Troll in a cheery voice.

Wake up? indeed, it was wake up! Had the thunder got into his wife's inside? Bang, bang, bang! It took but two steps for the Troll to cross the floor of his bothy in his rush for the door, where, forgetting just like the other two to bob his head, so great was his anxiety to leave the place, he dashed his brains out against the lintel and fell dead, crumpled up in an ugly mass on the threshold, and that was the end of him.

Well, it did not take Duncan long to find out where the treasure lay, for he knew well enough now where to look for it. In the four corners of the bothy were hidden gems and jewels, silver and gold, while, stowed away under the hearthstone, he found three bags of pearls, shining so clear and clean, they must have come from the mussel-beds of Leven, so pure were they.

So he filled his wallet and his pockets with the treasure, and, whistling to the Thunder-pig, he marched up the glen to where his brother Dougald was waiting for him at the bothy of the second green man, and, finding him, they passed on together to the bothy of the first green man, where the eldest, Donald, expected them.

Then with mutual congratulations, and in cheerful companionship, they all went up the glen homewards to Rannoch, and on the way Duncan could not help boasting of how cleverly he had managed the whole proceedings in this way and that way. And the two elder brothers did not contradict him, because, though Duncan was the youngest, he was so much the cleverest, and so—oh, but I beg your pardon! I have told you all that before.

Oh but they were glad when they saw once more the fair loch of Rannoch shining in the evening sun, and looked again upon the clachan, and the bothies of their old friends at home, and heard the robins singing in the fir-trees. There, too, they saw their old mother bringing in the washing she had hung out to dry on the rowan-bushes, for it had been a fine summer day after the thunderstorm, and the west wind blew softly.

She was surprised, you may be sure, to see them so soon returning with such queer companions and such full pouches. And they all three kissed her, and she kissed them, bidding them each a hearty welcome home.

So they told their tale, and showed her all their treasures, and they blessed themselves that they never need leave dear Rannoch and home again.

Well, what? you won't be satisfied till you hear what happened to the Thunder-creatures? Oh, ah! yes, I forget to tell you that.

The very next morning, when Duncan and his brothers went to the byre behind the bothy where they had lodged their companions for the night, what was their surprise to see a handsome young man, clad in tartan, standing by the door, and two fair maidens seated by him on the cheese-press.

"Your servant, sir," said the young man. "May I introduce myself as MacSwiney of Glen Muick, and these are my two sisters, Flora and Foula, both of whom you remember, I am sure, as the Thunder-plant and Thunder-fowl. I, I need hardly add, am the Thunder-pig, at your service. We were enchanted by the witch of Ben e Bhreac, from which thraldom you have released us, for which receive our thanks."

Having said this, the young man bowed again, and his sisters got up and curtsied their acknowledgments.

And Donald went up to Flora, and Dougald went

The next morning Duncan and his brothers found a handsome young man standing by the door and two fair maidens seated by him.—Page 64.

Scottish Fairy Tales.

up to Foula, and begged them to remain and be their wives, and both Flora and Foula said, " Thank you kindly; we will."

But Duncan, hearing all this, turned round on his heel and went back into the bothy, and sitting down

HID HIS FACE IN HER APRON.

by his mother, hid his face in her apron, and refused to say a word to anybody.

Then both Donald and Dougald laughed to themselves, because for the first time Duncan had made a mistake, and they had got sweet wives, and Duncan

5

had got none, for all his cleverness. But he looked so very unhappy about it, that MacSwiney came up to him and said, " Cheer up; I have a sister at home as beautiful as Flora or Foula. I will send for her, and she will make you a good wife, and you will be as happy as the others."

So it came to pass; and they were all married on the same day, MacSwiney giving his sisters away; and the wedding feast was a splendid one, for had not they the Trolls' treasure to buy provisions with?

One thing I do hope,—that the brides and their brother forgot their old tricks of thunder-making, nor played any such games on the wedding guests. I am certain it would have disturbed much the whole proceedings. I know for one, I should have felt, like the Trolls, most uncomfortable.

NURSERY STORIES.

THE STORY OF THE WHITE PET.[1]

THERE was a farmer before now who had a **White Pet**,[2] and when Christmas was drawing near, he thought that he would kill the White Pet. The White Pet heard that, and he thought he would run away and that is what he did.

He had not gone far when a bull met him. Said the bull to him, "All hail! White Pet, where art thou going?" "I," said the White Pet, "am going to seek my fortune; they were going to kill me for Christmas, and I thought I had better run away." "It is better for me," said the bull, "to go with thee, for they were going to do the very same with me."

"I am willing," said the White Pet; "the larger the party the better the fun."

They went forward till they fell in with a dog.

"All hail! White Pet," said the dog. "All hail! thou dog." "Where art thou going?" said the dog.

"I am running away, for I heard that they were threatening to kill me for Christmas."

"They were going to do the very same to me,"

* J. F. Campbell, *Popular Tales of the West Highlands.*
[1] A lamb brought up by hand.

said the dog, " and I will go with you." " Come, then," said the White Pet.

They went then, till a cat joined them. " All hail! White Pet," said the cat. " All hail! oh cat."

" Where art thou going?" said the cat. " I am going to seek my fortune," said the White Pet, because they were going to kill me at Christmas."

" They were talking about killing me too," said the cat, " and I had better go with you."

" Come on then," said the White Pet.

Then they went forward till a cock met them. " All hail! White Pet," said the cock. " All hail to thyself! oh cock," said the White Pet. " Where," said the cock, " art thou going?" " I," said the White Pet, " am going away, for they were threatening my death at Christmas."

" They were going to kill me at the very same time," said the cock, " and I will go with you."

" Come, then," said the White Pet.

They went forward till they fell in with a goose. " All hail! White Pet," said the goose. " All hail to thyself! oh goose," said the White Pet. " Where art thou going?" said the goose.

" I," said the White Pet, " am running away, because they were going to kill me at Christmas."

" They were going to do that to me too," said the goose, " and I will go with you."

The party went forward till the night was drawing on them, and they saw a little light far away; and, though far off, they were not long getting there. When they reached the house, they said to each other that they would look in at the window to see who was in the house, and they saw thieves counting money; and the White Pet said, " Let every one of us call his own call. I will call my own call; and let the bull call his own call; let the dog call his own call; and the cat her own call; and the cock his own call; and the goose his own call." With that they gave out one shout—GAIRE!

When the thieves heard the shouting that was without, they thought the mischief was there; and they fled out, and they went to a wood that was near them. When the White Pet and his company saw that the house was empty, they went in and they got the money that the thieves had been counting, and they divided it amongst themselves; and then they thought that they would settle to rest. Said the White Pet, " Where wilt thou sleep to-night, oh bull ? " " I will sleep," said the bull, " behind the door where I used " (to be). " Where wilt thou sleep thyself, White Pet ? " " I will sleep," said the White Pet, " in the middle of the floor where I used " (to be). " Where wilt thou sleep, oh dog ? " said the White Pet. " I will sleep beside the fire where I used " (to be), said the dog. " Where wilt thou sleep, oh cat ? " " I will sleep," said the cat, " in the candle press, where I like to be." " Where wilt thou sleep, oh cock ? " said the White Pet. " I," said the cock, " will sleep on the rafters where I used " (to be). " Where wilt thou sleep, oh goose ? " " I will sleep," said the goose, " on the midden,[1] where I was accustomed to be."

They were not long settled to rest, when one of the thieves returned to look in to see if he could perceive if any one at all was in the house. All things were still, and he went on forward to the candle press for a candle, that he might kindle to make him a light; but when he put his hand in the box the cat thrust her claws into his hand, but he took a candle with him, and he tried to light it. Then the dog got up, and he stuck his tail into a pot of water that was beside the fire; he shook his tail and put out the candle. Then the thief thought that the mischief was in the house, and he fled; but when he was passing the White Pet, he gave him a blow; before he got past the bull, he gave him a kick; and the cock began to crow; and when he went out, the goose began to belabour him with his wings about the shanks.

He went to the wood where his comrades were, as fast as was in his legs. They asked him how it had gone with him. " It went," said he, " but middling; when I went to the candle press, there was a man in it who thrust ten knives into my hand; and when I went to the fireside to light the candle, there was a big black man lying there, who was sprinkling water on it to put it out; and when I tried to go out, there was a big man in the middle of the floor, who gave me a shove; and another man behind the door who pushed me out; and there was a little brat on the loft calling out CUIR-ANEES-AN-SHAW-AY-S-FONI-MI-HAYN-

[1] Dung-heap.

DA—Send him up here and I'll do for him; and there was a shoemaker out on the midden, belabouring me about the shanks with his apron."

When the thieves heard that, they did not return to seek their lot of money; and the White Pet and his comrades got it to themselves and it kept them peaceably as long as they lived.

THE MILK-WHITE DOO.[1] [2]

THERE was once a man that wrought in the fields, and had a wife, and a son, and a dochter. One day he caught a hare, and took it hame to his wife, and bade her make it ready for his dinner. While it was on the fire, the good-wife aye tasted and tasted at it, till she had tasted it a' away, and then she didna ken what to do for her goodman's dinner. So she cried in Johnie her son to come and get his head kaimed; and when she was kaiming his head, she slew him, and put him into the pat. Well, the goodman cam hame to his dinner, and his wife set down Johnie well boiled to him; and when he was eating, he takes up a foot, and says: " That's surely my Johnie's fit."

" Sic nonsense! it's ane o' the hare's," says the goodwife.

Syne he took up a hand, and says: " That's surely my Johnie's hand."

[1] Robert Chambers, *Popular Rhymes of Scotland.*
[2] Pigeon.

" Ye're havering,[1] goodman; it's anither o' the hare's feet."

So when the goodman had eaten his dinner, little Katy, Johnie's sister, gathered a' the banes, and put them in below a stane at the cheek o' the door—

> Where they grew, and they grew,
> To a milk-white doo,
> That took its wings,
> And away it flew.

And it flew till it cam to where twa women were washing claes, and it sat down on a stane, and cried—

" Pew, pew,
   My minny me slew,
   My daddy me chew,
   My sister gathered my banes,
   And put them between twa milk-white stanes;
   And I grew, and I grew,
   To a milk-white doo,
   And I took to my wings, and away I flew."

" Say that owre again, my bonny bird, and we'll gie ye a' thir claes," says the women.

> " Pew, pew,
>   My minny me slew," etc.

And it got the claes; and then flew till it cam to a man counting a great heap o' siller, and it sat down and cried—

[1] Talking nonsense.

> " Pew, pew,
> My minny me slew," etc.

" Say that again, my bonny bird, and I'll gie ye a'
this siller," says the man.

> " Pew, pew,
> My minny me slew," etc.

And it got a' the siller; and syne it flew till it cam
to twa millers grinding corn, and it cried—

> " Pew, pew,
> My minny me slew," etc.

" Say that again, my bonny bird, and I'll gie ye this
millstane," says the miller.

> " Pew, pew,
> My minny me slew," etc.

And it gat the millstane; and syne it flew till it
lighted on its father's house-top. It threw sma'
stanes down the lum,[1] and Katy cam out to see what
was the matter; and the doo threw all the claes to
her. Syne the father cam out, and the doo' threw a'
the siller to him. And syne the mother cam out, and
the doo threw down the millstane upon her and killed
her. And at last it flew away; and the goodman and
his dochter after that

[1] Chimney.

Lived happy, and died happy,
And never drank out of a dry cappy.

———

THE CROONIN DOO.[1] [2]

" WHERE hae ye been a' the day,
My bonny wee croodin doo ? "
" O I hae been at my stepmother's house;
Make my bed, mammie, now!
Make my bed, mammie, now ! "

" Where did ye get your dinner,
My bonny wee croodin doo ? "
" I got it in my stepmother's;
Make my bed, mammie, now, now, now!
Make my bed, mammie, now ! "

" What did she gie ye to your dinner,
My bonny wee croodin doo ? "
" She ga'e me a little four-footed fish;
Make my bed, mammie, now, now, now!
Make my bed, mammie, now ! "

" Where got she the four-footed fish,
My bonny wee croodin doo ? "

[1] A term of endearment applied to a child ; literally, " cooing dove."
[2] Chambers, *Popular Rhymes of Scotland.*

" She got it down in yon well strand;
O make my bed, mammie, now, now, now!
Make my bed, mammie, now! "

" What did she do wi' the banes o't,
My bonny wee croodin doo ? "
" She ga'e them to the little dog;
Make my bed, mammie, now, now, now!
Make my bed, mammie, now! "

" O what became o' the little dog,
My bonny wee croodin doo ? "
" O it shot out its feet and died!
O make my bed, mammie, now, now, now!
O make my bed, mammie, now! "

THE CATTIE SITS IN THE KILN-RING
SPINNING.[1]

THE cattie sits in the kiln-ring,
   Spinning, spinning;
And by came a little wee mousie,
   Rinning, rinning.

" Oh, what's that you're spinning, my loesome,
  Loesome lady ? "

[1] Chambers, *Popular Rhymes of Scotland.*

" I'm spinning a sark[1] to my young son,"
  Said she, said she.

" Weel mot he brook it, my loesome,
  Loesome lady."
" Gif he dinna brook it weel, he may brook it ill,"
  Said she, said she.

" I soopit[2] my house, my loesome,
  Loesome lady."
" 'Twas a sign ye didna sit amang dirt then,"
  Said she, said she.

" I fand twall pennies, my winsome,
  Winsome lady."
" 'Twas a sign ye warna sillerless,"[3]
  Said she, said she.

" I gaed to the market, my loesome,
  Loesome lady."
" 'Twas a sign ye didna sit at hame then,"
  Said she, said she.

" I coft[4] a sheepie's head, my winsome,
  Winsome lady."
" 'Twas a sign ye warna kitchenless,"
  Said she, said she.

" I put it in my pottie to boil, my loesome,
  Loesome lady."

[1] Shirt. [2] Swept. [3] Without money. [4] Bought.

" 'Twas a sign ye didna eat it raw,"
    Said she, said she.

" I put it in my winnock[1] to cool, my winsome,
    Winsome lady."
" 'Twas a sign ye didna burn your chafts[2] then,"
    Said she, said she.

" By came a cattie, and ate it a' up, my loesome,
    Loesome lady."
"And sae will I you—worrie, worrie—gnash, gnash,"
    Said she, said she.

MARRIAGE OF ROBIN REDBREAST AND THE WREN.[3]

THERE was an auld grey Poussie Baudrons,[4] and she gaed awa' down by a water-side, and there she saw a wee Robin Redbreast happin' on a brier; and Poussie Baudrons says: " Where's tu gaun, wee Robin?" And wee Robin says: " I'm gaun awa' to the king to sing him a sang this guid Yule morning." And Poussie Baudrons says: " Come here, wee Robin, and I'll let you see a bonny white ring round my neck." But wee Robin says: " Na, na! grey Poussie Baudrons; na, na! Ye worry't the wee mousie; but ye'se no worry me." So wee Robin flew

---

[1] Window.   [3] Chambers, *Popular Rhymes of Scotland.*
[2] Chaps, mouth.   [4] Pussy cat.

awa' till he came to a fail fauld-dike,[1] and there he
saw a grey greedy gled[2] sitting.   And grey greedy
gled says: " Where's tu gaun, wee Robin ? "   And
wee Robin says: " I'm gaun awa' to the king to
sing him a sang this guid Yule morning."   And grey
greedy gled says: " Come here, wee Robin, and I'll
let you see a bonny feather in my wing."   But wee
Robin says: " Na, na! grey greedy gled; na, na!
Ye pookit[3] a' the wee lintie;[4] but ye'se no pook me."
So wee Robin flew awa' till he came to the cleuch o'
a craig,[5] and there he saw slee Tod Lowrie[6] sitting.
And slee Tod Lowrie says: " Where's tu gaun,
wee Robin ? "   And wee Robin says: " I'm
gaun awa' to the king to sing him a sang
this guid Yule morning."   And slee Tod Lowrie
says: " Come here, wee Robin, and I'll let ye see a
bonny spot on the tap o' my tail."   But wee Robin
says: " Na, na! slee Tod Lowrie; na, na!   Ye
worry't the wee lammie; but ye'se no worry me."   So
wee Robin flew awa' till he came to a bonny burn-
side, and there he saw a wee callant[7] sitting.   And
the wee callant says: " Where's tu gaun, wee Robin ? "   And wee Robin says: " I'm gaun awa' to the
king to sing him a sang this guid Yule morning."
And the wee callant says: " Come here, wee Robin,
and I'll gie ye a wheen grand moolins[8] out o' my
pooch."   But wee Robin says: " Na, na! wee callant;

---

[1] Turf wall enclosing a field.   [5] Face of a rock.
[2] Kite.   [6] Mister Fox.
[3] Pluck, strip.   [7] Boy.
[4] Linnet.   [8] Some crumbs.

na, na! Ye speldert the gowdspink; but ye'se no spelder me." So wee Robin flew awa' till he came to the king, and there he sat on a winnock sole,[1] and sang the king a bonny sang. And the king says to the queen: " What'll we gie to wee Robin for singing us this bonny sang? " And the queen says to the king: " I think we'll gie him the wee wran to be his wife." So wee Robin and the wee wran were married, and the king, and the queen, and a' the court danced at the waddin'; syne he flew awa' hame to his ain water-side, and happit on a brier.

THE TEMPTED LADY.[2]

" Noo, lasses, ye should never be owre proud; for ye see there was ance a leddy, and she was aye fond o' being brawer than other folk; so she gaed awa' to take a walk ae day, her and her brother: so she met wi' a gentleman—but it was nae gentleman in reality, but Auld Nick himsel', who can change himsel' brawly into a gentleman—a' but the cloven feet; but he keepit them out o' sight. So he began to make love to the young leddy :—

> ' I'll gie you a pennyworth o' preens,[3]
> That's aye the way that love begins;
> If ye'll walk with me, leddy, leddy,
> If ye'll walk with me, leddy.'

[1] Window sill.
[2] Chambers, *Popular Rhymes of Scotland.*
[3] Pins.

' I'll no hae your pennyworth o' preens,
That's no the way that love begins;
And I'll no walk with you, with you,
And I'll no walk with you.'

' O Johnie, O Johnie, what can the matter be,
That I love this leddy, and she loves na me?
And for her sake I must die, must die,
And for her sake I must die!

' I'll gie you a bonny silver box,
With seven silver hinges, and seven silver locks,
If ye'll walk,' etc.

' I'll no hae your bonny silver box,
With seven silver hinges, and seven silver locks,
And I'll no walk,' etc.

' O Johnie, O Johnie' [*as in third verse*].

' But I'll gie you a bonnier silver box,
With seven golden hinges, and seven golden locks,
If ye'll walk,' etc.

' I'll no hae' [*as in fifth verse*].

' O Johnie' [*as in third verse*].

' I'll gie you a pair o' bonny shoon,
The tane made in Sodom, the tother in Rome,
If ye'll walk,' etc.

'I'll no hae' [*as in fifth verse*].

'O Johnie' [*as in third verse*].

'I'll gie you the half o' Bristol town,
With coaches rolling up and down,
If ye'll walk,' etc.

'I'll no hae' [*as in fifth verse*].

'O Johnie' [*as in third verse*].

'I'll gie you the hale o' Bristol town,
With coaches rolling up and down,
If ye'll walk with me, leddy, leddy,
If ye'll walk with me, leddy.'

'If ye'll gie me the hale o' Bristol town,
With coaches rolling up and down,
I will walk with you, with you,
And I will walk with you."

And aff he flew wi' her! Noo, lasses, ye see ye maun
aye mind that."

THE FAUSE KNIGHT AND THE WEE BOY.[1]

" O WHERE are ye gaun?"
Quo' the fause knight upon the road;
" I'm gaun to the schule,"
Quo' the wee boy, and still he stude.

[1] Chambers, *Popular Rhymes of Scotland.*

6

" What is that upon your back ? "
  Quo' the fause knight upon the **road**;
" Atweel it is my bukes,"
  Quo' the wee boy, and still he stude.

" What's that ye've got in your arm ? "
  Quo' the fause knight upon the road;
" Atweel it is my peat," [1]
  Quo' the wee boy, and still he stude.

" Wha's aucht thae sheep ? "
  Quo' the fause knight upon the road;
" They're mine and my mother's,"
  Quo' the wee boy, and still he stude.

" How mony o' them are mine ? "
  Quo' the fause knight upon the road;
" A' they that hae blue tails,"
  Quo' the wee boy, and still he stude.

" I wiss ye were on yon tree,"
  Quo' the fause knight upon the road;
" And a guid ladder under me,"
  Quo' the wee boy, and still he stude.

" And the ladder for to break,"
  Quo' the fause knight upon the road;
" And you for to fa' down,"
  Quo' the wee boy, and still he stude.

[1] A contribution to the schoolmaster's stock of fuel.

" I wiss ye were in yon sea,"
  Quo' the fause knight upon the road;
" And a guid bottom under me,"
  Quo' the wee boy, and still he stude.

" And the bottom for to break,"
  Quo' the fause knight upon the road;
" And ye to be drownèd,"
  Quo' the wee boy, and still he stude.[1]

THE STRANGE VISITOR.[2]

A WIFE was sitting at her reel ae night;
  And aye she sat, and aye she reeled, and aye she
    wished for company.

In came a pair o' braid braid soles, and sat down at
    the fireside;
  And aye she sat, etc.

In came a pair o' sma' sma' legs, and sat down on the
    braid braid soles;
  And aye she sat, etc.

[1] Motherwell gives the above, in his *Minstrelsy Ancient and Modern*, as a nursery tale of Galloway, and a specimen of a class of compositions of great antiquity, representing the Enemy of man in the endeavour to confound some poor mortal with puzzling questions.

[2] Chambers, *Popular Rhymes of Scotland.*

In came a pair o' muckle muckle knees, **and sat down**
on the sma' sma' legs;
And aye she sat, etc.

In came a pair o' sma' sma' thees, and sat down on
the muckle muckle knees;
And aye she sat, etc.

In came a pair o' muckle muckle hips, and sat down
on the sma' sma' thees;
And aye she sat, etc.

In came a sma' sma' waist, and sat down on the
muckle muckle hips;
And aye she sat, etc.

In came a pair o' braid braid shouthers, and sat down
on the sma' sma' waist;
And aye she sat, etc.

In came a pair o' sma' sma' arms, and sat down on
the braid braid shouthers;
And aye she sat, etc.

In came a pair o' muckle muckle hands, **and sat down**
on the sma' sma' arms;
And aye she sat, etc.

In came a sma' sma' neck, and sat down on **the braid**
braid shouthers;
And aye she sat, etc.

In came a great big head, and sat down on the sma'
sma' neck.

" What way hae ye sic braid braid feet?" quo' the
wife.
" Muckle ganging, muckle ganging " (*gruffly*).
" What way hae ye sic sma' sma' legs? "
  " *Aih-h-h!*—late—and *wee-e-e*—moul " (*whining-ly*).
" What way hae ye sic muckle muckle knees? "
" Muckle praying, muckle praying " (*piously*).
" What way hae ye sic sma' sma' thees? "
" Aih-h-h!—late—and wee-e-e—moul " (*whining-ly*).
" What way hae ye sic big big hips? "
" Muckle sitting, muckle sitting " (*gruffly*).
" What way hae ye sic a sma' sma' waist? "
" Aih-h-h!—late—and wee-e-e—moul " (*whiningly*).
" What way hae ye sic braid braid shouthers? "
" Wi' carrying broom, wi' carrying broom " (*gruff-ly*).
" What way hae ye sic sma' sma' arms? "
" Aih-h-h!—late—and wee-e-e—moul " (*whiningly*).
" What way hae ye sic muckle muckle hands? "
" Threshing wi' an iron flail, threshing wi' an iron
  flail " (*gruffly.*)
" What way hae ye sic a sma' sma' neck? "
" Aih-h-h!—late—and wee-e-e—moul " (*pitifully*).
" What way hae ye sic a muckle muckle head? "
" Muckle wit, muckle wit " (*keenly*).
" What do you come for? "

" For you ! " (*At the top of the voice, with a wave of the arm and a stamp of the feet.*)[1]

RASHIN-COATIE.[2]

Once, a long time ago, there was a gentleman had two lassies. The oldest was ugly and ill-natured, but the youngest was a bonnie lassie and good; but the ugly one was the favourite with her father and mother. So they ill-used the youngest in every way, and they sent her into the woods to herd cattle, and all the food she got was a little porridge and whey.

Well, amongst the cattle was a red calf, and one day it said to the lassie, " Gee that porridge and whey to the doggie, and come wi' me."

So the lassie followed the calf through the wood, and they came to a bonnie hoosie, where there was a nice dinner ready for them; and after they had feasted on everything nice they went back to the herding.

Every day the calf took the lassie away, and feasted her on dainties; and every day she grew bonnier. This disappointed the father and mother and the ugly sister. They expected that the rough usage she was getting would take away her beauty; and they watched and watched until they saw the calf take the lassie away to the feast. So they resolved to kill

[1] The figure is meant for that of Death.
[2] *The Folk-Lore Journal.*

the calf; and not only that, but the lassie was to be compelled to kill him with an axe. Her ugly sister was to hold his head, and the lassie who loved him had to give the blow and kill him.

She could do nothing but greet;[1] but the calf told her not to greet, but to do as he bade her; and his plan was that instead of coming down on his head she was to come down on the lassie's head who was holding him, and then she was to jump on his back and they would run off. Well, the day came for the calf to be killed, and everything was ready—the ugly lassie holding his head, and the bonnie lassie armed with the axe. So she raised the axe, and came down on the ugly sister's head; and in the confusion that took place she got on the calf's back and they ran away. And they ran and better nor ran till they came to a meadow where grew a great lot of rashes; and, as the lassie had not on many clothes, they pu'ed rashes, and made a coatie for her. And they set off again and travelled, and travelled, till they came to the king's house. They went in, and asked if they wanted a servant. The mistress said she wanted a kitchen lassie, and she would take Rashin-coatie. So Rashin-coatie said she would stop, if they keepit the calf too. They were willing to do that. So the lassie and the calf stoppit in the king's house, and everybody was well pleased with her; and when Yule came, they said she was to stop at home and make the dinner, while all the rest went to the kirk. After they were away the calf asked if she would

[1] Weep.

like to go. She said she would, but she had no
clothes, and she could not leave the dinner. The calf
said he would give her clothes, and make the dinner
too. He went out, and came back with a grand
dress, all silk and satin, and such a nice pair of slippers. The lassie put on the dress, and before she
left she said—

> " Ilka peat gar anither burn,
>   An' ilka spit gar anither turn,
>   An' ilka pot gar anither play,
>   Till I come frae the kirk on gude Yule day."

So she went to the kirk, and nobody kent it was
Rashin-coatie. They wondered who the bonnie lady
could be; and, as soon as the young prince saw her,
he fell in love with her, and resolved he would find
out who she was, before she got home; but Rashin-
coatie left before the rest, so that she might get home
in time to take off her dress, and look after the dinner.

When the prince saw her leaving, he made for the
door to stop her; but she jumped past him, and in
the hurry lost one of her shoes. The prince kept the
shoe, and Rashin-coatie got home all right, and the
folk said the dinner was very nice.

Now the prince was resolved to find out who the
bonnie lady was, and he sent a servant through all the
land with the shoe. Every lady was to try it on, and
the prince promised to marry the one it would fit.
That servant went to a great many houses, but could
not find a lady that the shoe would go on, it was so

little and neat. At last he came to a henwife's house, and her daughter had little feet. At first the shoe would not go on, but she paret her feet, and slippit her toes, until the shoes went on. Now the prince was very angry. He knew it was not the lady that he wanted; but, because he had promised to marry whoever the shoe fitted, he had to keep his promise.

The marriage day came, and, as they were all riding to the kirk, a little bird flew through the air, and it sang—

> "Clippit feet an' paret taes is on the saidle set;
> But bonnie feet an' braw feet sits in the kitchen neuk."

"What's that ye say?" said the prince. "Oh," says the henwife, "would ye mind what a feel bird says?" But the prince said, "Sing that again, bonnie birdie." So the bird sings—

> "Clippit feet an' paret taes is on the saidle set;
> But bonnie feet an' braw feet sits in the kitchen neuk."

The prince turned his horse and rode home, and went straight to his father's kitchen, and there sat Rashin-coatie. He kent her at once, she was so bonnie; and when she tried on the shoe it fitted her, and so the prince married Rashin-coatie, and they lived happy, and built a house for the red calf, who had been so kind to her.

STORIES OF ANIMALS.[1]

THE FOX OUTWITTED.

ONE day the fox succeeded in catching a fine fat goose asleep by the side of a loch; he held her by the wing, and making a joke of her cackling, hissing, and fears, he said—

"Now, if you had me in your mouth as I have you, tell me what you would do?"

"Why," said the goose, "that is an easy question. I would fold my hands, shut my eyes, say a grace, and then eat you."

"Just what I mean to do," said Rory;[2] and folding his hands, and looking very demure, he said a pious grace with his eyes shut.

But while he did this the goose had spread her wings, and she was now half way over the loch; so the fox was left to lick his lips for supper.

"I will make a rule of this," he said in disgust, "never in all my life to say a grace again till after I feel the meat warm in my belly."

[1] J. F. Campbell, *Popular Tales of the West Highlands.*
[2] Rory is a corruption of a Gaelic proper name, which means, one whose hair is the color of the fox "Ruadh."

THE FOX TROUBLED WITH FLEAS.

THE fox is much troubled by fleas, and this is the way in which he gets rid of them. He hunts about till he finds a lock of wool, and then he takes it to the river, and holds it in his mouth, and so puts the end of his brush into the water, and down he goes slowly. The fleas run away from the water, and at last they all run over the fox's nose into the wool, and then the fox dips his nose under and lets the wool go off with the stream.[1]

THE FOX AND THE BAG-PIPES.

THE fox, being hungry one day, found a bag-pipe, and proceeded to eat the bag, which is generally, or was till lately, made of hide. There was still a remnant of breath in the bag, and when the fox bit it the drone gave a groan, when the fox, surprised but not frightened, said—

"Here is meat and music!"[2]

THE FOX'S STRATAGEM.

THE fox is very wise indeed. I don't know whether it is true or not, but an old fellow told me that he had seen him go to a loch where there were

[1] This is told as a fact.
[2] A popular saying in the West Highlands.

wild ducks, and take a bunch of heather in his mouth, then go into the water, and swim down with the wind till he got into the middle of the ducks, and then he let go the heather and killed two of them.

THE FOX AND THE WRENS.

A fox had noticed for some days a family of wrens, off which he wished to dine. He might have been satisfied with one, but he was determined to have the whole lot—father and eighteen sons,—and all so like that he could not tell one from the other, or the father from the children.

"It is no use to kill one son," he said to himself, "because the old cock will take warning and fly away with the seventeen. I wish I knew which is the old gentleman."

He set his wits to work to find out, and one day, seeing them all threshing in a barn, he sat down to watch them; still he could not be sure.

"Now I have it," he said; "well done the old man's stroke! He hits true," he cried.

"Oh!" replied the one he suspected of being the head of the family; "if you had seen my grandfather's strokes you might have said that."

The sly fox pounced on the cock, ate him up in a trice, and then soon caught and disposed of the eighteen sons, all flying in terror about the barn.

THE FOX AND THE COCK.

A fox one day met a cock, and they began talking.

" How many tricks canst thou do ? " said the fox.

" Well," said the cock, " I could do three; how many canst thou do thyself ? "

" I could do three score and thirteen," said the fox.

" What tricks canst thou do ? " said the cock.

" Well," said the fox, " my grandfather used to shut one eye and give a great shout."

" I could do that myself," said the cock.

" Do it," said the fox. And the cock shut one eye and crowed as loud as ever he could, but he shut the eye that was next the fox, and the fox gripped him by the neck and ran away with him. But the wife to whom the cock belonged saw him and cried out, " Let go the cock; he's mine."

" Say thou, SE MO CHOILEACH FHEIN A TH' ANN " (it is my own cock), said the cock to the fox.

Then the fox opened his mouth to say as the cock did, and he dropped the cock, and he sprung up on the top of a house, and shut one eye and gave a loud crow; and that's all there is of that sgeulachd.[1]

HOW THE WOLF LOST HIS TAIL.

One day the wolf and the fox were out together, and they stole a dish of crowdie. Now the wolf was

[1] Tale.

the biggest beast of the two, and he had a long tail like a greyhound, and great teeth.

The fox was afraid of him, and did not dare to say a word when the wolf ate the most of the crowdie, and left only a little at the bottom of the dish for him, but he determined to punish him for it; so the next night when they were out together the fox said—

"I smell a very nice cheese, and" (pointing to the moonshine on the ice) "there it is too."

"And how will you get it?" said the wolf.

"Well, stop you here till I see if the farmer is asleep, and if you keep your tail on it, nobody will see you or know that it is there. Keep it steady. I may be some time coming back."

So the wolf lay down and laid his tail on the moonshine in the ice, and kept it for an hour till it was fast. Then the fox, who had been watching him, ran in to the farmer and said: "The wolf is there; he will eat up the children,—the wolf! the wolf!"

Then the farmer and his wife came out with sticks to kill the wolf, but the wolf ran off leaving his tail behind him, and that's why the wolf is stumpy-tailed to this day, though the fox has a long brush.[1]

FROG AND CROW.

HERE is a bit of crow language,—a conversation with a frog. When it is repeated in Gaelic it can be made absurdly like the notes of the creatures.

[1] The story errs in ascribing a stumpy tail to the wolf.

" Ghille Criosda mhic Dhughail cuir a nois do mhàg."

Christ's servant, son of Dugald, put up thy paw.

" Tha eagal orm, tha eagal orm, tha eagal orm."

I fear.

" Gheibh thu còta gorm a's léine. Gheibh thu còta gorm a's léine."

Thou shalt have a blue coat and a shirt.

Then the frog put up his hand and the hoodie took him to a hillock and began to eat him, saying,

" Biadh dona lom ! 's bu dona riabh thu."

Bad bare meat and bad wert thou ever.

" Caite bheil do ghealladh math a nis ? " said the frog.

Where is thy good promise now ?

" Sann ag ol a bha sinn an latha sin. Sann ag ol a bha sinn an latha sin."

It is drinking we were on that day.

" Toll ort a ruid ghrannda gur beag feola tha air do chramhan."

" Toll ort ! " said the hoodie.

A hole in thee, ugly thing ! how little flesh is on thy bones.

THE GROUSE COCK AND HIS WIFE.

THE Grouse Cock and his wife are always disput-ing, and may be heard on any fine evening or early morning quarreling and scolding about the stock of food.

This is what the hen says—
" FAIC THUSA 'N LA UD 'S AN LA UD EILE."
And the cock, with his deeper voice, replies—
" FAIC THUSA 'N CNOC UD 'S AN CNOC UD EILE."
See thou yonder day, and yon other day.
See thou yonder hill, and yon other hill.

THE EAGLE AND THE WREN.[1]

THE Eagle and the Wren once tried who could fly highest, and the victor was to be king of the birds. So the Wren flew straight up, and the Eagle flew in great circles, and when the Wren was tired he settled on the Eagle's back.

When the Eagle was tired he stopped, and—
" Where art thou, Wren ? " said the Eagle.
" I am here above thee," said the Wren.
And so the Wren won the match.

THE WREN'S PRESUMPTION.

THOU'RT lessened by that, said the Wren, when he dipped his beak in the sea.

THE TWO FOXES.

A MAN was one day walking along the road with a creel of herrings on his back, and two foxes saw him,

[1] This story describes the flight of eagle and wren correctly enough.

and the one, who was the biggest, said to the other, " Stop thou here, and follow the man, and I will run round and pretend that I am dead." So he ran round, and stretched himself on the road. The man came on, and when he saw the fox, he was well pleased to find so fine a beast, and he picked him up, and threw him into the creel, and he walked on. But the fox threw the herrings out of the creel, and the other followed and picked them up; and when the creel was empty, the big fox leaped out and ran away, and that is how they got the herrings.

Well, they went on together till they came to a smith's house, and there was a horse tied at the door, and he had a golden shoe, and there was a name on it.

" I will go and read what is written on that shoe," said the big fox, and he went; but the horse lifted his foot, and struck a kick on him, and drove his brains out.

" Lad, lad," said the little fox, " no scholar me, nor wish I to be; " and, of course, he got the herrings.

THE BEE AND THE MOUSE.

A BEE met a mouse and said—
" Come over till we make a house."
" I will not," said Luchag, the mousie.
He to whom thou gavest thy summer honey,
Let him make a winter house for thee;
I have a little house under the ground,

That can reach neither cold nor breeze,
Thou wilt be a ragged creature,
Running on the tops of the trees.

THE TWO MICE.

THERE was a mouse in the hill, and a mouse in a farm.

"It were well," said the hill mouse, "to be in the farm, where one might get things."

Said the farm mouse, "Better is peace."

ALEXANDER JONES.

" JEAN, sit a wee bit east," requested the town-clerk, between the puffs of his pipe, as he sat on the corner of the bench before his fire one chilly evening. " You're taking ower muckle room, and mair than your share o' the settle."

But Jean, his wife, had just got her knitting into a nasty tangle, and was not in the best of humours, so declined to move one inch, or to attend to what her husband was saying.

" Jean," said her husband again, " sit a wee bit east; it's no decent to sit sae selfish. Sit a bit east, d'ye hear?" and the town-clerk gave his wife a rude shove to her end of the bench.

"Wha' d'ye mean by that? and wha' d'ye mean by east?" cried his wife. "There's nae sic thing as east to begin with, and——"

"Nae sic thing as east?" shouted the town-clerk. "Will ye no' believe the sun himsel'?" and then in a loud voice he declaimed that, as the sun went round the earth every day, and was always rising every moment somewhere in the east, which thing he hoped no one was fool enough to deny, everywhere was the east, all over the place; and if there was anything ridiculous, it was to talk about west. If everywhere was east, there was nowhere where west could be. So he hoped his wife would not make a goose of herself, and talk nonsense.

But then his wife got up and said he did not look at it in the right way at all. On the contrary, the sun was all the day setting somewhere in the west, which thing she hoped no one was fool enough to contradict; and as he was always setting somewhere, and doing it every moment, everywhere was west, and if everywhere was west, there was no room for east to be anywhere. So she trusted her husband would not make an ass of himself, and mention east again.

But he shook his head, just like a dog that has been bitten behind the ear, and was going to reply, when she kilted her petticoats, and ran round the room in one direction to show how it was done, crying, "West, west, west!"

This made the town-clerk very angry, and he got

They all ran around, getting very giddy and banging their heads together.
Page 101.   *Scottish Fairy Tales.*

up also, and hitched his trousers, and ran round the table in the opposite direction, yelling out, " East, east, east! " to show how he thought it was done.

Yet it only ended by their getting very giddy, and banging their heads together, a thing which hurt very much, and did not conduce to good-temper or the solving of the difficulty, you may be sure.

But Alexander Jones sat quiet in the corner, and said nothing.

Still, they agreed in one thing, namely, that the question was of too deep importance to rest there. So they went to the grocer, who had a good-sized house up the street, and told him all about the thing, with the ins and outs of the question; and the grocer and the grocer's wife, and the grocer's maiden aunt by marriage on the mother's side, and the grocer's wife's youngest married sister, and the grocer's wife's youngest married sister's little girl, were all naturally much interested, to say the least. But one took one view, and another took another, and they ran round the table, some this way and some that, to explain how in their opinion it was done. It only ended in their getting very giddy and banging their heads together, a thing which hurt, and did not conduce to good-temper or the solving of the difficulty, you may be sure.

But Alexander Jones sat quiet in the corner all the time, and said nothing.

Still, they agreed in one thing, that the question was of too deep importance to rest there. So the whole lot went to the innkeeper, who had a much larger house than the grocer, down the street, and told him all about the thing, with the ins and outs of the matter; and the innkeeper, and the innkeeper's wife, and the innkeeper's maiden aunt by marriage on the mother's side, and the innkeeper's wife's youngest married sister, and the innkeeper's youngest married sister's little girl, were all naturally much interested, to say the least. But one took one view, and another took another, and they ran round the table, some this way and some that, to explain how in their opinion it was done. And it only ended by their all getting very giddy and banging their heads together, a thing which hurt, and did not conduce to good-temper or the solving of the difficulty, you may be sure.

But Alexander Jones sat all the time quiet in the corner, and said nothing.

Still, they agreed in one thing, that the question was of too deep importance to rest there. So the whole lot went to the chief magistrate, who had the very largest house in the burgh, in the middle of the street by the market-place, and they told him all about the thing, and the ins and outs of the matter; and the magistrate, and the magistrate's wife, and the magistrate's maiden aunt by marriage on the mother's side, and the magistrate's wife's youngest married sister, and the magistrate's wife's youngest married sister's little girl, were all naturally much interested in the matter, to say the least. But one took one view, and another took another, and they ran round the magistrate's table, some this way and some that, to explain how in their opinion it was done; and it only ended by their all getting very giddy and banging their heads together, a thing which hurt, and did not conduce to good-temper or the solving of the difficulty, you may be sure.

But Alexander Jones sat quiet in the corner, and said nothing.

Still, they agreed in one thing, that the question was of too deep importance to rest there. So the magistrate called a meeting of the whole populace in the town-hall.

And when the populace came to the town-hall, the chief magistrate told them all about it, and the ins and outs of the matter; and the populace, and the populace's wife, and the populace's maiden aunt by marriage on the mother's side, and the populace's wife's youngest married sister, and the populace's wife's youngest married sister's little girl, were all naturally much interested, to say the least. But one took one view, and another took another.

And they all wanted then to run round a table to explain how each thought it was done; but here a difficulty arose, for, alas! there was no table in the town-hall to run round, and what then were they to do? Yet they were not going to be balked for a trifle like that, not they? So they requested the chief magistrate to stand in the middle, and let them all run round him in the direction it pleased them.

But the chief magistrate objected strongly, for he said it would make him worse than giddy to see some folk going one way round him and some going the other; indeed, it would be certain to make him sick. So he suggested instead that Alexander Jones should be placed in the middle. Yes, why could they not run round him? Better make use of him, he was so stupid, and said nothing; besides, the chief magistrate wanted to run round with the best of them himself, and why should he be cut out more than any one else?

" No, no," cried they all. " Alexander Jones is too small, and would be certain to be trod upon." It would not do at all, and the chief magistrate must really do what he was asked. Hadn't they, only the other day, given him an imitation gold badge to wear on his stom——well, never mind—and he must do something for them in return, or they'd take it away, that they would.

So the poor man had to give in, but he insisted upon having his eyes bandaged, and also on having a good chair to sit in, otherwise he knew he would be sick; of that he felt certain.

Then they bandaged his eyes with an old dishclout they got from somewhere; for a handkerchief would not go round his face, he had such a very big nose; and, having seated him in a chair, they all ran round him in a circle, some this way, some another; but they all only got very giddy and banged each other's heads, a thing which hurt, and did not conduce to good-temper or to the solving of the difficulty; and, worse than all, just at the end, when they could run no longer, and were quite out of breath, Eliza M'Diarmed, the fat widow who kept the confectionery-shop, fell plump against the chief magistrate, and sent him and his chair flying all along the floor.

But Alexander Jones sat quiet in the corner, and said nothing.

THEY SEATED HIM IN A CHAIR.

Then the chief magistrate pulled the bandage off his eyes in a towering passion, and said something must and should be settled there and then. No, he would stand it no longer. He threatened, also, if they did not agree, he would put a tax on buttons;

which was rather clever of him, for you see, both
sexes would feel that tax equally, and he, inasmuch
as his robes were all fastened by a buckle at his neck,
and a jewelled girdle round his stom——well, never
mind—it would not affect him at all.

At this the town-clerk rose, and said they must,
in that case, devise some other way of discovering
the answer to this terrible riddle, and he proposed
to call in from the street Peter the roadman, for he
was up and about at all hours, late and early, and
would know more than most about the sun's move-
ments; only, if they asked him, they must ask also
his one-eyed sister, Jessica—she, you must know, took
in the chief magistrate's washing, and so was a person
of importance in the burgh—for Peter would certainly decline to come in unless she came with him.

Now this was, indeed, most provoking for me.
Because, you see, there was not another square inch
of room left in the town-hall for another person, and
two people would have to go out to let Peter the roadman and his sister Jessica come in.

So they turned me out for one, as being a stranger
from the country, only asked there in courtesy; and
Alexander Jones for the other, because he was so
stupid, and said nothing.

Thus, you see, I never knew what decision the
meeting came to, though I am certain it did come to
some, as next morning people's clothes were still
worn as usual, and buttons were at the same price in
the shops as before.

And, though disappointed greatly for my own sake,

I am still more for yours, my friends, who I must say have listened to this long story most patiently.

But why was Alexander Jones so stupid as to sit still in the corner and say nothing?

Oh! hush, hush now! how silly you are! Why, how on earth could he do anything else? Alexander Jones was the town-clerk's

TOM CAT.

FAIRY TALES.

THE FAIRIES OF SCOTLAND.[1]

THE Fairies of Scotland are represented as a diminutive race of beings, of a mixed, or rather dubious nature, capricious in their dispositions, and mischievous in their resentment. They inhabit the interior of green hills, chiefly those of a conical form, in Gaelic termed Sighan, on which they lead their dances by moonlight; impressing upon the surface the marks of circles, which sometimes appear yellow and blasted, sometimes of a deep green hue; and within which it is dangerous to sleep, or to be found after sunset. The removal of those large portions of turf, which thunder-bolts sometimes scoop out of the ground with singular regularity, is also ascribed to their agency. Cattle, which are suddenly seized with the cramp, or some similar disorder, are said to be elf-shot, and the approved cure is, to chafe the parts affected with a blue bonnet, which, it may be readily believed, often restores the circulation. The triangular flints, frequently found in Scotland, with which the ancient inhabitants probably barbed their shafts,

[1] Sir Walter Scott, *Minstrelsy of the Scottish Border.*

are supposed to be the weapons of Fairy resentment, and are termed elf arrow-heads. The rude brazen battle-axes of the ancients, commonly called celts, are also ascribed to their manufacture. But, like the Gothic duergar, their skill is not confined to the fabrication of arms; for they are heard sedulously hammering in linns, precipices, and rocky or cavernous situations, where, like the dwarfs of the mines, mentioned by Georg. Agricola, they busy themselves in imitating, the actions and the various employments of men. The Brook of Beaumont, for example, which passes, in its course, by numerous linns and caverns, is notorious for being haunted by the Fairies and the perforated and rounded stones which are formed by trituration in its channel, are termed, by the vulgar, fairy cups and dishes.

It is sometimes accounted unlucky to pass such places, without performing some ceremony to avert the displeasure of the elves. There is, upon the top of Minchmuir, a mountain in Peeblesshire, a spring called the Cheese Well, because, anciently, those who passed that way were wont to throw into it a piece of cheese, as an offering to the Fairies, to whom it was consecrated.

The usual dress of the Fairies is green; though on the moors they have been sometimes observed in heath-brown, or in weeds dyed with the stoneraw, or lichen. They often ride in invisible procession, when their presence is discovered by the shrill ringing of their bridles. On these occasions they sometimes borrow mortal steeds; and when such are found at morning, panting and fatigued in their stalls, with their manes and tails dishevelled and entangled, the grooms, I presume, often find this a convenient excuse for their situation; as the common belief of the elves quaffing the choicest liquors in the cellars of the rich might occasionally cloak the delinquencies of an unfaithful butler.

THE FAIRY AND THE MILLER'S WIFE.[1]

ONE day as a mother was sitting rocking her baby to sleep, she was surprised, on looking up, to see a lady of elegant and courtly demeanour, so unlike any one she had ever seen in that part of the country, standing in the middle of the room. She had not heard any one enter, therefore you may judge it was with no little surprise, not unmingled with curiosity, that she rose to welcome her strange visitor. She handed her a chair, but she very politely declined to · be seated. She was very magnificently attired; her dress was of the richest green, embroidered round with spangles of gold, and on her head was a small coronet of pearls. The woman was still more surprised at her strange request. She asked, in a rich musical voice, if she would oblige her with a basin of oatmeal. A basin full to overflowing was immediately handed to her, for the woman's husband, being both a farmer and miller, had plenty of meal at

[1] Campbell, *Tales of the West Highlands.*

command. The lady promised to return it, and named the day she would do so. One of the children put out her hand to get hold of the grand lady's spangles, but told her mother afterwards that she felt nothing. The mother was afraid the child would lose the use of her hands, but no such calamity ensued. It would have been very ungrateful in her fairy majesty if she had struck the child powerless for touching her dress, if indeed such power were hers. But to return to our story. The very day mentioned the oatmeal was returned, not by the same lady, but by a curious little figure with a yelping voice; she was likewise dressed in green. After handing the meal, she yelped out, " Braw meal; it's the top pickle of the sin corn." It was excellent; and what was very strange, all the family were advised to partake of it but one servant lad, who spurned the fairy's meal; and he dying shortly after, the miller and his wife firmly believed it was because he refused to eat of the meal. They also firmly believed their first visitor was no less a personage than the Queen of the Fairies, who, having dismissed her court, had not one maid of honour in waiting to obey her commands. A few nights after this strange visit, as the miller was going to bed, a gentle tap was heard at the door, and on its being opened by him, with a light in his hand, there stood a little figure dressed in green, who, in a shrill voice, but very polite manner, requested him to let on the water and set the mill in order, for she was going to grind some corn. The miller did not dare to refuse, so did as she desired him. She told him to go to bed again, and he would find all as he had left it. He found everything in the morning as she said he would. So much for the honesty of fairies.

SIR GODFREY MACCULLOCH.[1]

THE Scottish Fairies, in like manner, sometimes reside in subterranean abodes, in the vicinity of human habitations, or, according to the popular phrase, under the " door-stane," or threshold; in which situation they sometimes establish an intercourse with men, by borrowing and lending, and other kindly offices. In this capacity they are termed "the good neighbours," from supplying privately the wants of their friends, and assisting them in all their transactions, while their favours are concealed. Of this the traditionary story of Sir Godfrey Macculloch forms a curious example.

As this Gallovidian gentleman was taking the air on horseback, near his own house he was suddenly accosted by a little old man arrayed in green, and mounted upon a white palfrey. After mutual salutation, the old man gave Sir Godfrey to understand that he resided under his habitation, and that he had great reason to complain of the direction of a drain, or common sewer, which emptied itself directly into his chamber of daïs.[2] Sir Godfrey Macculloch was

[1] Sir Walter Scott, *Minstrelsy of the Scottish Border.*
[2] Or, best room.

a good deal startled at this extraordinary complaint; but, guessing the nature of the being he had to deal with, he assured the old man, with great courtesy, that the direction of the drain should be altered; and caused it to be done accordingly. Many years afterwards Sir Godfrey had the misfortune to kill, in a fray, a gentleman of the neighbourhood. He was apprehanded, tried, and condemned. The scaffold upon which his head was to be struck off was erected on the Castle Hill of Edinburgh; but hardly had he reached the fatal spot when the old man, upon his white palfrey, pressed through the crowd with the rapidity of lightning. Sir Godfrey, at his command, sprung on behind him; the " good neighbour " spurred his horse down the steep bank, and neither he nor the criminal was ever again seen.

THE LAIRD O' CO'.[1]

In the days of yore, the proprietors of Colzean, in Ayrshire, were known in that country by the title of *Lairds o' Co'*, a name bestowed on Colzean from some co's (or coves) in the rock underneath the castle.

One morning, a very little boy, carrying a small wooden can, addressed the laird near the castle gate, begging for a little ale for his mother, who was sick: the laird directed him to go to the butler and get his can filled; so away he went as ordered. The butler had a barrel of ale on tap, but about half full, out of

[1] Chambers, *Popular Rhymes of Scotland.*

8

which he proceeded to fill the boy's can; but, to his extreme surprise, he emptied the cask, and still the little can was not nearly full. The butler was unwilling to broach another barrel; but the little fellow insisted on the fulfilment of the laird's order, and a reference was made to him by the butler, who stated the miraculously large capacity of the tiny can, and received instant orders to fill it if all the ale in the cellar would suffice. Obedient to this command, he broached another cask, but had scarcely drawn a drop, when the can was full, and the dwarf departed with expressions of gratitude.

Some years afterwards, the laird, being at the wars in Flanders, was taken prisoner, and for some reason or other (probably as a spy) condemned to die a felon's death. The night prior to the day appointed for his execution, being confined in a dungeon strongly barricaded, the doors suddenly flew open, and the dwarf reappeared, saying—

> "Laird o' Co',
> Rise an' go "—

a summons too welcome to require repetition.

On emerging from prison, the boy caused him to mount on his shoulders, and in a short time set him down at his own gate, on the very spot where they had first met, saying—

> "Ae guid turn deserves anither—
> Tak ye that for bein' sae kind to my auld mither,"

and vanished.

HABITROT.[1]

In the old days, when spinning was the constant employment of women, the spinning-wheel had its presiding genius or fairy. Her Border name was Habitrot, and Mr. Wilkie tells the following legend about her:—

A Selkirkshire matron had one fair daughter, who loved play better than work, wandering in the meadows and lanes better than the spinning-wheel and distaff. The mother was heartily vexed at this taste, for in those days no lassie had any chance of a good husband unless she was an industrious spinster. So she cajoled, threatened, even beat her daughter, but all to no purpose; the girl remained what her mother called her, " an idle cuttie."

At last, one spring morning, the gudewife gave her seven heads of lint, saying she would take no excuse; they must be returned in three days spun into yarn. The girl saw her mother was in earnest, so she plied her distaff as well as she could; but her little hands were all untaught, and by the evening of the second day a very small part of her task was accomplished. She cried herself to sleep that night, and in the morning, throwing aside her work in despair, she strolled out into the fields, all sparkling with dew. At last she reached a flowery knoll, at whose foot ran a little burn, shaded with woodbine and wild roses; and there she sat down, burying her face in her hands. When

[1] From the Wilkie MS.

she looked up, she was surprised to see by the margin of the stream an old woman, quite unknown to her, " drawing out the thread " as she basked in the sun. There was nothing very remarkable in her appearance, except the length and thickness of her lips, only she was seated on a self-bored stone. The girl rose, went to the good dame, and gave her a friendly greeting, but could not help inquiring what made her so " long lippit." " Spinning thread, ma hinnie," said the old woman, pleased with her friendliness, and by no means resenting the personal remark. It must be noticed that spinners used constantly to wet their fingers with their lips, as they drew the thread from the rock or distaff. " Ah! " said the girl, " I should be spinning too, but it's a' to no purpose, I sall ne'er do my task;" on which the old woman proposed to do it for her. Overjoyed, the maiden ran to fetch her lint, and placed it in her new friend's hand, asking her name, and where she should call for the yarn in the evening; but she received no reply; the old woman's form passed away from her among the trees and bushes, and disappeared. The girl, much bewildered, wandered about a little, sat down to rest, and finally fell asleep by the little knoll.

When she awoke she was surprised to find that it was evening. The glories of the western sky were passing into twilight grey. Causleen, the evening star, was beaming with silvery light, soon to be lost in the moon's increasing splendour. While watching these changes, the maiden was startled by the sound of an uncouth voice, which seemed to issue from below a self-bored stone, close beside her. She laid her ear to the stone, and distinctly heard these words: "Little kens the wee lassie on yon brae-head that ma name's Habitrot." Then, looking down the hole, she saw her friend, the old dame, walking backwards and forwards in a deep cavern among a group of spinsters all seated on colludie stones (a kind of white pebble found in rivers), and busy with distaff and spindle. An unsightly company they were, with lips more or less disfigured by their employment, as were old Habitrot's. The same peculiarity extended to another of the sisterhood, who sat in a distant corner reeling the yarn; and she was marked, in addition, by grey eyes, which seemed staring from her head, and a long hooked nose.

As she reeled, she counted thus, " Ae cribbie, twa cribbie, haith cribbie thou's ane; ae cribbie, twa cribbie, haith cribbie thou's twa," and so on. After this manner she continued till she had counted a cut, hank slip,—a cribbie being once round the reel, or a measure of about three feet, the reel being about eighteen inches long.

While the girl was still watching, she heard Habitrot address this singular being by the name of Scantlie Mab, and tell her to bundle up the yarn, for it was time the young lassie should give it to her mother. Delighted to hear this, our listener got up and turned homewards, nor was she long kept in suspense. Habitrot soon overtook her, and placed the yarn in her hands. " Oh, what can I do for ye in return?" exclaimed she, in delight. " Naething—naething," replied the dame; " but dinna tell yer mither whae spun the yarn."

Scarcely crediting her good fortune, our heroine went home, where she found her mother had been busy making sausters, or black puddings, and hanging them up in the lum to dry, and then, tired out, had retired to rest. Finding herself very hungry after her long day on the knoll, the girl took down pudding after pudding, fried and ate them, and at last went to bed too. The mother was up first the next morning, and when she came into the kitchen and found her sausters all gone, and the seven hanks of yarn lying beautifully smooth and bright upon the table, her mingled feelings of vexation and delight were too much for her. She ran out of the house wildly, crying out—

> " Ma daughter's spun se'en, se'en, se'en,
> Ma daughter's eaten se'en, se'en, se'en,
> And all before daylight!"

A laird, who chanced to be riding by, heard the exclamation, but could not understand it; so he rode up and asked the gudewife what was the matter, on which she broke out again—

> " Ma daughter's spun se'en, se'en, se'en,
> Ma daughter's eaten se'en, se'en, se'en

before daylight; and if ye dinna believe me, why come in and see it." The laird's curiosity was aroused; he alighted and went into the cottage, where he saw the yarn, and admired it so much, he begged to see the spinner.

The mother dragged in the blushing girl. Her rustic grace soon won his heart, and he avowed he was lonely without a wife, and had long been in search of one who was a good spinner. So their troth was plighted, and the wedding took place soon afterwards, the bride stifling her apprehensions that she should not prove so deft at her spinning-wheel as her lover expected. And once more old Habitrot came to her aid. Whether the good dame, herself so notable, was as indulgent to all idle damsels does not appear —certainly she did not fail this little pet of hers. " Bring your bonny bridegroom to my cell," said she to the young bride soon after her marriage; " he shall see what comes o' spinning, and never will he tie you to the spinning-wheel."

Accordingly the bride led her husband the next day to the flowery knoll, and bade him look through the self-bored stone. Great was his surprise to behold Habitrot dancing and jumping over her rock,[1] singing all the time this ditty to her sisterhood, while they kept time with their spindles :—

> " We who live in dreary den
>   Are both rank and foul to see,
> Hidden frae the glorious sun
>   That teems the fair earth's canopie :
> Ever must our evenings lone
> Be spent on the colludie stone.
>
> Cheerless in the evening grey
>   When Causleen hath died away,

[1] Spinning-wheel.

But ever bright and ever fair
   Are they who breathe this evening air;
And lean upon the self-bored stone
Unseen by all but me alone."

The song ended, Scantlie Mab asked Habitrot what she meant by her last line, " Unseen by all but me alone." " There is ane," replied Habitrot, " whom I bid to come here at this hour, and he has heard my song through the self-bored stone." So saying she rose, opened another door, which was concealed by the roots of an old tree, and invited the bridal pair to come in and see her family.

The laird was astonished at the weird-looking com-pany, as he well might be, and enquired of one after another the cause of the strange distortion of their lips. In a different tone of voice, and with a differ-ent twist of the mouth, each answered that it was oc-casioned by spinning. At least they tried to say so, but one grunted out, " Nakasind," and another " Owkasaänd," while a third murmured " O-a-a-send." All, however, conveyed the fact to the bride-groom's understanding; while Habitrot slyly hinted that if his wife were allowed to spin, her pretty lips would grow out of shape too, and her pretty face get an ugsome look. So before he left the cave he pro-tested his little wife should never touch a spinning-wheel, and he kept his word. She used to wander in the meadows by his side, or ride behind him over the hills, and all the flax grown on his land was sent to old Habitrot to be converted into yarn.

THE TULMAN.[1]

THERE was a woman in Baile Thangusdail, and she was out seeking a couple of calves; and the night and lateness caught her, and there came rain and tempest, and she was seeking shelter. She went to a knoll with the couple of calves, and she was striking a tether-peg into it. The knoll opened. She heard a gleegashing as if a pot-hook were clashing beside a pot. She took wonder, and she stopped striking the tether-pig. A woman put out her head and all above her middle, and she said, " What business hast thou to be troubling this tulman in which I make my dwelling?" "I am taking care of this couple of calves, and I am but weak. Where shall I go with them?" "Thou shalt go with them to that breast down yonder. Thou wilt see a tuft of grass. If thy couple of calves eat that tuft of grass, thou wilt not be a day without a milk cow as long as thou art alive, because thou hast taken my counsel."

As she said, she never was without a milk cow after that, and she was alive fourscore and fifteen years after the night that was there.

THE ISLE OF PABAIDH.[1]

THERE came a woman of peace (a fairy) the way of the house of a man in the island of Pabaidh, and

[1] Campbell, *Popular Tales of the West Highlands.*

she had the hunger of motherhood on her. He gave her food, and that went well with her. She stayed that night. When she went away she said to him, " I am making a desire that none of the people of this island may go in childbed after this." None of these people, and none others that would make their dwelling in the island, ever departed in childbed from that time.

SANNTRAIGH.[1]

THERE was a herd's wife in the island of Sanntraigh, and she had a kettle. A woman of peace would come every day to seek the kettle. She would not say a word when she came, but she would catch hold of the kettle. When she would catch the kettle, the woman of the house would say—

> " A smith is able to make
>   Cold iron hot with coal.
>   The due of a kettle is bones,
>   And to bring it back again whole."

The woman of peace would come back every day with the kettle, and flesh and bones in it. On a day that was there, the housewife was for going over the ferry to Baile a Chaisteil, and she said to her man, " If thou wilt say to the woman of peace as I say, I will go to Baile Castle." " Oo! I will say it. Surely it's I that will say it." He was spinning a heather rope to

[1] The same.

be set on the house. He saw a woman coming and a
shadow from her feet, and he took fear of her. He
shut the door. He stopped his work. When she
came to the door she did not find the door open, and
he did not open it for her. She went above a hole
that was in the house. The kettle gave two jumps,
and at the third leap it went out at the ridge of the
house. The night came, and the kettle came not.
The wife came back over the ferry, and she did not
see a bit of the kettle within, and she asked, " Where
was the kettle ? " " Well, then, I don't care where it
is," said the man ; " I never took such a fright as I
took at it. I shut the door, and she did not come any
more with it." " Good-for-nothing wretch, what
didst thou do ? There are two that will be ill off—
thyself and I." " She will come to-morrow with it."
" She will not come."

She hasted herself and she went away. She
reached the knoll, and there was no man within. It
was after dinner, and they were out in the mouth of
the night. She went in. She saw the kettle, and
she lifted it with her. It was heavy for her with the
remnants that they left in it. When the old carle
that was within saw her going out, he said—

> " Silent wife, silent wife,
>   That came on us from the land of chase,
>   Thou man on the surface of the ' Bruth,'
>   Loose the black, and slip the Fierce."

The two dogs were let loose ; and she was not long
away when she heard the clatter of the dogs coming.

She kept the remnant that was in the kettle, so that
if she could get it with her, well, and if the dogs
should come that she might throw it at them. She
perceived the dogs coming. She put her hand in the
kettle. She took the board out of it, and she threw
at them a quarter of what was in it. They noticed it
there for a while. She perceived them again, and she
threw another piece at them when they closed upon
her. She went away walking as well as she might;
when she came near the farm, she threw the mouth
of the pot downwards, and there she left them all that
was in it. The dogs of the town struck up a barking
when they saw the dogs of peace stopping. The woman of peace never came more to seek the kettle.

WATER FAIRIES.[1]

THE Dracæ are a sort of water-spirits who inveigle
women and children into the recesses which they inhabit, beneath lakes and rivers, by floating past them,
on the surface of the water, in the shape of gold rings
or cups. The women thus seized are employed as
nurses, and after seven years are permitted to revisit
earth. Gervase of Tilbury mentions one woman in
particular who had been allured by observing a
wooden dish, or cup, float by her, while she was washing clothes in the river. Being seized as soon as she
reached the depths, she was conducted into one of the
subterranean recesses, which she described as very

[1] Sir Walter Scott, *Minstrelsy of the Scottish Border.*

magnificent, and employed as nurse to one of the
brood of the hag who had allured her. During her residence in this capacity, having accidentally touched
one of her eyes with an ointment of serpent's grease,
she perceived, at her return to the world, that she had
acquired the faculty of seeing the *Dracæ*, when they
intermingle themselves with men. Of this power
she was, however, deprived by the touch of her
ghostly mistress, whom she had one day incautiously
addressed. It is a curious fact that this story, in
almost all its parts, is current in both the Highlands
and Lowlands of Scotland, with no other variation
than the substitution of Fairies for Dracæ, and the
cavern of a hill for that of a river. Indeed many of
the vulgar account it extremely dangerous to touch
anything which they may happen to find without
saining (blessing) it, the snares of the enemy being
notorious and well-attested. A poor woman of Te-
viotdale having been fortunate enough, as she thought
herself, to find a wooden beetle, at the very time
when she needed such an implement, seized it without
pronouncing a proper blessing, and, carrying it home,
laid it above her bed to be ready for employment in
the morning. At midnight the window of her cottage
opened, and a loud voice was heard calling up some
one within by a strange and uncouth name. The ter-
refied cottager ejaculated a prayer, which, we may
suppose, ensured her personal safety; while the enchanted implement of housewifery, tumbling from
the bedstead, departed by the window with no small
noise and precipitation,

FAIRY TRANSPORTATION.[1]

THE power of the fairies was not confined to un-christened children alone; it was supposed frequently to be extended to full-grown persons, especially such as in an unlucky hour were devoted to the devil by the execration of parents and of masters; or those who were found asleep under a rock, or on a green hill, belonging to the fairies, after sunset, or, finally, to those who unwarily joined their orgies. A tradition existed, during the seventeenth century, concerning an ancestor of the noble family of Duffus, who, " walking abroad in the fields, near to his own house, was suddenly carried away, and found the next day at Paris, in the French king's cellar, with a silver cup in his hand. Being brought into the king's presence, and questioned by him who he was, and how he came thither, he told his name, his country, and the place of his residence! and that on such a day of the month, which proved to be the day immediately preceding, being in the fields, he heard the noise of a whirlwind, and of voices, crying '*Horse and Hattock!*' (this is the word which the fairies are said to use when they remove from any place), whereupon he cried '*Horse and Hattock*' also, and was immediately caught up and transported through the air by the fairies, to that place, where, after he had drunk heartily, he fell asleep, and before he woke, the rest of the company were gone, and had left

[1] Sir Walter Scott, *Minstrelsy of the Scottish Border.*

him in the posture wherein he was found. It is said the king gave him the cup which was found in his hand, and dismissed him." The narrator affirms " that the cup was still preserved, and known by the name of the *Fairy Cup*." He adds that Mr. Steward, tutor to the then Lord Duffus, had informed him that, " when a boy at the school of Forres, he and his school-fellows were upon a time whipping their tops in the churchyard, before the door of the church, when, though the day was calm, they heard a noise of a wind, and at some distance saw the small dust begin to rise and turn round, which motion continued advancing till it came to the place where they were, whereupon they began to bless themselves ; but one of their number being, it seems, a little more bold and confident than his companions, said, ' *Horse and Hattock with my top,*' and immediately they all saw the top lifted up from the ground, but could not see which way it was carried, by reason of a cloud of dust which was raised at the same time. They sought for the top all about the place where it was taken up, but in vain ; and it was found afterwards in the churchyard, on the other side of the church."

THE POOR MAN OF PEATLAW.[1]

THE following is an account of a fairy frolic said to have happened late in the last century :—The victim of elfin sport was a poor man, who, being em-

[1] Sir Walter Scott, *Minstrelsy of the Scottish Border.*

ployed in pulling heather upon Peatlaw, a hill in
Selkirkshire, had tired of his labour, and laid
him down to sleep upon a fairy ring. When he awakened, he was amazed to find himself in the midst of
a populous city, to which, as well as to the means
of his transportation, he was an utter stranger. His
coat was left upon the Peatlaw; and his bonnet,
which had fallen off in the course of his aërial journey, was afterwards found hanging upon the steeple
of the church of Lanark. The distress of the poor
man was, in some degree, relieved by meeting a car-
rier, whom he had formerly known, and who conducted him back to Selkirk, by a slower conveyance
than had whirled him to Glasgow. That he had been
carried off by the fairies was implicitly believed by
all who did not reflect that a man may have private
reasons for leaving his own country, and for dis-
guising his having intentionally done so.

THE FAIRY BOY OF ·LEITH.[1]

THE worthy Captain George Burton communi-
cated to Richard Bovet, gentleman, author of the interesting work entitled *Pandæmonium, or the Devil's
Cloister Opened*,[2] the following singular account of
a lad called the Fairy Boy of Leith, who, it seems,
acted as a drummer to the elves, who weekly held
rendezvous in the Calton Hill, near Edinburgh.

[1] The same.   [2] London, 1684.

" About fifteen years since, having business that detained me for some time at Leith, which is near Edinburgh, in the kingdom of Scotland, I often met some of my acquaintance at a certain house there, where we used to drink a glass of wine for our refection ; the woman which kept the house was of honest reputation among the neighbours, which made me give the more attention to what she told me one day about a fairy boy (as they called him), who lived about that town. She had given me so strange an account of him that I desired her I might see him the first opportunity, which she promised ; and not long after, passing that way, she told me there was the fairy boy but a little before I came by ; and, casting her eye into the street, said, Look you, sir, yonder he is at play with those other boys ; and, designing him to me, I went, and, by smooth words, and a piece of money, got him to come into the house with me ; where, in the presence of divers people, I demanded of him several astrological questions, which he answered with great subtilty ; and, through all his discourse, carried it with a cunning much above his years, which seemed not to exceed ten or eleven.

" He seemed to make a motion like drumming upon the table with his fingers, upon which I asked him whether he could beat a drum ? To which he replied, Yes, sir, as well as any man in Scotland ; for every Thursday night I beat all points to a sort of people that used to meet under yonder hill (pointing to the great hill between Edenborough and Leith.) How, boy ? quoth I, what company have you there ?

9

There are, sir, said he, a great company both of men and women, and they are entertained with many sorts of musick, besides my drum; they have, besides, plenty of variety of meats and wine, and many times we are carried into France or Holland in a night, and return again, and whilst we are there we enjoy all the pleasures the country doth afford. I demanded of him how they got under that hill? To which he replied that there was a great pair of gates that opened to them, though they were invisible to others; and that within there were brave large rooms, as well accommodated as most in Scotland. I then asked him how I should know what he said to be true? Upon which he told me he would read my fortune, saying I should have two wives, and that he saw the forms of them sitting on my shoulders; that both would be very handsome women. As he was thus speaking, a woman of the neighbourhood, coming into the room, demanded of him what her fortune should be? He told her that she had two bastards before she was married, which put her in such a rage that she desired not to hear the rest.

" The woman of the house told me that all the people in Scotland could not keep him from the rendezvous on Thursday night; upon which, by promising him some more money, I got a promise of him to meet me at the same place, in the afternoon, the Thursday following, and so dismist him at that time. The boy came again, at the place and time appointed, and I had prevailed with some friends to continue with me, if possible, to prevent his moving that night.

He was placed between us, and answered many questions, until, about eleven of the clock, he was got away unperceived by the company; but I, suddenly missing him, hasted to the door, and took hold of him, and so returned him into the same room; we all watched him, and, of a sudden, he was again got out of doors; I followed him close, and he made a noise in the street as if he had been set upon; but from that time I could never see him.

" George Burton."

" MIND THE CROOKED FINGER."[1]

Bill Robertson, æt. 71, residing in Lerwick, soberly narrated this trowy story:—

" My midder, God rest her soul, tauld me this, and she nedder could nor wid ha' tauld me a lee. Shü wis staying wi' freends at Kirgood-a-Weisdale; an' ee nicht about da hüming (twilight) da guidman was sair fashed, for da honest wife haed just haed a pirie baby. An' noo, my lamb 'at ye ir (are), what sud he hear juist as he was gaein' ta leave the lamb-house, but three most unearthly knocks, da sam as it haed a been frae onder da grund. Noo, he kent na what dis could be, but he made a' fast, an' gangs up intil de corn yard, and as he comes in sight of the screws he hears a voice 'at said tree times, ' Mind da crooked finger.' Noo, his wife haed a crooked finger, and he

[1] Mr. J. G. Ollason's MS.

kent ower weel 'at something wis gaen ta happen, for his *grey neebors* wis apon da watch for da helpless infant, or midder, or baith. So he comes into da hoose, an' lichts a candle, taks doon da Bible, an' a steel knife. He opens da buik an' da knife, when such a roaring and *trüling,* an' onerthly stamping an' rattling, an' confusion comes frae da byre as made da whole hoose shak. An' a' body tell a-whaaking (quaking). Noo, he taks da open Bible, and maks for da byre, an' dem 'at wis i' da hoos follows him trimbling an' whaaking, only da wise-woman bein' left with da poor wife an' infant. Noo, whin he gets ta da door, he heaves in de Bible afore him, sticks da open knife in his mouth, edge ootwards, and da lowin' candle in een o' his hands. Da instant yon was dune da trülin' an' noise an' din ceased all of a sudden, and da image 'at haed been prepared for ta pit i' da place i' da poor wife an' innocent pirie lamb was a' 'at was left i' da byre. 'Weel,' says da guidman, as he gripped in his airms da very likeness o' his wife 'at da trows had left i' da byre, ' I've taen dee, and I'll use dee.' Weel, he tuk in ta da hoose da image left by da trows, an' it haed every joint an' pairt of a woman. An' my midder tauld me shü saw it, an' da honest folk for mony a year, an' der children after dem, sat upon da stock, or image, or likeness; an' things was set on it, and wood was sawn on it. An' dat's as true as I'm spekin' to you, and no a borrowed or handed story; for my midder tauld me it wi' her ain lips, an' she wid no a tauld me a lee."

THE TWO YOUNG PLOUGHMEN.[1]

"You have been often at the Gatehouse," said Johnny Nicholson; "well, you'll mind a flat piece of land near Enrick farm; well, that was once a large loch; a long way down from there is still the ruin of a mill, which at that time was fed from this loch. Well, one night about the Hallowe'en times, two young ploughmen went to a smiddy to get their socks (of their ploughs) and colters repaired, and in passing the said mill on their way home again they heard music and dancing, and fiddling, and singing, and laughing, and talking; so one of the lads would be in to see what was going on; the other waited outside for hours, but his companion never came out again, so he went home, assured that the brownies had got hold of him. About the same time the following year, the same lad went again to the smiddy on the same errand, and this time he took another lad with him, but had the precaution to put the Bible in his pocket. Well, in passing the mill the second time, he heard the same sounds of music and dancing. This time, having the Bible in his hand, he ventured to look in, when who should he see but his companion whom he had left standing there that day twelvemonths. He handed him the Bible, and the moment he did so the music and dancing ceased, the lights went out, and all was darkness."

[1] Campbell, *Popular Tales of the West Highlands.*

THE SMITH AND THE FAIRIES.[1]

YEARS ago there lived in Crossbrig a smith of the name of MacEachern. This man had an only child, a boy of about thirteen or fourteen years of age, cheerful, strong, and healthy. All of a sudden he fell ill, took to his bed, and moped whole days away. No one could tell what was the matter with him, and the boy himself could not, or would not, tell how he felt. He was wasting away fast; getting thin, old, and yellow; and his father and all his friends were afraid that he would die.

At last one day, after the boy had been lying in this condition for a long time, getting neither better nor worse, always confined to bed, but with an extraordinary appetite,—one day, while sadly revolving these things, and standing idly at his forge, with no heart to work, the smith was agreeably surprised to see an old man, well known to him for his sagacity and knowledge of out-of-the-way things, walk into his workshop. Forthwith he told him the occurrence which had clouded his life.

The old man looked grave as he listened; and after sitting a long time pondering over all he had heard, gave his opinion thus—" It is not your son you have got. The boy has been carried away by the ' Daoine Sith,' and they have left a *Sibhreach* in his place." " Alas! and what then am I to do?" said the smith. " How am I ever to see my own son again?" " I

[1] Campbell, *Popular Tales of the West Highlands.*

will tell you how," answered the old man. " But, first, to make sure that it is not your own son you have got, take as many empty egg-shells as you can get, go with them into the room, spread them out carefully before his sight, then proceed to draw water with them, carrying them two and two in your hands as if they were a great weight, and arrange when full, with every sort of earnestness, round the fire." The smith accordingly gathered as many broken egg-shells as he could get, went into the room, and proceeded to carry out all his instructions.

He had not been long at work before there arose from the bed a shout of laughter, and the voice of the seeming sick boy exclaimed, " I am now 800 years of age, and I have never seen the like of that before."

The smith returned and told the old man. " Well, now," said the sage to him, " did I not tell you that it was not your son you had: your son is in Brorra-cheill in a digh there (that is, a round green hill frequented by fairies). Get rid as soon as possible of this intruder, and I think I may promise you your son.

" You must light a very large and bright fire before the bed on which this stranger is lying. He will ask you, ' What is the use of such a fire as that?' Answer him at once, ' You will see that presently!' and then seize him, and throw him into the middle of it. If it is your own son you have got, he will call out to save him; but if not, this thing will fly through the roof."

The smith again followed the old man's advice;

kindled a large fire, answered the question put to him as he had been directed to do, and seizing the child flung him in without hesitation. The " Sibh-reach " gave an awful yell, and sprung through the roof, where a hole was left to let the smoke out.

On a certain night the old man told him the green round hill, where the fairies kept the boy, would be open. And on that night the smith, having provided himself with a Bible, a dirk, and a crowing cock, was to proceed to the hill. He would hear singing and dancing and much merriment going on, but he was to advance boldly; the Bible he carried would be a certain safeguard to him against any danger from the fairies. On entering the hill he was to stick the dirk in the threshold, to prevent the hill from closing upon him; " and then," continued the old man, " on entering you will see a spacious apartment before you, beautifully clean, and there, standing far within, working at a forge, you will also see your own son. When you are questioned, say you come to seek him, and will not go without him."

Not long after this the time came round, and the smith sallied forth, prepared as instructed. Sure enough, as he approached the hill, there was a light where light was seldom seen before. Soon after a sound of piping, dancing, and joyous merriment reached the anxious father on the night wind.

Overcoming every impulse to fear, the smith ap-proached the threshold steadily, stuck the dirk into it as directed, and entered. Protected by the Bible he carried on his breast, the fairies could not touch him; but they asked him, with a good deal of displeasure, what he wanted there. He answered, " I want my son, whom I see down there, and I will not go without him."

Upon hearing this the whole company before him gave a loud laugh, which wakened up the cock he carried dozing in his arms, who at once leaped up on his shoulders, clapped his wings lustily, and crowed loud and long.

The fairies, incensed, seized the smith and his son, and, throwing them out of the hill, flung the dirk after them, and in an instant all was dark.

For a year and a day the boy never did a turn of work, and hardly ever spoke a word; but at last one day, sitting by his father and watching him finishing a sword he was making for some chief, and which he was very particular about, he suddenly exclaimed, " That is not the way to do it; " and, taking the tools from his father's hands, he set to work himself in his place, and soon fashioned a sword the like of which was never seen in the country before.

From that day the young man wrought constantly with his father, and became the inventor of a peculiarly fine and well-tempered weapon, the making of which kept the two smiths, father and son, in constant employment, spread their fame far and wide, and gave them the means in abundance, as they before had the disposition, to live content with all the world and very happily with one another.

THE LOTHIAN FARMER'S WIFE.[1]

THE wife of a farmer in Lothian had been carried off by the fairies, and, during the year of probation, repeatedly appeared on Sunday, in the midst of her children, combing their hair. On one of these occasions she was accosted by her husband; when she related to him the unfortunate event which had separated them, instructed him by what means he might *win* her, and exhorted him to exert all his courage, since her temporal and eternal happiness depended on the success of his attempt. The farmer, who ardently loved his wife, set out on Hallowe'en, and, in the midst of a plot of furze, waited impatiently for the procession of the fairies. At the ringing of the fairy bridles, and the wild, unearthly sound which accompanied the cavalcade, his heart failed him, and he suffered the ghostly train to pass by without interruption. When the last had rode past, the whole troop vanished, with loud shouts of laughter and exultation; among which he plainly discovered the voice of his wife, lamenting that he had lost her for ever.

REDEMPTION FROM FAIRY LAND.[2]

NEAR the town of Aberdeen, in Scotland, lived James Campbell, who had one daughter, named

[1] Sir Walter Scott, *Minstrelsy of the Scottish Border.*
[2] Sir Walter Scott, *ibid.*, " from a broadside still popular in Ireland."

Mary, who was married to John Nelson, a young man of that neighbourhood. Shortly after their marriage, they being a young couple, they went to live in the town of Aberdeen, where he followed his trade, being a goldsmith; they lived loving and agreeable together until the time of her lying-in, when there was female attendants prepared suitable to her situation; when near the hour of twelve at night they were alarmed with a dreadful noise, at which of a sudden the candles went out, which drove the attendants in the utmost confusion; soon as the women regained their half-lost senses, they called in their neighbours who, after striking up lights, and looking towards the lying-in woman, found her a corpse, which caused great confusion in the family. There was no grief could exceed that of her husband, who, next morning, prepared ornaments for her funeral; people of all sects came to her wake, amongst others came the Rev. Mr. Dodd, who, at first sight of the corpse, said, "It's not the body of any Christian, but that Mrs. Nelson was taken away by the fairies, and what they took for her was only some substance left in her place." He was not believed, so he refused attending her funeral; they kept her in the following night, and the next day she was interred.

Her husband, one evening after sunset, being riding in his own field, heard a most pleasant concert of music, and soon after espied a woman coming towards him dressed in white; she being veiled, he could not observe her face, yet he rode near her, and asked very friendly who she was that chose to walk alone so late in the evening? at which she unveiled her face, and burst into tears, saying, I am not permitted to tell you who I am. He knowing her to be his wife, asked her in the name of God, what disturbed her, or what occasioned her to appear at that hour? She said her appearing at any hour was of no consequence; for though you believe me to be dead and buried, I am not, but was taken away by the fairies the night of my delivery; you only buried a piece of wood in my place; I can be recovered if you take proper means; as for my child, it has three nurses to attend it, but I fear it cannot be brought home; the greatest dependence I have on any person is my brother Robert, who is a captain of a merchant ship, and will be home in ten days hence. Her husband asked her what means he should take to win her? She told him he should find a letter the Sunday morning following, on the desk in his own room, directed to her brother, wherein there would be directions for winning her. Since my being taken from you I have had the attendance of a queen or empress, and if you look over my right shoulder you will see several of my companions; he then did as she desired, when, at a small distance, he saw a king and queen sitting, beside a moat,[1] on a throne, in splendour.

She then desired him to look right and left, which he did, and observed other kings on each side of the king and queen, well guarded. He said, I fear it is an impossibility to win you from such a place. No,

---

[1] A rising ground, a knoll.

says she, were my brother Robert here in your place, he would bring me home; but let it not encourage you to attempt the like, for that would occasion the loss of me for ever; there is now severe punishment threatened to me for speaking to you; but, to prevent that, do you ride up to the moat, where (suppose you will see no person) all you now see will be near you, and do you threaten to burn all the old thorns and brambles that is round the moat, if you do not get a firm promise that I shall get no punishment; I shall be forgiven; which he promised. She then disappeared, and he lost sight of all he had seen; he then rode very resolutely up to the moat, and went round it, vowing he would burn all about it if he would not get a promise that his wife should get no hurt. A voice desired him to cast away a book that was in his pocket, and then demand his request; he answered he would not part with his book, but grant his request, or they should find the effect of his rage. The voice answered, that upon honour she should be forgave her fault, but for him to suffer no prejudice to come to the moat, which he promised to fulfil, at which he heard most pleasant music. He then returned home, and sent for the Rev. Mr. Dodd, and related to him what he had seen; Mr. Dodd stayed with him till Sunday morning following, when as Mr. Nelson looked on the desk in his room, he espied a letter, which he took up, it being directed to her brother, who in a few days came home; on his receiving the letter he opened it, wherein he found the following :—

"Dear Brother,—My husband can relate to you
my present circumstances. I request that you will
(the first night after you see this) come to the moat
where I parted from my husband: let nothing daunt
you, but stand in the centre of the moat at the hour
of twelve at night, and call me, when I, with several
others, will surround you; I shall have on the whitest
dress of any in company; then take hold of me, and
do not forsake me; all the frightful methods they
shall use let it not surprise you, but keep your hold,
suppose they continue till cock crow, when they shall
vanish all of a sudden, and I shall be safe, when I
will return home and live with my husband. If you
succeed in your attempt, you will gain applause from
all your friends, and have the blessing of your ever-
loving and affectionate sister,

"Mary Nelson."

No sooner had he read the letter than he vowed to
win his sister and her child, or perish in the attempt;
he returned to the ship, and related to his sailors the
contents of the letter; he delayed till ten at night,
when his loyal sailors offered to go with him, which
he refused, thinking it best to go alone. As he left his
ship a frightful lion came roaring towards him; he
drew his sword and struck at the lion, which he observed was of no substance, it being only the appearance of one, to terrify him in his attempt; it only
encouraged him, so that he proceeded to the moat, in
the centre of which he observed a white handkerchief

spread; on which he was surrounded with a number
of women, the cries of whom were the most frightful
he ever heard; his sister being in the whitest dress of
any round him, he seized her by the right hand, and
said, With the help of God, I will preserve you from
all infernal imps: when of a sudden, the moat seemed
to be on fire around him. He likewise heard the
most dreadful thunder could be imagined; frightful
birds and beasts seemed to make towards him out of
the fire, which he knew was not real; nothing daunted
his courage; he kept hold of his sister for the space
of an hour and three-quarters, when the cocks began
to crow; then the fire disappeared, and all the frightful imps vanished. He held her in his arms, and fell
on his knees, and gave God thanks for his proceedings
that night: he believing her clothing to be light, put
his outside coat on her; she then embraced him, saying she was now safe, as he put any of his clothing
on her; he then brought her home to her husband,
which occasioned great rejoicing. Her husband and
he began to conclude to destroy the moat in revenge
of the child they had away, when instantly they heard
a voice, which said, you shall have your son safe, and
well, on condition that you will not till the ground
within three perches of the moat, nor damage bushes
or brambles round that place, which they agreed to,
when, in a few minutes, the child was left on his
mother's knee, which caused them to kneel and return
thanks to God.

The circumstance of this terrifying affair was occasioned by leaving Mrs. Nelson, the night of her

lying-in, in the care of women who were mostly in-toxicated with liquor!

THE FAIRY AND THE BIBLE-READER.[1]

On a still Sabbath evening in summer, an old man was seated, reading his Bible in the open air, at a quiet spot upon the Ross-shire coast. A beautiful lit-tle lady, clad in green, drew near, and addressing him in a silvery voice, sought to know if for such as she Holy Scripture held out any hope of salvation. The old man spoke kindly to her; but said that in those pages there was no mention of salvation for any but the sinful sons of Adam. On hearing this, the fairy flung her arms despairingly above her head, and with a shriek plunged into the sea.

THOM AND WILLIE.[2]

Thom and Willie, two young fisher-mates of Lunna, in Shetland, were rivals for the hand of the fair Osla, daughter of Jarm. Now it so happened that, one October afternoon, they took their hand-lines and went out fishing together in their boat.

[1] Campbell, *Popular Tales of the West Highlands.*
[2] Arranged from Mr. J. G. Ollason's MS.

Towards dusk the wind rose, and it soon blew so hard as to compel the young men to run for the nearest shelter—a haven in the islet of Linga in Whalsay Sound, which they happily reached in safety. The islet was uninhabited, and the fishermen had with them neither food nor the means of kindling a fire. They had, however, a roof over their heads; for there was a hut, or lodge, on the island, used by fishermen in the fair weather season, but deserted since the close of that period. For two days the storm raged without ceasing, and at last the situation of the castaways began to grow very serious. However, on the morning of the third day, a little before daybreak, Willie, who was awake before his companion, discovered that the weather had faired, and that the wind blew in a favouring direction. Upon this, without rousing Thom, he proceeded to the boat, which lay safely hauled up upon the shore, and by dint of great exertion managed to launch her singlehanded. Meantime Thom had awoke; and, at last, as Willie did not come back, he followed him to the noust, or place where boats are drawn up. And here a sight met his view which filled him with dismay. The yawl had disappeared from her place; but, raising his eyes, he beheld her already far out at sea and speeding before the breeze in the direction of Lunna. At this sight poor Thom gave way to despair. He realised that his comrade had basely and heartlessly deserted him; he knew that it was not likely that the islet would be visited until the fishing-season should have come round again; and he had small hopes of

10

help from any exertions on his behalf which might be
made by his friends, seeing that they would be in ignorance where to look for him. Amid melancholy
thoughts and forebodings the day passed slowly, and
at nightfall he betook himself to his shake-down of
straw within the lodge. Darkness closed in, and he
slept. But, towards the small hours of the morning,
he was suddenly awakened; when great was his astonishment to see that the hut was lighted up with a
strange illumination, whilst a queer inhuman hum
and chatter, accompanied by the patter of many pairs
of little feet and the jingle of gold and silver vessels,
smote upon his ear. A fairy banquet was, in fact,
in course of preparation in the lodge. Thom raised
himself noiselessly upon his elbow,· and watched the
proceedings. With infinite bustle and clatter, the
table was at last laid. Then there entered a party
of trows, who bore between them in a chair, or litter,
a female fairy, to whom all appeared to pay honour.
The company took seats, and the banquet was on the
point of commencing, when in a moment the scene of
festivity was changed to one of wild alarm and confusion. A moment more, and Thom learnt to his
cost the cause of the sudden change. The presence
of a human being had been detected, and at a word
from their queen the " grey people," swarming together, were about to rush upon the intruder. But in
this trying juncture Thom did not lose his presence
of mind. His loaded fowling-piece lay by his side,
and, as the fairies rushed upon him, he raised it to
his shoulder and fired. In an instant the light was

extinguished, and all was darkness, silence, and solitude.

Let us now return to the perfidious Willie. Reaching Lunna in safety, he related a tragic tale (which he had invented on the voyage), to account for the absence of his comrade; and, finding that his story was believed, he began anew, without much loss of time, to urge his suit with the fair Osla. Her father, Jarm, regarded him with favour; but the maiden herself turned a deaf ear to all his entreaties. She felt that she could not love him; and, besides, she was haunted by a suspicion that Thom, in whose welfare she felt a tender interest, had been the victim of foul play. Pressure was, however, put upon her, and in spite of her objections, an early day was fixed for the wedding. The poor girl was in great distress. However, one night, when she had cried herself to sleep, she dreamed a dream, the result of which was that next morning she proceeded to the house of Thom's parents, and begged them to join her in a search for their missing son. This, notwithstanding their love for him, they were somewhat reluctant to do; arguing that, even supposing him to have been abandoned, as she divined, upon one of the rocky islets of the coast, he must ere now have perished from exposure and starvation. But the girl persisted in her entreaties, which at last prevailed. A boat was manned, and by Osla's direction was steered towards Linga, upon approaching which, sure enough, as the girl had predicted, it was discovered that the islet had a human tenant. Thom met his friends on the beach, and when the first eager greetings had passed, surprise was expressed at the freshness and robustness of his appearance. But this surprise increased tenfold when, in recounting his adventures, he explained that, during the latter days of his isolation, he had supported life upon the remains of the scarcely-tasted fairy banquet, adding that never in his life before had he fared so delicately. On their return to Lunna, the party were received with rejoicings; and it is scarcely necessary to add that Thom and Osla were soon made man and wife. From that time forward Willie prospered no more. The loss of his health and fortune followed that of his good name, and he sank ere long into an early and unregretted grave.

THE GLOAMING BUCHT.[1]

" SPEAKIN ' o' fairies," quoth Robbie Oliver (an old shepherd, who lived at Southdean in Jedwater, and died about 1830), " I can tell ye about the vera last fairy that was seen hereaway. When my faither, Peter Oliver, was a young man, he lived at Hyndlee, an' herdit the Brocklaw. Weel, it was the custom to milk the yowes in thae days, an' my faither was buchtin'[2] the Brocklaw yowes to twae young, lish, clever hizzies ae nicht i' the gloamin'. Nae little daffin'

---

[1] *Old Friends with Newe Faces.* Field & Tuer.
[2] Folding.

an' gabbin'[1] gaed on amang the threesome, I'se warrant ye, till at last, just as it chanced to get darkish, my faither chancit to luik alang the lea at the head o' the bucht, an' what did he see but a wee little creaturie a' clad i' green, an' wi' lang hair, yellow as gowd, hingin' round its shoulders, comin' straight for him, whiles gi'en a whink o' a greet,[2] an' aye atween its hands raisin' a queer, unyirthly cry, ' Hae ye seen Hewie Milburn? Oh! hae ye seen Hewie Milburn?' Instead of answering the creature, my faither sprang owre the bucht flake,[3] to be near the lasses, saying, ' Bliss us a'—what's that?' ' Ha, ha! Patie lad,' quo' Bessie Elliot, a free-spoken Liddesdale hempy; ' theer a wife com'd for ye the nicht, Patie lad.' ' A wife!' said my faither; ' may the Lord keep me frae sic a wife as that,' an' he confessed till his deein' day, he was in sic a fear that the hairs o' his heed stuid up like the birses of a hurcheon.[4] The creature was nae bigger than a three-year-auld lassie, but feat an' tight, lith o' limb, as ony grown woman, an' its face was the downright perfection o' beauty, only there was something wild an' unyirthly in its e'en that couldna be lookit at, faur less describit: it didna molest them, but aye taigilt[5] on about the bucht, now an' then repeatin' its cry, ' Hae ye seen Hewie Milburn?' Sae they cam' to nae ither conclusion than that it had tint[6] its companion. When my faither an' the lasses left the

[1] Romping and " chaffing."
[2] Whimper.
[8] Movable gate of the fold.
[4] Bristles of a hedgehog.
[5] Lingered.
[6] Lost.

bucht, it followed them hame to the Hyndlee kitchen, where they offered it yowe brose, but it wad na tak' onything, till at last a neer-do-weel callant made as if he wad grip it wi' a pair o' reed-het tangs, an' it appeared to be offendit, an' gaed awa' doon the burn-side, cryin' its auld cry eerier an' waesomer than ever, and disappeared in a bush o' seggs."[1]

THE FAIRY'S SONG.[2]

" O where is tiny Hew?
　And where is little Len?
And where is bonnie Lu,
　And Menie of the Glen?
And where's the place of rest—
　The ever changing hame?
Is it the gowan's breast,
　Or 'neath the bells of faem?
　　Ay lu lan dil y'u.

" The fairest rose you find
　May have a taint within;
The flower of womankind
　May not be free from sin,—
The fox-glove cup go bring,
　The tail of shooting sterne,

[1] Sedge.

[2] The song is taken from a poem founded upon the above story, and entitled the *Gloamyne Buchte*. The author was James Telfer, schoolmaster at Saughtree, in Liddesdale; born 1800, died 1862.

And round our grassy ring
　　We'll pledge the pith o' fern.
　　　　Ay lu lan dil y'u.

" And when the yellow moon
　　Is gliding down the sky,
On wings of wishes boun',
　　Our band to her can fly;
Her highest horn we'll ride,
　　And quaff her honey dew;
Then in her shadowy side
　　Our gambollings renew!
　　　　Ay lu lan dil y'u."

THE FAITHFUL PURSE-BEARER.

A TALE of the times of old. Far away in the north, where the purple heath spreads as thick on the hills in summer as the snow lies white in winter, where the streams flow down the granite-strewn corries of the mountains, brown gold as the topaz lying hid in their bosoms, a powerful chief ruled his clan.

Over hill and glen his domain spread far and wide, and his name was law itself in peace, and power in warfare. 'Twas said the Spey and the Garry both contributed to his table, and Cairn Gorm and Ben Alder furnished him with sport; which would mean that over much country, and by many men, his sway was known and acknowledged.

Now, upon two things the chief prided himself more than all else—more than his prowess in war, yes, more than the extent of his domains and power—

the beauty of his wife and his own justice. What his clansmen thought of these two things is not to the point; what he thought of them was enough for himself and for us.

It must also be added that he possessed something seldom vouchsafed to men in authority, but an invaluable blessing when procurable, and that was a faithful steward, who had charge of his purse, his farm, and his treasures, with which may be included a charge not the least, you may be sure, in importance at that period—the complete control of his cellar.

Ian na Sporran was faithful to his chief, and was trusted by him in return.

Yet is any one so good or so faithful as to be safe from the dart of jealousy? I trow not. The very fact of Ian na Sporran being so faithful and so trusted was enough to create in the malignant heart of Ian na Piob, the chief bard, the most inveterate and overwhelming hatred. Rent with jealousy of Ian na Sporran, the one question for his evil heart to solve was how to contrive the steward's downfall.

" It is no use," said the chief to Ian na Piob; " it is no use to come howling to me about the falseness of your fellow-servants. Just show me if I have lost any of my corn, any of my gold, any of my wine, any of my jewels, and then I'll see into the matter. I am quite ready to attend to anything reasonable; for you know I am a just man, and my wife is beautiful."

Well, for a whole year Ian na Sporran served the

chief faithfully, and for a whole year Ian na Piob thought how he might bring him low.

Now, it wanted three days to the New Year, when all the first men in the clan came yearly together before their chief to offer homage and congratulations, and Ian na Piob, pondering more desperately than ever how he could circumvent Ian na Sporran, was walking in the glen alone, kicking at every root and stone that came in his way, and giving vent from time to time to his feelings in envious groans. " Kera kaw," croaked the grey hoodie of Rothiemurchus. " What's the meaning of this ado? Have you eaten too many blaeberries? or what is it that pains you so ? "

And Ian na Piob looked up, and saw the hoodie; and he considered her evil eye spoke a heart as wicked as his own, so he told his tale.

" Is that all? " quoth the hoodie. " Why don't you say he stole the chief's golden barley ? "

" Just because I cannot get at the barley; and, what's more, I have no witness to support me if I lie about it," answered Ian na Piob.

" Silly fool! " croaked the hoodie; " what will you give me if I appear as a witness in your behalf ? "

" A measure of beans willingly from my own garden, and some sweetmeats I will steal from the chief's table," eagerly exclaimed Ian na Piob.

" Kera kaw! I strike that bargain," crowed the hoodie. " Bring the beans and sweetmeats to me to-morrow. Call on me when I'm wanted, and I shall be there without fail."

So the beans and sweemeats were given, and the morn of the New Year arrived.

And indeed it was a crowd that filled the great hall of the castle that same day, as the folk came to deliver compliments to the chief and his lady, to make their statements, and to receive orders. Jauntily among them came Ian na Piob, and, pushing to the front, bowed in low obiesance.

"IS THAT ALL?" QUOTH THE HOODIE.

"How now?" said the chief. "Any complaints? any advice? any wish? I am a just man, and my wife is beautiful; say on without fear."

"Ian na Sporran has been stealing your golden barley, O chief!" cried Ian na Piob, "and he should be put to death."

"Who is your witness?" said the chief. "Remember I am a just man, and my wife is beautiful, and I must have proof."

" Just the hoodie of Rothiemurchus," answered Ian na Piob; " none other than he."

" Well, in that case, Ian na Sporran," remarked the chief, turning towards him, " you must die."

" Would not your highness call the witness, and prove his truthfulness before condemning me?" asked Ian na Sporran. " If I am guilty, I am willing to die! if I am innocent, your own justice and your wife's beauty forbid that I should suffer."

" I am a just man, and my wife is beautiful," answered the chief. " You are right. Ian na Piob, call your witness."

Thrice whistled Ian na Piob, and in a trice there stood in the window the hoodie of Rothiemurchus.

" Do you take oath, O hoodie," said the chief, " that Ian na Sporran stole my golden barley?"

" I do," said the hoodie.

" How so?" asked the chief.

" Because," croaked the hoodie, without hesitation, " Ian na Sporran gave me some to eat this very morning to keep me from declaring his offence; for he knew I saw him do it. Look you how my crop is distended full, full, full!"

" Oh!" said the chief, looking at Ian na Sporran, " you must certainly die!"

" I pray you cut the witness open, and see if he speaks the truth," said Ian na Sporran.

" Do so," said the chief; " for I am a just man, and my wife is beautiful."

Thrice whistled Ian na Piob, and there stood in the window the hoodie of
Rothiemurchus.—Page 156.   *Scottish Fairy Tales.*

So they cut the hoodie open, and found nothing in his inside but some sugar and broad beans. Then they flung the carcass out of the window into the loch below, where Spottie Face, the great salmon, had his residence, who ate him up at one gulp, and that was the end of him.

" This is just nonsense! " roared the chief. " The case is dismissed; let us go in to supper." So the chief and his vassals went in to supper, and in the delights of the feast-room forgot all about the evil of the morning.

If there was an angry man in the whole district that man was Ian na Piob; nor did the sense of this failure make him give up his evil intentions, but he pondered again from that day the whole year through how he might bring Ian na Sporran to the gallows.

It was again three days before the New Year that Ian na Piob was walking through the pinewoods of Dalwhinnie, and he crushed the fallen cones of last year savagely beneath his feet into the frosty ground, while from time to time he raised his voice in angry exclamation.

" What's all this to-do about? " said the black witch of Loch Ericht, as she sat at the entrance of the dark cave, blinking with her red een in the blue reek of the peat fire that whirled in puffs out of the cavern, like smoke from some fell dragon's jaws.

At that Ian na Piob looked up; and thinking she appeared as black and as evil as himself, he lost no time in telling her his tale.

"Why don't you say he stole the chief's gold? That's easy enough, I'm sure," said she.

"Because I can't get at the gold, and I have no witness to swear for me, should I need one."

"Silly rabbit!" scornfully cried the witch. "What will you give me if the sun appears as your witness?"

"My best," said Ian na Piob.

"Well, if we want the sun," answered she, "I must brew trolls' broth to attract him. Give me the little toe of your right foot and the little toe of your left foot, and I will do the trick."

Now it must be confessed that Ian na Piob was grieved to lose any of his limbs, and to suffer pain; but what will not an envious man do or suffer to get the better of an enemy?

So he cut off the little toe from his right foot, and the little toe from his left foot, and gave them to the witch of Loch Ericht to make trolls' broth.

"Now," said Ian na Piob, "I can't walk."

"Pooh! nonsense!" replied the witch; "you shall have my crutch and get on well enough with it." Then he gave a grunt, and snorted twice like a trumpet, and at that a queer thing came out from behind the juniper -bushes, and gave him the hag's crutch.

"Now, come here again to-morrow, and the broth will be brewed; then take it on New Year morning, and, walking withershins round the standing-stones of Trium, cast it on the ground as the sun rises, and he will come that day as a witness to the

Ian na Piob cut off the little toe from his right foot, and the little toe from his left foot and gave them to the witch to make trolls' broth.—Page 158.

Scottish Fairy Tales.

council." So the witch went into the cave, and Ian na Piob hobbled away lame. Let us hope the vision of revenge was a good plaster to his sore feet.

The next morning he came very, very early, you may be sure, and called on the witch, and the queer thing came out from behind the juniper bushes and gave him the bowl filled with trolls' broth, and he took it away and did just as the old hag directed him.

Oh, there was no doubt at all that it was a large crowd which came at the New Year, and gathered together in the hall of the castle, to offer congratulations to their chief and his wife, and to taste good things at his board!

And after many had spoken, and much business had been transacted, Ian na Piob, seeing his turn had come, hobbled forward, leaning on the crutch he had received from the old hag.

"How now, Ian na Piob?" said the chief. "If you have anything to say, say on. I am wearying for my supper, so be quick about it."

"Oh," answered Ian na Piob, "that fellow over there—Ian na Sporran—has been at it again! He has stolen your golden coins, and he should die."

"I am a just man, and my wife is beautiful, so I can't take your word for it alone, you know. Any witnesses! No hoodies, or any of that crew, for me this time, mind that!"

"Sir, my witness is none other than the sun himself," answered Ian na Piob.

"Oh," said the chief, turning to Ian na Sporran,

" if that is so, you certainly must have your head chopped off."

" Sir," said Ian na Sporran humbly, " order him, I beg, to produce his witness. If I am guilty, then let me die."

" I am a just man, and my wife is—— What the plague are you hobbling about in that way for ? " said the chief to Ian na Piob, breaking off suddenly in the middle of the well-known sentence.

" Frost-bite! " grunted Ian na Piob. " But follow me, chief and gentlemen all, to the chamber that looks towards the south-west, and then I will prove my accusation true."

" Why to the chamber at the south-west ? " asked the chief.

" Because," replied Ian na Piob, " there the stolen money lies, and my witness shall attend."

" Lead on," cried the chief, " and be quick about it, for I am very hungry indeed."

So Ian na Piob led the way to the chamber looking to the south-west, and as they entered the chamber, sure enough the sun streamed in through the window, and shone and glittered on many a golden coin that lay there in rich confusion on the floor.

" Headsman, do your duty! " cried the chief, pointing to Ian na Sporran.

" Sir chief, I beg you, before I die, take up one of these coins and look at it narrowly in the shade, and see if it is really a golden one or not! "

" I am a just man, and my wife is beautiful," said the chief. " Hand me one of those golden coins."

So they handed him a coin, and taking it into a corner out of the sunlight, he saw it was a common coin, and not a golden one at all.

"If I had yon witness in my power," said the chief to Ian na Piob, " I'd thrash him! As for you, your punishment shall come after supper."

Then the chief took the arm of Ian na Sporran, and hurried away to the banqueting-hall, for he was very hungry indeed, and would brook no more delay.

And for that time again Ian na Piob got off his well-merited punishment, for in the delights of the feast the evil of the morning was forgotten, and indeed, the whole thing was so silly, it was scarcely worth noticing or remembering.

How savage Ian na Piob was at this second failure, you who are now acquainted with him can well imagine. He had gained nothing in the war of revenge, and had lost two toes into the bargain. " I'll have it out with that old witch at any rate!" said he. " If she won't help me again better than last time, she shall be burnt, or my name isn't what it is!"

So as the next New Year came round, when, he knew, was his only opportunity, he sought the cavern, and called loudly on the witch: but when she answered, and came to the mouth of the cave, she looked so evil that his courage oozed out of his finger-tips (he had not toes enough for it to ooze out at that end), and his angry words dwindled away to a feeble whine of complaint.

11

"Well," quoth the hag, "what brings you here again?"

"The wretched failure of your scheme," sobbed Ian na Piob, and he then told her all that had occurred.

"And whose fault was that, I should like to know?" growled she. "I can't think of another plan fit for such a goose as you. Stay, though—no! you're so great a fool, it would be no good, so be off, I shan't take any more trouble."

"Tell me your plan, I beseech you!" cried Ian na Piob, all pain and disappointment lost in the expectation of revenge. "I'll give anything to bring Ian na Sporran to a bad end!"

"Well, you must bring me some more sweetmeats from the chief's table, and we will prove that he stole the chief's wine this time."

"But I've no witness," wailed he. "The hoodie is dead, and the sun is no use at all; what am I to do?"

"Silly rabbit!" grunted the witch. "We'll get the moon to come, but we must brew her trolls' broth, or it can't be managed at all. Give me the big toe off your right foot, and the big toe off your left foot, and I will do the trick; or else be off, and don't bother!"

Well, Ian na Piob thought that as he had lost his little toes, his big ones might just as well go the same road, so he cut them off and gave them to the witch.

"Wow, wow, wow!" he squealed in pain. "There

now, I can't walk, no, not even with the crutch!"
and he sat down on the ground and waved his toeless
feet in the air.

"Now, now," said the hag, "don't lie here roaring
like a baby." And she gave a grunt and snorted twice
like a trumpet, and the queer thing came from behind the juniper bushes, and handed him a long,
broad petticoat made of stiff hog bristles, and when
he had tied it round his middle with some leather
thongs, it supported him on all sides.

"You look vastly pretty," said the hag, with a
horrid leer.

"I wish you were made just as pretty yourself!"
said he, as he waddled down the road as best he could.
"I shall come to-morrow before sunset for the
broth."

And that morrow's evening, before the shadows
crept out of the fir-wood, and spread over the hillsides, Ian na Piob was at the cavern mouth again.

And the queer thing came from behind the juniper
bushes, and gave into his hands the bowl of trolls'
broth that the hag had in the meantime prepared.

"Go to the rock of Osinn," said the hag, "where
the withered pine spreads its bare branches to the
sky. There, as the moon rises, walk three times
withershins round the riven trunk, and cast the broth
on the ground before her."

And Ian na Piob painfully went away to the rock
of Osinn, carrying the bowl of broth in one hand, and
struggling with the crutch in the other, his body supported by the bristle petticoat. And he did as the

hag bade him, and as the moon rose over the crags of Braeriach, he cast the broth on the ground before her, bidding her come the next day at even to be his witness when he should call.

The next day, when the New Year came, and all the retainers and vassals flocked to the castle to give greeting and receive advice, Ian na Piob came with them, clad in his petticoat of hog bristles, looking his worst, and thinking his cruelest.

" What mountebank have we here ? " quoth the chief, as, at the end of the council, Ian na Piob tottered forward to make his statement.

" Alas ! noble sir, 'tis the frost-bite has taken possession of my limbs completely—yea, has gotten a bit higher up than last year; but regardless of the pain I am suffering, I have come here to denounce that villain Ian na Sporran, and demand, in the name of justice, that he be put to death at once."

" How now ! " cried the chief, " I am a just man, and my wife is beautiful, and I will not condemn a man without proof or witness. Say on, but beware how you trifle with me this time ! "

" He has stolen your wine, and I can prove it," said Ian na Piob.

" Stolen my wine ! oh, indeed, that must be put a stop to, and you," said the chief, turning to Ian na Sporran, " must be put an end to."

" Again, O chief," said Ian na Sporran, " will you listen to my enemy without certain proof ? "

" Nay," answered the chief, " that is to doubt my own justice and my wife's beauty. Where is your witness?" continued he sharply, looking at Ian na Piob.

"The moon," said he, "and none other. The deed was done during the night, and she will come at eventide and give proof of it."

"The moon be praised!" ejaculated the chief, "that she don't want to come now, and that I can have my supper first." So without more ado, the chief walked out of the hall to the chamber where the feast was laid out, and in the delight of the feast forgot soon the business of the morning.

But when they had all drunk quite as much as was good for them, and had eaten, in my opinion, more than was necessary, Ian na Piob scrambled up to the chief, and begged him to step up to the chamber in the north-west tower, for there his witness was waiting to prove his accusation.

"Oh, bother!" said the chief. "Cut his head off! I don't care, and I don't want proof."

"Noble master," said Ian na Sporran, "remember you are a just man, and your wife is beautiful."

"Pest take the whole affair!" roared the chief, getting up. "I can't even have my meals in peace! I suppose, then, I must. But whoever trifles with me now is a dead man!"

So, in a fume, he bounced off after Ian na Piob, kicking him occasionally from behind to make him move faster, and followed by his lady and the rest of the vassals, who were all agog to see what would happen now.

Well, when they arrived at the north-west tower,

and had entered the room, there, sure enough, were basins and goblets and beakers set about the floor and tables, and filled to overflowing with dark red wine. No doubt about it at all, for the moon was shining in at the window, and it was almost as bright as noon-day.

"I have seen enough!" cried the chief. "Ian na Sporran, down on your knees, and, sword-bearer, give me my claymore! You'll take my drink, will you? I'll have your head off; you won't feel thirsty much longer!"

"I beseech you, my lord," said Ian na Sporran, falling on his knee, "taste but a drop of that wine. Grant me this one last request before I die. I will make no resistance to your demands; only grant me this one little boon."

"Well, you don't deserve it, but I will do that," replied the chief, taking up one of the cups, and placing it to his lips, "for I am a just man, and my wife is—— Ah, auch, phew, bach!!" and with a fearful grimace he spat the liquid out all over the floor.

"Give me some water, wine, brose, anything to take the taste out of my mouth! Oh, ach! phew! I'm poisoned as sure as death!" yelled the chief, rushing out of the room, and scattering them all on this side and on that in his wild dart at the door. "Secure Ian na Piob! He shall die to-morrow before cockcrow!" and he was down the stairs and his nose into a beaker of brose before any one could

"I beseech you, my lord," said Ian na Sporran, falling on his knees, "taste but a drop of that wine."—Page 166. *Scottish Fairy Tales.*

say " How d'ye do ? " or had recovered from the start he had given them.

But the chief was not poisoned at all, for it was only brown burn water that Ian na Piob had poured into the goblets, and that looked so purple in the moonlight. So Ian na Piob was placed under lock and key in the dungeon below the moat, and as he was to be executed the next morning without fail, a guard was set over him to make sure of his not escaping.

But, somehow, Ian na Piob contrived to get a message sent to the chief's lady that he had something of great moment to confide to her ear alone, saying that, though he must die, it was a real pity so great a secret should be lost, especially when she could listen so easily at the keyhole, while he spoke to her on the other side of the door, and nobody would be any the wiser or any the worse.

So the chief's lady thought it could do no harm to any one, and besides, the chief need not know anything about it; moreover, she was like every other woman, as inquisitive as an ape, and could not deny her curiosity. Thus it was that at midnight she bribed the gaoler, and repaired to the dungeon where Ian na Piob was confined. There, giving three raps upon the oaken beams, she applied her ear to the keyhole of the great door.

Now what Ian na Piob told that lady is no business of yours or mine; but what he did tell her must have been of deep consequence, and it seems to have been a secret the full explanation of which he could

not give her for three days at least, inasmuch as she
went straightway to the chief, her husband, and
begged him to defer the execution of Ian na Piob
for three days; and the chief, who by this time had
recovered his temper, consented after a little demur,

APPLIED HER EAR TO THE KEYHOLE.

for his wife not only was beautiful, but when her
mind was set on anything, he knew she would worry
the inside out of a pig before she gave it up. Yes,
poor man! he knew this only too well, from long
experience! Hence his consent.

And it happened, since it was impossible for Ian
na Piob to escape with the frost-bite in his limbs,

as he said he had, the gaoler allowed him to go about the castle at liberty, for he did not want to be bothered to sit opposite that dungeon three whole days, and was pleased, too, to be saved the trouble of carrying food to his prisoner from time to time.

Sharp though the pain proved that Ian na Piob was suffering, and deep his fear of the doom that was hanging over him, revenge still was the undying fire that burned in his heart.

"Oh, if I could only compass somehow that fellow's death," cried he, "I should die happy!" and he bit his finger to the bone as he crouched on the stair and thought and thought and thought.

And as he sat thinking on the stairs, he happened to glance up, and the moon sailing in the frosty blue sky looked down at him through the open lattice, and he shook his fist at her and called her an evil name; and the stars came out one by one, and winked and blinked, so shocked were they at such conduct. But as he watched them, a thought, novel and crafty, struck him, and he suddenly rose, and with an evil grin on his face he took in his hand a goblet of crystal that stood on the table by his side, and with the help of the crutch and the stiff petticoat, painfully climbed the winding stairs. Then, making his way to a chamber that looked towards the south, he went in, and after locking the door on the inside, he sat down on a stool in front of the open windows. Then he closed the pine-shutters that hung on each side of the casement, and taking a sharp-pointed awl from his pouch, for two hours by the dial without ceasing he laboured to bore holes through them, some large, small. He pierced them in straight lines and circles, so as to portray, as best he could, the sets of stars he had noticed often in the winter heavens.

Next, he broke the goblet of crystal with his crutch into small pieces, and strewing them on the table beneath the closed window, and on the floor below, he left the room with a self-satisfied grimace, shutting the door behind him, locking it, and taking the key away with him.

"Now for the key," muttered he.

"Spottie Face! Spottie Face! Spottie Face!" he cried, getting up as best he could on the sill of the passage window, and stretching his neck out as far as possible over the water of the loch below. "Spottie Face, come hither!"

And Spottie Face, the great salmon that had its residence in the pool below, looked up, expecting some food to be thrown him from above.

"Spottie Face! O Spottie Face!" continued Ian na Piob, "if I give you some sweetmeats from the chief's table, will you do me a favour?"

Now Spottie Face was a nasty, cruel thing, and did not like doing favours for anybody; but you remember it was winter, and there was not much food going or any green meat on the banks, and so he put his nose above the water and waved assent with his tail.

"Then take this key, and cast it up on the bank below the window of Ian na Sporran. You know it; it is on the other side of the castle. This is not much to ask, you must allow; and I will throw the sweetmeats out of this window after the chief has left the banqueting-hall in the evening."

So Ian na Piob threw the key out to Spottie Face, and went his way down the staircase.

But Spottie Face, when he had seized the key, found it bitter cold to the jaws, for the frost had kissed the chill metal, and he spat it up again on to the bank just where he received it, and there it lay, a dark object on the frozen snow under Ian na Piob's own window. And Spottie Face sank to the bottom of the pool.

Now the fatal day arrived when Ian na Piob was to suffer for his evil deception of the chief, and the gaoler came, and led him into the hall of the castle, where all were assembled, and the chief and his wife sat in state to see the sentence carried out.

"I am a just man, and my wife is beautiful," spoke the chief. "You deceived me, and you tried to poison me: you shall die now, that's settled!"

"A boon I crave, one boon before I die!" cried Ian na Piob. "Let me but whisper a secret of utmost value into your lady's ear."

"Nothing of the sort!" roared the chief. "Go and have your head cut off! I won't hear of any delay."

But his good lady was not going to miss knowing that secret, whatever it might be; for she had been thinking about it for the last two days, and had fretted herself a good deal, besides, on the subject. So she gave her husband one of her looks, and he knew too well to say no when she looked yes.

Then Ian na Piob whispered in her ear.

"What? what? My jewels, my shining jewels?" screamed that lady, and, clenching her fists, she ran

GIVE ME BACK MY JEWELS.

up to Ian na Sporran and, shaking them in his astonished face, cried: "Give me my jewels back, you thieving villain you! give back my shining jewels that you have stolen!"

" Come along," cried his wife, seizing the chief by the sleeve and pulling him toward the door.—Page 173. *Scottish Fairy Tales.*

"What's all this fuss about!" asked the chief, jumping up with a bounce from his chair of state.

"Why, Ian na Piob says that Ian na Sporran has stolen my jewels! O husband dear! you must send Ian na Sporran at once to the gallows."

"Hush, softly, my love!" said he. "You are beautiful, but remember, be just as well. In fact, I don't believe a word you're saying; and as to Ian na Piob, witness or no witness, I'll never put trust in him again, that's flat!"

"How many witnesses would make you believe my word!" said Ian na Piob. "Will ten please you?"

"No!" roared the chief. "Nothing under twenty, so be off and be hung!"

"There are twenty waiting to prove this at this moment in the castle," cried Ian na Piob.

Then the chief found he was caught, and knew that if he would keep up his character for justice, he must consent to hear the case.

"And who may these witnesses be?" growled he.

"None other than the stars of heaven," answered Ian na Piob.

"That's a low trick to escape your doom till the evening!" said the chief.

"Nay, but they are waiting you at this very moment in the south chamber," said Ian na Piob; "and what's more, the jewels are there too," whispered he in the lady's ear.

"Come along, come along!" cried she, seizing the chief by the sleeve, and the whole party, headed by

Ian na Piob, made towards the door, for the chief saw he must go, willy nilly, as his wife seemed quite out of her mind.

" Now where's the key ? " said he when he got to the door and found it fast locked, " that's the next thing."

" Those who hide can find ! He's got it, of course," said Ian na Piob pointing to Ian na Sporran, " search him. If he has it not, depend upon it he has hid it in his chamber; and if it's not there, he's cast it out of his window. Oh, I know his tricks ! "

" Why, there it is on the bank ! " said one of the chief's followers, looking out of the window. And sure enough, there it was, lying on the bank just under the chamber window belonging to Ian na Piob.

So they ran down and fetched it; but Ian na Piob nearly fainted with rage, for he saw that Spottie Face the salmon had deceived him.

But now the door was opened wide, and there within without doubt the jewels lay on the table and on the floor glittering in the light of the stars that shone brightly through the window into the darkened room.

" My jewels, my jewels ! " cried the chief's wife, running forward.

" O Ian na Sporran," said the chief, shaking his head, " you must this time without doubt be put an end to ! "

" Yes, yes," cried his wife, " at once ! at once ! for he deserves it."

" I pray you, noble chief," said Ian na Sporran, " question those witnesses, and ask them the truth."

"What nonsense you're talking! Why, they are thousands of miles off," said the chief. "How can they hear me?"

"They are not further than the other side of the window," answered Ian na Sporran. "Permit me to go and beckon to them."

"Don't let him, don't let him!" shrieked Ian na Piob, hobbling forward in his petticoat to prevent him. "He's going to play some nasty trick!"

"You forget yourself, Ian na Piob!" thundered the chief; "and you forget also that I am a just man, and my wife is beautiful. Ian na Sporran, go and beckon to them."

Then Ian na Sporran went to the casement and flung the shutter wide, and the bright daylight filled the chamber, and all put up their hands to their eyes, for they were dazzled at the sudden change.

"Dear lady," said Ian na Sporran, "look now at your jewels! Nought but glass are they, you see; and where are my enemy's witnesses? I trow they are still sleeping in the dark coffers of the night, the other side of the ocean."

"Ian na Sporran, forgive me and all of us!" said the chief coming forward, and giving him his hand. "We will never, never, never distrust you again, as long as we live. Ask me any favour, and it shall be granted."

"Then give me the life of Ian na Piob," cried Ian na Sporran; "for as I am the happiest man to-day in the country, I would have none sorrow while I am glad."

" On one condition," answered the chief. " **Ian na Piob**, stand forth, and with both hands **uplifted**, swear you will never try to give **false-witness and** lie to me again."

Then Ian na Piob waddled forward, and **flung** both his hands up over his head, but leaving **go of the** crutch, he overbalanced himself and fell flat on his face before the chief, and by no effort could **he raise** himself up again.

" You have signed your own doom," said the chief. " To the loch with him! hanging is too good! "

Then they flung Ian na Piob, petticoat, **crutch** and all, out of the window into the loch below, **where** Spottie Face the great salmon had his residence, **and** he had not reached the bottom before Spottie **Face** had him fast, and with one great gulp swallowed **him,** petticoat and all.

" My dear," said his wife to the chief, " I think **you** are as clever as you are just," and she gave **him a** good kiss on his brown cheek.

" And you, my love," said he, vastly **pleased,** " you are as sensible as you are beautiful."

And with these words he gave her a good kiss on the left cheek, which was real good of him, don't **you** think, for turn and turn about is but **fair play.**

THE BROWNIE, THE BOGLE, THE KELPY, MERMEN, DEMONS.

THE SCOTTISH BROWNIE.[1]

THE Scottish Brownie formed a class of beings distinct in habit and disposition from the freakish and mischievous elves. He was meagre, shaggy, and wild in his appearance.

In the daytime he lurked in remote recesses of the old houses which he delighted to haunt; and in the night sedulously employed himself in discharging any laborious task which he thought might be acceptable to the family to whose service he had devoted himself. But the Brownie does not drudge from the hope of recompense. On the contrary, so delicate is his attachment that the offer of reward, but particularly of food, infallibly occasions his disappearance for ever. It is told of a Brownie, who haunted a Border family now extinct, that the lady having fallen unexpectedly in labour, and the servant, who was ordered to ride to Jedburgh for the *sage-femme*, showing no great alertness in setting out, the familiar spirit slipt on the great-coat of the lingering domes-

[1] Sir Walter Scott, *Minstrelsy of the Scottish Border.*

tic, rode to the town on the laird's best horse, and returned with the midwife *en croupe*. During the short space of his absence, the Tweed, which they must necessarily ford, rose to a dangerous height. Brownie, who transported his charge with all rapidity, was not to be stopped by this obstacle. He plunged in with the terrified old lady, and landed her in safety where her services were wanted. Having put the horse into the stable (where it was afterwards found in a woful plight), he proceeded to the room of the servant whose duty he had discharged, and, finding him just in the act of drawing on his boots, administered to him a most merciless drubbing with his own horsewhip. Such an important service excited the gratitude of the laird, who, understanding that Brownie had been heard to express a wish to have a green coat, ordered a vestment of that colour to be made and left in his haunts. Brownie took away the green coat, but was never seen more. We may suppose that, tired of his domestic drudgery, he went in his new livery to join the fairies.

THE BROWNIE OF BODSBECK.[1]

The brownie of the farmhouse of Bodsbeck, in Moffatdale, left his employment upwards of a century ago, on a similar account. He had exerted himself so much in the farm labour, both in and out of

[1] Chambers, *Popular Rhymes of Scotland.*

doors, that Bodsbeck became the most prosperous
farm in the district. He always took his meat as it
pleased himself, usually in very moderate quantities,
and of the most humble description. During a time
of very hard labour, perhaps harvest, when a little
better fare than ordinary might have been judged acceptable, the goodman took the liberty of leaving out
a mess of bread and milk, thinking it but fair that
at a time when some improvement, both in quantity
and quality, was made upon the fare of the human
servants, the useful brownie should obtain a share
in the blessing. He, however, found his error, for
the result was that the brownie left the house for
ever, exclaiming—

> "Ca', brownie, ca'
> A' the luck o' Bodsbeck away to Leithenha'.''

The luck of Bodsbeck accordingly departed with its
brownie, and settled in the neighbouring farmhouse,
called Leithenhall, whither the brownie transferred
his friendship and services.

THE BROWNIE AND THE THIEVISH MAIDS.[1]

ONE of the principal characteristics of the brownie
was his anxiety about the moral conduct of the household to which he was attached. He was a spirit very

[1] Chambers, *Popular Rhymes of Scotland.*

much inclined to prick up his ears at the first appearance of any impropriety in the manners of his
fellow-servants. The least delinquency committed
either in barn, or cow-house, or larder, he was sure
to report to his master, whose interests he seemed to
consider paramount to every other thing in this world,
and from whom no bribe could induce him to conceal
the offences which fell under his notice. The men,
therefore, and not less the maids, of the establishment usually regarded him with a mixture of fear,
hatred, and respect; and though he might not often
find occasion to do his duty as a spy, yet the firm belief that he would be relentless in doing so, provided
that he did find occasion, had a salutary effect. A
ludicrous instance of his zeal as guardian of the
household morals is told in Peeblesshire. Two dairy-
maids, who were stinted in their food by a too frugal
mistress, found themselves one day compelled by
hunger to have recourse to the highly improper expedient of stealing a bowl of milk and a bannock,
which they proceeded to devour, as they thought, in
secret. They sat upon a form, with a space between,
whereon they placed the bowl and the bread, and they
took *bite and sip* alternately, each putting down the
bowl upon the seat for a moment's space after taking
a draught, and the other then taking it up in her
hands, and treating herself in the same way. They
had no sooner commenced their mess than the
brownie came between the two, invisible, and whenever the bowl was set down upon the seat took also a
draught; by which means, as he devoured fully as

much as both put together, the milk was speedily exhausted. The surprise of the famished girls at finding the bowl so soon empty was extreme, and they began to question each other very sharply upon the subject, with mutual suspicion of unfair play, when the brownie undeceived them by exclaiming, with malicious glee—

> " Ha ! ha ! ha !
> Brownie has't a' ! "

THE BOGLE.[1]

THIS is a freakish spirit, who delights rather to perplex and frighten mankind than either to serve or seriously to hurt them. *Shellycoat,* a spirit who resides in the waters, and has given his name to many a rock and stone upon the Scottish coast, belongs to the class of bogles. When he appeared, he seemed to be decked with marine productions, and in particular with shells, whose clattering announced his approach. From this circumstance he derived his name. One of his pranks is thus narrated :—Two men, on a very dark night, approaching the banks of the Ettrick, heard a doleful voice from its waves repeatedly exclaim, " Lost ! Lost ! " They followed the sound, which seemed to be the voice of a drowning person, and, to their infinite astonishment, they found that it ascended the river. Still they continued, during

[1] Sir Walter Scott, *Minstrelsy of the Scottish Border.*

a long and tempestuous night, to follow the cry of the
malicious sprite; and arriving, before morning's
dawn, at the very sources of the river, the voice was
now heard descending the opposite side of the mountain in which they arise. The fatigued and deluded
travellers now relinquished the pursuit, and had no
sooner done so than they heard Shellycoat applaud-
ing, in loud bursts of laughter, his successful roguery.
The spirit was supposed particularly to haunt the old
house of Gorinberry, situated on the river Hermi-
tage, in Liddesdale.

THE DOOMED RIDER.[1]

" THE Conan is as bonny a river as we hae in a'
the north country. There's mony a sweet sunny spot
on its banks, an' mony a time an' aft hae I waded
through its shallows, whan a boy, to set my little
scauting-line for the trouts an' the eels, or to gather
the big pearl-mussels that lie sae thick in the fords.
But its bonny wooded banks are places for enjoying
the day in—no for passing the nicht. I kenna how
it is; it's nane o' your wild streams that wander des-
olate through a desert country, like the Avon, or that
come rushing down in foam and thunder, ower
broken rocks, like the Foyers, or that wallow in darkness, deep, deep in the bowels o' the earth, like the
fearfu' Auldgraunt; an' yet no ane o' these rivers

[1] *Folk-Lore and Legends, Scotland.* **W. W. Gibbings.**

has mair or frightfuller stories connected wi' it than
the Conan. Ane can hardly saunter ower half-a-mile
in its course, frae where it leaves Contin till where it
enters the sea, without passing ower the scene o'
some frightful auld legend o' the kelpie or the water-
wraith. And ane o' the most frightful looking o'
these places is to be found among the woods of Conan
House. Ye enter a swampy meadow that waves wi'
flags an' rushes like a cornfield in harvest, an' see
a hillock covered wi' willows rising like an island in
the midst. There are thick mirk-woods on ilka side;
the river, dark an' awesome, an' whirling round an'
round in mossy eddies, sweeps away behind it; an'
there is an auld burying-ground, wi' the broken ruins
o' an auld Papist kirk, on the tap. Ane can see
amang the rougher stanes the rose-wrought mullions
of an arched window, an' the trough that ance held
the holy water. About twa hunder years ago—a wee
mair maybe, or a wee less, for ane canna be very sure
o' the date o' thae old stories—the building was en-
tire; an' a spot near it, whar the wood now grows
thickest, was laid out in a corn-field. The marks o'
the furrows may still be seen amang the trees.

" A party o' Highlanders were busily engaged, ae
day in harvest, in cutting down the corn o' that field;
an' just aboot noon, when the sun shone brightest an'
they were busiest in the work, they heard a voice
frae the river exclaim, ' The hour but not the man
has come.' Sure enough, on looking round, there
was the kelpie stan'in' in what they ca' a fause ford,
just fornent the auld kirk. There is a deep black

pool baith aboon an' below, but i' the ford there's a bonny ripple, that shows, as ane might think, but little depth o' water; an' just i' the middle o' that, in a place where a horse might swim, stood the kelpie. An' it again repeated its words, 'The hour but not the man has come,' an' then flashing through the water like a drake, it disappeared in the lower pool. When the folk stood wondering what the creature might mean, they saw a man on horseback come spurring down the hill in hot haste, making straight for the fause ford. They could then understand her words at ance; an' four o' the stoutest o' them sprang oot frae amang the corn to warn him o' his danger, an' keep him back. An' sae they tauld him what they had seen an' heard, an' urged him either to turn back an' tak' anither road, or stay for an hour or sae where he was. But he just wadna hear them, for he was baith unbelieving an' in haste, an' wauld hae taen the ford for a' they could say, hadna the Highlanders, determined on saving him whether he would or no, gathered round him an' pulled him frae his horse, an' then, to mak' sure of him, locked him up in the auld kirk. Weel, when the hour had gone by—the fatal hour o' the kelpie—they flung open the door, an' cried to him that he might noo gang on his journey. Ah! but there was nae answer, though; an' sae they cried a second time, an' there was nae answer still; and then they went in, an' found him lying stiff an' cauld on the floor, wi' his face buried in the water o' the very stone trough that we may still see amang the ruins. His hour had come, an' he had fallen in a fit, as 'twould seem, head-foremost amang the water o' the trough, where he had been smothered, —an' sae ye see, the prophecy o' the kelpie availed naething."

GRAHAM OF MORPHIE.[1]

The old family of the Grahams of Morphie was in former times very powerful, but at length they sunk in fortune, and finally the original male line became extinct. Among the old women of the Mearns, their decay is attributed to a supernatural cause. When one of the lairds, say they, built the old castle, he secured the assistance of the water-kelpy or river-horse, by the accredited means of throwing a pair of branks[2] over his head. He then compelled the robust spirit to carry prodigious loads of stones for the building, and did not relieve him till the whole was finished. The poor kelpy was glad of his deliverance, but at the same time felt himself so galled with the hard labour, that on being permitted to escape from the branks, and just before he disappeared in the water, he turned about, and expressed, in the following words, at once his own grievances and the destiny of his taskmaster's family—

> "Sair back and sair banes,
> Drivin' the laird o' Morphie's stanes !
> The laird o' Morphie 'll never thrive
> As lang's the kelpy is alive ! "

---

[1] Chambers, *Popular Rhymes of Scotland.*   [2] Shafts.

THE FISHERMAN AND THE MERMAN.[1]

OF mermen and merwomen many strange stories
are told in the Shetland Isles.   Beneath the depths
of the ocean, according to these stories, an atmosphere
exists adapted to the respiratory organs of certain
beings, resembling in form the human race, possessed
of surpassing beauty, of limited supernatural powers,
and liable to the incident of death.   They dwell in a
wide territory of the globe, far below the region of
fishes, over which the sea, like the cloudy canopy of
our sky, loftily rolls, and they possess habitations con-
structed of the pearl and coral productions of the
ocean.   Having lungs not adapted to a watery me-
dium, but to the nature of atmospheric air, it would
be impossible for them to pass through the volume of
waters that intervenes between the submarine and
supramarine world, if it were not for the extraordinary power they inherit of entering the skin of some
animal capable of existing in the sea, which they are
enabled to occupy by a sort of demoniacal possession.
One shape they put on is that of an animal human
above the waist, yet terminating below in the tail
and fins of a fish, but the most favourite form is that
of the larger seal or Haaf-fish; for, in possessing an
amphibious nature, they are enabled not only to exist
in the ocean, but to land on some rock, where they
frequently lighten themselves of their sea-dress, resume their proper shape, and with much curiosity

[1] *Folk-Lore and Legends, Scotland.*   W. W. Gibbings.

examine the nature of the upper world belonging to the human race. Unfortunately, however, each merman or merwoman possesses but one skin, enabling the individual to ascend the seas, and if, on visiting the abode of man, the garb be lost, the hapless being must unavoidably become an inhabitant of the earth.

A story is told of a boat's crew who landed for the purpose of attacking the seals lying in the hollows of the crags at one of the stacks. The men stunned a number of the animals, and while they were in this state stripped them of their skins, with the fat attached to them. Leaving the carcases on the rock, the crew were about to set off for the shore of Papa Stour, when such a tremendous swell arose that every one flew quickly to the boat. All succeeded in entering it except one man, who had imprudently lingered behind. The crew were unwilling to leave a companion to perish on the skerries,[1] but the surge increased so fast that after many unsuccessful attempts to bring the boat close in to the stack the unfortunate wight was left to his fate. A stormy night came on, and the deserted Shetlander saw no prospect before him but that of perishing from cold and hunger, or of being washed into the sea by the breakers which threatened to dash over the rocks. At length he perceived many of the seals, who in their flight had escaped the attack of the boatmen, approach the skerry, disrobe themselves of their amphibious hides, and resume the shape of the sons and daughters of the ocean. Their first object was to assist in the re-

[1] Rocks which are submerged at high tide.

covery of their friends, who, having been stunned by clubs, had, while in that state, been deprived of their skins. When the flayed animals had regained their sensibility, they assumed their proper form of mermen or merwomen, and began to lament in a mournful lay, wildly accompanied by the storm that was raging around, the loss of their sea-dress, which would prevent them from again enjoying their native azure atmosphere and coral mansions that lay below the deep waters of the Atlantic. But their chief lamentation was for Ollavitinus, the son of Gioga, who, having been stripped of his seal's skin, would be for ever parted from his mates, and condemned to become an outcast inhabitant of the upper world. Their song was at length broken off by observing one of their enemies viewing, with shivering limbs and looks of comfortless despair, the wild waves that dashed over the stack. Gioga immediately conceived the idea of rendering subservient to the advantage of her son the perilous situation of the man. She addressed him with mildness, proposing to carry him safe on her back across the sea to Papa Stour, on condition of receiving the seal-skin of Ollavitinus. A bargain was struck, and Gioga clad herself in her amphibious garb; but the Shetlander, alarmed at the sight of the stormy main that he was to ride through, prudently begged leave of the matron, for his better preservation, that he might be allowed to cut a few holes in her shoulders and flanks, in order to procure, between the skin and the flesh, a better fastening for his hands and feet. The request being complied with, the man grasped the neck of the seal, and committing himself to her care, she landed him safely at Acres Gio in Papa Stour; from which place he immediately repaired to a skeo[1] at Hamna Voe, where the skin was deposited, and honourably fulfilled his part of the contract by affording Gioga the means whereby her son could again revisit the ethereal space over which the sea spread its green mantle.

THE MERMAID WIFE.[2]

A STORY is told of an inhabitant of Unst, who, in walking on the sandy margin of a voe,[3] saw a number of mermen and mermaids dancing by moonlight, and several seal-skins strewed beside them on the ground. At his approach they immediately fled to secure their garbs, and, taking upon themselves the form of seals, plunged immediately into the sea. But as the Shetlander perceived that one skin lay close to his feet, he snatched it up, bore it swiftly away, and placed it in concealment. On returning to the shore he met the fairest damsel that was ever gazed upon by mortal eyes, lamenting the robbery, by which she had become an exile from her submarine friends, and a tenant of the upper world. Vainly she implored the restitution of her property; the man had drunk

[1] Hut for drying fish.
[2] *Folk-Lore and Legends, Scotland.* W. W. Gibbings.
[3] A deep inlet, or creek.

deeply of love, and was inexorable; but he offered her protection beneath his roof as his betrothed spouse. The merlady, perceiving that she must become an inhabitant of the earth, found that she could not do better than accept of the offer. This strange attachment subsisted for many years, and the couple had several children. The Shetlander's love for his merwife was unbounded, but his affection was coldly returned. The lady would often steal alone to the desert strand, and, on a signal being given, a large seal would make his appearance, with whom she would hold, in an unknown tongue, an anxious conference. Years had thus glided away, when it happened that one of the children, in the course of his play, found concealed beneath a stack of corn a seal's skin; and, delighted with the prize, he ran with it to his mother. Her eyes glistened with rapture— she gazed upon it as her own—as the means by which she could pass through the ocean that led to her native home. She burst forth into an ecstacy of joy, which was only moderated when she beheld her children, whom she was now about to leave; and, after hastily embracing them, she fled with all speed towards the seaside. The husband immediately returned, learned the discovery that had taken place, ran to overtake his wife, but only arrived in time to see her transformation of shape completed—to see her, in the form of a seal, bound from the ledge of a rock into the sea. The large animal of the same kind with whom she had held a secret converse soon appeared, and evidently congratulated her, in the most tender manner, on her escape. But before she dived to unknown depths, she cast a parting glance at the wretched Shetlander, whose despairing looks excited in her breast a few transient feelings of commiseration.

" Farewell! " said she to him, " and may all good attend you. I loved you very well when I resided upon earth, but I always loved my first husband much better."

THE SEAL-CATCHER'S ADVENTURE.[1]

THERE was once upon a time a man who lived upon the northern coasts, not far from " Taigh Jan Crot Callow " (John-o'-Groat's House), and he gained his livelihood by catching and killing fish, of all sizes and denominations. He had a particular liking for the killing of those wonderful beasts, half dog and half fish, called " Roane," or seals, no doubt because he got a long price for their skins, which are not less curious than they are valuable. The truth is, that the most of these animals are neither dogs nor cods, but downright fairies, as this narration will show. It happened one day, as this notable fisher had returned from the prosecution of his calling, that he was called upon by a man who seemed a great stranger, and who said he had been despatched for him by a person who wished to contract for a quan-

[1] W. Grant Stewart, *Highland Superstitions and Amusements.*

tity of seal-skins, and that the fisher must accompany him (the stranger) immediately to see the person who wished to contract for the skins, as it was necessary that he should be served that evening. Happy in the prospect of making a good bargain, and never suspecting any duplicity, he instantly complied. They both mounted a steed belonging to the stranger, and took the road with such velocity that, although the direction of the wind was towards their backs, yet the fleetness of their movement made it appear as if it had been in their faces. On reaching a stupendous precipice which overhung the sea, his guide told him they had now reached their destination.

" Where is the person you spoke of ? " inquired the astonished seal-killer.

" You shall see that presently," replied the guide.

With that they immediately alighted, and, without allowing the seal-killer much time to indulge the frightful suspicions that began to pervade his mind, the stranger seized him with irresistible force, and plunged headlong with him into the sea. After sinking down, down, nobody knows how far, they at length reached a door, which, being open, led them into a range of apartments, filled with inhabitants —not people, but seals, who could nevertheless speak and feel like human folk; and how much was the seal-killer surprised to find that he himself had been unconsciously transformed into the like image. If it were not so, he would probably have died from the want of breath. The nature of the poor fisher's thoughts may be more easily conceived than described. Looking at the nature of the quarters into which he had landed, all hopes of escape from them appeared wholly chimerical, whilst the degree of comfort and length of life which the barren scene promised him were far from being flattering. The "Roane," who all seemed in very low spirits, appeared to feel for him, and endeavoured to soothe the distress which he evinced by the amplest assurances of personal safety. Involved in sad meditation on his evil fate, he was quickly roused from his stupor by his guide's producing a huge gully or joctaleg,[1] the object of which he supposed was to put an end to all his earthly cares. Forlorn as was his situation, however, he did not wish to be killed; and, apprehending instant destruction, he fell down, and earnestly implored for mercy. The poor generous animals did not mean him any harm, however much his former conduct deserved it, and he was accordingly desired to pacify himself, and cease his cries.

"Did you ever see that knife before?" said the stranger to the fisher.

The latter instantly recognised his own knife, which he had that day stuck into a seal, and with which it had escaped, and acknowledged it was formerly his own, for what would be the use of denying it?

"Well," rejoined the guide, "the apparent seal which made away with it is my father, who has lain dangerously ill ever since, and no means can stay his fleeting breath without your aid. I have been obliged

---

[1] A clasp-knife.

13

to resort to the artifice I have practised to bring you hither, and I trust that my filial duty to my father will readily excuse me."

Having said this, he led into another apartment the trembling seal-killer, who expected every minute to be punished for his own ill-treatment of the father. There he found the identical seal with which he had had the encounter in the morning, suffering most grievously from a tremendous cut in its hind-quarter. The seal-killer was then desired, with his hand, to cicatrise the wound, upon doing which it immediately healed, and the seal arose from its bed in perfect health. Upon this the scene changed from mourning to rejoicing—all was mirth and glee. Very different, however, were the feelings of the unfortunate seal-catcher, who expected no doubt to be metamorphosed into a seal for the remainder of his life. However, his late guide accosting him, said—

" Now, sir, you are at liberty to return to your wife and family, to whom I am about to conduct you; but it is on this express condition, to which you must bind yourself by a solemn oath—that you will never maim or kill a seal in all your life-time hereafter."

To this condition, hard as it was, he joyfully acceded; and the oath being administered in all due form, he bade his new acquaintance most heartily and sincerely a long farewell. Taking hold of his guide, they issued from the place, and swam up till they regained the surface of the sea, and, landing at the said stupendous pinnacle, they found their former steed ready for a second canter. The guide breathed upon the fisher, and they became like men. They mounted their horse, and fleet as had been their course towards the precipice, their return from it was doubly swift; and the honest seal-killer was laid down at his own door-cheek, where his guide made him such a present as would have almost reconciled him to another similar expedition—such as rendered his loss of profession, in so far as regarded the seals, a far less intolerable hardship than he had at first considered it.

THE MERMAID OF KNOCKDOLION.[1]

THE old house of Knockdolion stood near the water of Girvan, with a black stone at the end of it. A mermaid used to come from the water at night, and taking her seat upon this stone, would sing for hours, at the same time combing her long yellow hair. The lady of Knockdolion found that this serenade was an annoyance to her baby, and she thought proper to attempt getting quit of it, by causing the stone to be broken by her servants. The mermaid, coming next night, and finding her favourite seat gone, sang thus—

> " Ye may think on your cradle—I'll think on my stane ;
> And there'll never be an heir to Knockdolion again."

---

[1] Chambers, *Popular Rhymes of Scotland.*

Soon after, the cradle was found overturned, and the baby dead under it. It is added that the family soon after became extinct.

THE YOUNG LAIRD OF LORNTIE.[1]

THE young Laird of Lorntie, in Forfarshire, was one evening returning from a hunting excursion, attended by a single servant and two greyhounds, when, in passing a solitary lake, which lies about three miles south from Lorntie, and was in those times closely surrounded with natural wood, his ears were suddenly assailed by the shrieks of a female apparently drowning. Being of a fearless character, he instantly spurred his horse forward to the side of the lake, and there saw a beautiful female struggling with the water, and, as it seemed to him, just in the act of sinking. "Help, help, Lorntie!" she exclaimed. "Help, Lorntie—help, Lor——," and the waters seemed to choke the last sounds of her voice as they gurgled in her throat. The laird, unable to resist the impulse of humanity, rushed into the lake, and was about to grasp the long yellow locks of the lady, which lay like hanks of gold upon the water, when he was suddenly seized behind, and forced out of the lake by his servant, who, farther-sighted than his master, perceived the whole affair to be the feint of a water-spirit. "Bide, Lorntie—bide a blink!" cried the faithful creature, as the laird was about to

[1] Chambers, *Popular Rhymes of Scotland.*

dash him to the earth; "that wauling madam was nae other, God sauf us! than the mermaid." Lorntie instantly acknowledged the truth of this asseveration, which, as he preparing to mount his horse, was confirmed by the mermaid raising herself half out of the water, and exclaiming, in a voice of fiendish disappointment and ferocity,—

> " Lorntie, Lorntie,
>> Were it na your man,
> I had got your heart's bluid
>> Skirl[1] in my pan."

NUCKELAVEE.[2]

NUCKELAVEE was a monster of unmixed malignity, never willingly resting from doing evil to mankind. He was a spirit in flesh. His home was the sea; and whatever his means of transit were in that element, when he moved on land he rode a horse as terrible in aspect as himself. Some thought that rider and horse were really one, and that this was the shape of the monster. Nuckelavee's head was like a man's, only ten times larger, and his mouth projected like that of a pig, and was enormously wide. There was not a hair on the monster's body, for the very good reason that he had no skin.

If crops were blighted by sea-gust or mildew, if live stock fell over high rocks that skirt the shores, or if an epidemic raged among men, or among the

[1] Sing.   [2] Mr. W. Traill Dennison in the *Scottish Antiquary.*

lower animals, Nuckelavee was the cause of all. His breath was venom, falling like blight on vegetable, and with deadly disease on animal life. He was also blamed for long-continued droughts; for some unknown reason he had serious objections to fresh water, and was never known to visit the land during rain.

I knew an old man who was credited with having once encountered Nuckelavee, and with having made a narrow escape from the monster's clutches. This man was very reticent on the subject. However, after much higgling and persuasion, the following narrative was extracted:—

Tammas, like his namesake Tam o' Shanter, was out late one night. It was, though moonless, a fine starlit night. Tammas's road lay close by the sea-shore, and as he entered a part of the road that was hemmed in on one side by the sea, and on the other by a deep fresh-water loch, he saw some huge object in front of, and moving towards him. What was he to do? He was sure it was no earthly thing that was steadily coming towards him. He could not go to either side, and to turn his back to an evil thing he had heard was the most dangerous position of all; so Tammie said to himself, " The Lord be aboot me, an' tak' care o' me, as I am oot on no evil intent this night! " Tammie was always regarded as rough and foolhardy. Anyway, he determined, as the best of two evils, to face the foe, and so walked resolutely yet slowly forward. He soon discovered to his horror that the gruesome creature approaching him was no other than the dreaded Nuckelavee. The lower part of this terrible monster, as seen by Tammie, was like a great horse with flappers like fins about his legs, with a mouth as wide as a whale's, from whence came breath like steam from a brewing-kettle. He had but one eye, and that as red as fire. On him sat, or rather seemed to grow from his back, a huge man with no legs, and arms that reached nearly to the ground. His head was as big as a clue of simmons (a clue of straw ropes, generally about three feet in diameter), and this huge head kept rolling from one shoulder to the other as if it meant to tumble off. But what to Tammie appeared most horrible of all, was that the monster was skinless; this utter want of skin adding much to the terrific appearance of the creature's naked body,—the whole surface of it showing only red raw flesh, in which Tammie saw blood, black as tar, running through yellow veins, and great white sinews, thick as horse tethers, twisting, stretching, and contracting as the monster moved. Tammie went slowly on in mortal terror, his hair on end, a cold sensation like a film of ice between his scalp and his skull, and a cold sweat bursting from every pore. But he knew it was useless to flee, and he said, if he had to die, he would rather see who killed him than die with his back to the foe. In all his terror Tammie remembered what he had heard of Nuckelavee's dislike to fresh water, and, therefore, took that side of the road nearest to the loch. The awful moment came when the lower part of the head of the monster got abreast of Tammie. The mouth of the

monster yawned like a bottomless pit. **Tammie**
found its hot breath like fire on his face: the long
arms were stretched out to seize the unhappy man.
To avoid, if possible, the monster's clutch, Tammie
swerved as near as he could to the loch; in doing so
one of his feet went into the loch, splashing up some
water on the foreleg of the monster, whereat the
horse gave a snort like thunder and shied over to the
other side of the road, and Tammie felt the wind of
Nuckelavee's clutches as he narrowly escaped the
monster's grip. Tammie saw his opportunity, and
ran with all his might; and sore need had he to run,
for Nuckelavee had turned and was galloping after
him, and bellowing with a sound like the roaring of
the sea. In front of Tammie lay a rivulet, through
which the surplus water of the loch found its way to
the sea, and Tammie knew, if he could only cross the
running water, he was safe; so he strained every
nerve. As he reached the near bank another clutch
was made at him by the long arms. Tammie made
a desperate spring and reached the other side, leaving his bonnet in the monster's clutches. Nuckelavee
gave a wild unearthly yell of disappointed rage as
Tammie fell senseless on the safe side of the water.

THE TWO SHEPHERDS.[1]

THERE were out between Lochaber and Baidea-
nach two shepherds who were neighbours to each

[1] Campbell, *Popular Tales of the West Highlands.*

other, and the cne would often be going to see the other. One was on the east side of a river, and another on the west. The one who was on the west side of the river came to the house of the one who was on the east of it on an evening visit. He stayed till it was pretty late, and then he wished to go home. " It is time to go home," said he. " It is not that which thou shalt do, but thou shalt stay to-night," said the other, " since it is so long in the night." " I will not stay at all events; if I were over the river I don't care more." The houseman had a pretty strong son, and he said, " I will go with thee, and I will set thee over the river, but thou hadst better stay." " I will not stay at all events." " If thou wilt not stay I will go with thee." The son of the houseman called a dog which he had herding. The dog went with him. When he set the man on the other side of the river, the man said to him, " Be returning now; I am far in thy debt." The strong lad returned, and the dog with him. When he reached the river as he was returning back home, he was thinking whether he should take the stepping-stones, or put off his foot-clothes and take below. He put off his foot-clothes for fear of taking the stepping-stones, and when he was over there in the river the dog that was with him leaped at the back of his head. He threw her off him; she leaped again; he did the same thing. When he was on the other side of the river he put his hand on his head, and there was not a bit of a bonnet on it. He was saying, whether should he return to seek the bonnet, or should he go home without it." " It's

disgusting for me to return home without my bonnet;
I will return over yet to the place where I put my
foot-clothes off me; I doubt it is there that I left it."
So he returned to the other side of the river. He
saw a right big man seated where he had been, and
his own bonnet in his hand. He caught hold of the
bonnet, and he took it from him. " What business
hast thou there with that?—It is mine, and thou
hadst no business to take it from me, though thou
hast got it." Over the river then they went, without
a word for each other, fiercely, hatingly. When they
went over, then, on the river, the big man put his
hand under the arm of the shepherd, and he began to
drag the lad down to a loch that was there, against his
will and against his strength. They stood front to
front, bravely, firmly on either side. In spite of the
strength of the shepherd's son, the big man was about
to conquer. It was so that the shepherd's son thought
of putting his hand about an oak tree that was in the
place. The big man was striving to take him with
him, and the tree was bending and twisting. At last
the tree was loosening in the earth. She loosened all
but one of her roots. At the time when the last root
of the tree slipped, the cocks that were about the
wood crowed. The shepherd's son understood when he
heard the cocks crowing that it was on the short side
of day. When they heard between them the cocks
crowing, the big man said, " Thou hast stood well,
and thou hadst need, or thy bonnet had been dear for
thee." The big man left him, and they never more
noticed a thing near the river.

FATLIPS.[1]

ABOUT fifty years ago, an unfortunate female wanderer took up her residence in a dark vault, among the ruins of Dryburgh Abbey, which during the day, she never quitted. When night fell, she issued from this miserable habitation, and went to the house of Mr. Haliburton, of Newmains, or to that of Mr. Erskine, of Shielfield, two gentlemen of the neighbourhood. From their charity she obtained such necessaries as she could be prevailed upon to accept. At twelve, each night, she lighted her candle, and returned to her vault; assuring her friendly neighbours that, during her absence, her habitation was arranged by a spirit, to whom she gave the uncouth name of *Fatlips,* describing him as a little man, wearing heavy iron shoes, with which he trampled the clay floor of the vault, to dispel the damps. This circumstance caused her to be regarded, by the well-informed, with compassion, as deranged in her understanding; and by the vulgar, with some degree of terror. The cause of her adopting this extraordinary mode of life she would never explain. It was, however, believed to have been occasioned by a vow that, during the absence of a man to whom she was attached, she would never look upon the sun. Her lover never returned. He fell during the civil war of 1745-46, and she never more would behold the light of day.

[1] Sir Walter Scott, *Minstrelsy of the Scottish Border.*

The vault, or rather dungeon, in which this unfortunate woman lived and died, passes still by the name of the supernatural being with which its gloom was tenanted by her disturbed imagination, and few of the neighbouring peasants dare enter it by night.

THE SILLY MUTTON.

Come, draw your chairs up to the fire, and listen to the tale I am about to tell. But mind and put three pocket-handkerchiefs on the table beside me, neither more nor less, and don't forget your own, for sad, sad is the telling, and tearful the conclusion of the story; and I should like us to be prepared for every emergency.

" What a smell of cooking! " said the auld wife, as she came home from the village to the foot of the brae. " Farmer M'Nab must be having a rare feast to-night! "

Stay a minute; I am beginning at the wrong end of the story. Let us commence properly at the first line. You would not understand it otherwise, I know, though, of course, you are all so very clever.

It was a silly mutton that got behind the flock that summer's day, and lost itself on the road. No one was to blame but itself, neither the shepherd nor the collie dog was in fault, for,—greedy thing,—as the flock was being driven over the moor, the silly mutton saw a bit of nice, tasty grass by the roadside, and determined to have it at any price. So it hid behind a boulder of granite till the flock and shepherd and collie dog had gone past, and then, with a low " baa, baa " of satisfaction, it proceeded to browse on the coveted pasture.

But it was not long before it began to repent its folly, for the sky grew suddenly dark and lowering, rain began to fall, and night-time to approach. Where was the silly mutton to find refuge now, or seek companionship? The flock was far away, and the shepherd and kind collie dog out of sight and call. With anxious heart the silly mutton wandered all over the moorland waste in a rare fright, hopeful that some friend might take pity upon it, for it was young, and had never been really alone before in its life. Ah! it was such a lonely spot. A nasty growl of thunder increased the fears of the silly animal, while the hideous and ominous croak of a raven from a neighbouring pine-tree nearly drove all the little sense it had left out of its head.

" Baa, baa, baa! " moaned the silly mutton, as it galloped hither and thither; " Baa, baa, baa! where shall I seek refuge? baa, baa! Oh, there's something at last!" it cried, as it spied the smoke of a bothy curling up from behind a heathery hillock, and, turning a corner, it ran through a little wicket gate up between a patch of kale and potatoes, and never rested till, with a butt of its head, it burst open the low door, and entered the humble abode.

"Good life and sour scones!" exclaimed the auld wife, as she started up in a fright at the sudden intrusion; but she soon recovered herself when she saw what it was, and in another moment was congratulating herself upon such a lucky treasure-trove. "Come in, come in, my pretty mutton," quoth she. "Good luck has fallen to me to-day, I must admit. Before long I shall make some money out of this visitor, I feel sure. I will feed it and look after it till the good time comes; it will repay me all my trouble." So the silly mutton had a rare time of it— shelter overhead, and enough to eat and drink in all conscience, and the only thing it had to do was to eat, sleep, chew the cud, and grow fat at the auld wife's fireside.

The silly mutton was not quite lost to all sense of gratitude: perhaps it would have been better if it had been; and it thought one day, as it lay before the hearth and considered what good quarters it had, "Let me see; how can I do the kind auld wife a favour? Truly, I would like to do her one, if it was in my power. I will listen carefully, and, the first time I see a chance, I will do my best to please her."

I told you the silly mutton was lying before the fire at the moment of which I am speaking. It was evening, and the auld wife had just finished her supper—a good meal of porridge, with just a taste of herring, potatoes, and salt, to make it go down, while a bowl of fresh milk, half emptied, was by her side, to be put away in the press with the remains of the feast, for next morning's breakfast.

"Oh, dearie me!" said the auld wife, yawning, for she was very tired, having been out all day in the turnip-field till her back ached; "oh, dearie me!" how I do wish the supper would clear itself off the table by itself! and that I could find myself bedded just as I am, without having to get up and undress!"

"Ah!" thought the silly mutton, "now is my chance to do the auld wife a favour. I've grown so and filled out so the last month, I'm sure I'm strong enough for that." And, would you believe it? before the auld wife could say "Gizzard," the silly mutton had butted the table upside down, so that all the supper was cleared off it on to the floor, and the auld wife found herself pitched slap on her back in the bed, for the silly mutton had deftly put his head between her legs, and, with a kick out behind, sent her flying across the room!

"Baa, baa, baa!" said the silly mutton, grinning from ear to ear at his success; "baa, baa, baa! what d'ye think o' that, auld wife?"

"Baa, baa, baa!" yelled the auld wife from the bed. "Just wait a minute, and I'll baa, baa you!" Then, painfully crawling from the bed, she reached out her hand for the broomstick and made for the silly mutton. "Now comes the reward," thought the

silly mutton, and, indeed, it never knew how it happened, but in less than a minute it found himself out
of the door, down the road, with many a sore place
on its hide.

"Well, there's no accounting for the ingratitude

PITCHED INTO THE BED.

of some folks;" moaned the silly mutton. "I shall
certainly be careful how I do a kindness next time,
if I ever get a chance! Let's hope I shall get the
chance;" and it disconsolately wandered along the
moorland road.

14

" Baa, baa, baa! Will no one take pity upon a
poor silly mutton that has lost its way? Baa, baa,
baa! Ah, there's something at last!" said the silly
mutton, as it saw another auld wife carrying her
spinning-wheel up a narrow path that seemed to
enter a wood by the side of the highway. "I'll follow her. She can't carry that thing far; I fancy
we must be near her home." So it followed the auld
wife at a short distance.

" Holloa!" said the auld wife, turning round as
she heard footsteps after her; "my patience me!
why, here's a mutton coming up the road! Well, if
we only wait long enough luck will come surely to
our doors, and a good fleece into the bargain. The
poor thing looks a bit banged about; but still, a day
or two of combing will put that all to rights. I shall
shear a good fleece. Come in, silly mutton, come
in and welcome!" And saying this, she held the
low door of the bothy open, and the silly mutton,
nothing loth, went in and sat down by the peat-fire.

And since it knew how to behave well in the
house, this auld wife and the silly mutton got on
capitally, and she chuckled to herself over her luck,
for her stock of wool was getting very low, and here
was enough to keep her wheel going again for a long
time to come. So the silly mutton throve, and got
quite fat, and its fleece shone bright, so silky was it;
for the auld wife took great care of it, combing and
washing it daily, till the mutton could not help wishing it could do something in return. The wife was
so very kind, that the mutton looked out daily for an

opportunity to repay her, until one fine morning quite unexpectedly, just before shearing-time, the chance came.

" One never can get all one wants," muttered the auld wife out loud, just as she was starting for a walk. " What a trouble it will be for me to have that mutton sheared! I must go, I suppose, this very day to Farmer M'Nab up the valley, and see if one of his gillies can lend me a hand, or I shall be late. Oh, how I do wish the fleece would come off of itself, and save me all the bother! But there, I must not complain." So off she started up the valley.

" Ah, auld wife," muttered the silly mutton, " I think I can do that job for you without troubling any Farmer M'Nabs or tiresome gillies. You really have been so kind, that, however much it hurts, I will try my very best; and, when I get my fleece off, it will be nice and cool, the weather is so sultry, so I shall gain too by the good action, I'm sure."

The garden of the auld wife, I may tell you, was full of groset bushes; there was also a quickset hedge round the patch, and some very prickly old whins one side the fence. " This is the very thing for me," said the silly mutton; and there and then it rolled about on the top of the whins, it capered in and out of the quickset hedge, and it danced the Flowers of Edinburgh round and between the groset bushes. In less than ten minutes there were left on the silly mutton's back but a few wretched shreds of wool, hanging down in a miserable tangle here and there, while with scratches and cuts from head to tail it presented a most deplorable appearance. And there on the whins, the hedge, and the groset bushes hung scraps of fleece in festoons of every length, till a west wind springing up sent a good half of them flying along the road like bits of foam, a pleasant surprise to meet the auld wife on her return from the farmer's.

Now came the auld wife. She had been longer than she had expected, having been detained picking up a few scraps of the wool which she spied on the road, thinking, poor soul, they were shed from a passing flock, and, though not of much worth, were still useful to make up in odds and ends. But, when she arrived at the bothy and saw the hideous desolation, and the wretched object standing making faces at her in the pathway, though her mouth flew wide open in surprise, she was absolutely dumb with her astonishment and rage.

"Baa, baa, baa! see what I have done for you!" cried the silly mutton; "baa, baa, baa! Ah, here comes the reward!" For now it saw the auld wife striding up towards him along the pathway at a great rate.

The silly mutton never knew how it was done, but the next moment it found itself shot through the quickset hedge into the road beyond, smarting behind with the most dreadful pain it had ever felt, for there the auld wife's uplifted boot had struck it, disappointment and rage lending power to the blow!

"Oh dear, oh dear! the auld wife's brogues must have been shod with iron spikes!" moaned the silly

"Baa, baa, baa! see what I have done for you!" cried the silly mutton as it saw the auld wife striding up the pathway toward him.—Page 212.

Scottish Fairy Tales.

mutton, as it galloped down the road as fast as three legs could carry it. The fourth leg, let me remark in passing, was of no use: it was so sore, so very sore. " The auld brute, to behave so! Well, there's certainly no accounting for the ingratitude of some people," said the silly mutton. " I shall certainly be very careful how I do a favour next time, if I ever get the chance. Let's hope I shall get the chance; " and he painfully wandered down the moorland road.

" Baa, baa, baa! will no one take pity upon a poor silly mutton that has lost his way? Baa, baa, baa! Ah! there's something at last, surely," as he saw another auld wife picking up sticks in a little copse beside the way. " I'll just sit down in the ditch here till she's finished her gathering, and then follow her home."

And the silly mutton had not long to wait, for the auld wife's bundle was soon gathered, and, as she toddled off home, the silly mutton followed at a respectful distance until she arrived at her bothy; and, just as she opened the door, it slipped past her quickly and lay down by the peat-fire. Oh! it knew how to behave prettily by this time, you may take that for sure.

" Holloa! " said the auld wife, " a mutton in my bothy! Where in the wide world did that come from? Can it be Farmer M'Nab has sent it to me for my larder during the winter? At any rate, I'll think so until he, or whoever it belongs to, sends for it, which, I do hope sincerely, will never be. Oh, mercy me! what a state the poor thing is in! But it is fat, for all that, and that's all I want." So she patched up the silly mutton's scars and tears, and cut off the ragged bits of fleece that still hung about him, and washed the bruise where the last auld wife had given such a gruesome kick, and then, having fed the mutton with every good thing she could think of, sat down by the fire and congratulated herself on her good luck.

CUT OFF THE RAGGED BITS.

And from day to day she fed the silly mutton on all there was good and nourishing, and the silly mutton grew fat and sleek, so that now it barely cared to move from his seat by the hearth, but ate and slept, and slept and ate all day long.

And so delighted was the silly mutton with his new quarters and new mistress, that all former misfortunes were forgotten, and it thought: " Sure, so kind

an auld wife cannot be ungrateful. I will try and
do her a favour if it is in my power, and if I only can
discover what she wants."

And now the dark nights of November approached,
when the auld wife thought it was time to salt the
mutton and hang it up in the larder for winter use.
So it happened one afternoon, while she sat consider-
ing how much of the mutton would do fresh for her
present use, and how much was to be salted for the
winter's store, she put out her hand and stroked the
silly mutton tenderly down his sides. " Ah ! " said
she out loud, " what lovely chops ! what bonnie chops
are here ! Oh, dearie me ! if they only could be
roasted without any bother on my part, what a lucky
woman I should be, to be sure ! " and she sighed as
she put on her shawl and daundered off, for she had
something that afternoon to do down in the village,
and wanted to get back home before it was quite dark.

Now, I must tell you, when the auld wife put out
her hand and stroked the silly mutton, though she
did it very tenderly and softly, it awoke, and, looking
up, heard the auld wife's last words. If it had heard
all about the salting and the larder, perhaps it would
not have been so precious obliging. But, said the
silly mutton, " She wants my chops roasted without
any trouble, does she ? Dear old lass ! so she shall ; it
is not very difficult, and only a step from this corner
to the fire. As my fleece came again soon after I
gave that away, it won't take much longer till I get
my chops back again, I suppose. It is little enough
she asks after all her trouble and attention to me, I

must say." So he got up and sat slap down in the midst of the burning embers in the centre of the hearth.

"Holloa!" said the silly mutton, "what a smell of cooking there is! Where's it coming from, I wonder?"

"Holloa!" said the silly mutton, "I'm getting a bit too hot; I hope the chops will be done soon!"

"Holloa!" said the silly mutton, "the smoke is choking me! Why can't the auld wife have better peats?"

"Holloa!" said the silly mutton. But it said no more, for it was a great deal too fat to move up when once it had sat down; and, choked with the smoke, it fell back suffocated on the auld wife's hearth.

.   .   .   .   .   .

"What a smell of cooking!" said the auld wife, as she came from the village to the foot of the brae. "Farmer M'Nab must be having a grand feast! Why has he not asked me to it? the stingy old hunks! Dearie me! but it makes my mouth water. But I'll have as good a feast myself sooner or later, and I won't ask him to that—no, no, not I!" and she stopped for a moment to laugh as she thought of the silly mutton at home and his fat chops.

"What a smell of cooking!" said the auld wife, when at last she got to the top of the brae, and she turned her face to the wind and sniffed again. "It can't come from Farmer M'Nab for he is down to the right, and this good smell comes from further up the valley, and there is only my house further on.

It must be some strolling tinkers in the wood hard by making their supper. I do hope they have not been helping themselves to any of mine in my absence. They are nasty fellows, those tinkers!" and she picked up her petticoats and went on faster.

" What a smell of cooking!" said the auld wife, as she turned the corner of the pine wood by her bothy. " Oh! oh! oh! oh! what do I see?"

Ah! how can I describe the spectacle that met her gaze—smoke in volumes pouring from the door and windows; at the top a burning roof-tree, and the frizzling remains of an animal lying in the middle of the blazing furniture!

And then it was, believe me, the auld wife opened her mouth and began,—no, I won't tell you what she said; it won't make the story any better to listen to, or the conclusion any less sad to relate. Suffice it to say it was neither pretty nor polite.

But, as the silly mutton said, there is no accounting for the ingratitude of some folk; and that's not such a silly remark if you look at it sideways, is it?

WITCHCRAFT.

MACGILLICHALLUM OF RAZAY.[1]

JOHN GARVE MACGILLICHALLUM, of Razay, was an ancient hero of great celebrity. Distinguished in the age in which he lived for the gallantry of his exploits, he has often been selected by the bard as the theme of his poems and songs. Along with a constitution of body naturally vigorous and powerful, Razay was gifted with all those noble qualities of the mind which a true hero is supposed to possess. And what reflected additional lustre on his character was that he never failed to apply his talents and powers to the best uses. He was the active and inexorable enemy of the weird sisterhood, many of whom he was the auspicious instrument of sending to their " black inheritance " much sooner than they either expected or desired. It was not therefore to be supposed that, while those amiable actions endeared Razay to all good people, they were at all calculated to win him the regard of those infernal hags to whom he was so deadly a foe. As might be naturally expected, they cherished towards him the most

[1] W. Grant Stewart, *Highland Superstitions.*

218

implacable thirst of revenge, and sought, with unre-
mitting vigilance, for an opportunity of quenching
it. That such an opportunity did unhappily occur,
and that the meditated revenge of these hags was too
well accomplished, will speedily appear from this
melancholy story.

It happened upon a time that Razay and a number
of friends planned an expedition to the island of
Lewis, for the purpose of hunting the deer of that
place. They accordingly embarked on board the chieftain's yacht, manned by the flower of the young men
of Razay, and in a few hours they chased the fleet-
bounding hart on the mountains of Lewis. Their
sport proved excellent. Hart after hart, and hind
after hind, were soon levelled to the ground by the
unerring hand of Razay; and when night terminated
the chase they retired to their shooting quarters,
where they spent the night with joviality and mirth,
little dreaming of their melancholy fate in the morning.

In the morning of next day, the chief of Razay
and his followers rose with the sun, with the view of
returning to Razay. The day was squally and occasionally boisterous, and the billows raged with great
violence. But Razay was determined to cross the
channel to his residence, and ordered his yacht to
prepare for the voyage. The more cautious and less
courageous of his suite, however, urged on him to
defer the expedition till the weather should somewhat
settle,—an advice which Razay, with a courage which
knew no fear, rejected, and expressed his firm de-

termination to proceed without delay. Probably with a view to inspire his company with the necessary degree of courage to induce them all to concur in the undertaking, he adjourned with them to the ferry-house, where they had recourse to that supporter of spirits under every trial, the usquebaugh, a few bottles of which added vastly to the resolution of the company. Just as the party were disputing the practicability of the proposed adventure, an old woman, with wrinkled front, bending on a crutch, entered the ferry-house; and Razay, in the heat of argument, appealed to the old woman, whether the passage of the channel on such a day was not perfectly practicable and free from danger. The woman, without hesitation, replied in the affirmative, adding such observations, reflecting on their courage, as immediately silenced every opposition to the voyage; and accordingly the whole party embarked in the yacht for Razay. But, alas! what were the consequences? No sooner were they abandoned to the mercy of the waves than the elements seemed to conspire to their destruction. All attempts to put back the vessel proved unavailing, and she was speedily driven out before the wind in the direction of Razay. The heroic chieftain laboured hard to animate his company, and to dispel the despair which begun to seize them, by the most exemplary courage and resolution. He took charge of the helm, and in spite of the combined efforts of the sea, wind, and lightning, he kept the vessel steadily on her course towards the lofty point of Aird, in Skye. The drooping spirits of his crew be-

gan to revive, and hope began to smile upon them,—
when lo! to their great astonishment, a large cat was
seen to climb the rigging. This cat was soon followed by another of equal size, and the last by a suc-
cessor, until at length the shrouds, masts, and whole
tackle were actually covered with them. Nor did the
sight of all those cats, although he knew well enough
their real character, intimidate the resolute Razay,
until a large black cat, larger than any of the rest, appeared on the mast-head, as commander-in-chief of
the whole legion. Razay, on observing him, instantly
foresaw the result; he, however, determined to sell
his life as dearly as possible, and immediately com-
manded an attack upon the cats; but, alas! it soon
proved abortive. With a simultaneous effort the cats
overturned the vessel on her leeward wale, and every
soul on board was precipitated into a watery grave.
Thus ended the glorious life of *Jan Garbh Macgillichallum,* of Razay, to the lasting regret of the brave
clan Leod and all good people, and to the great satisfaction of the abominable witches who thus accomplished his lamentable doom.

THE WITCH OF LAGGAN.[1]

THE same day, another hero, celebrated for his
hatred of witchcraft, was warming himself in his
hunting hut, in the forest of Gaick, in Badenoch.

[1] W. Grant Steward, *Highland Superstitions.*

His faithful hounds, fatigued with the morning chase, lay stretched on the turf by his side,—his gun, that would not miss, reclined in the neuk of the bothy,—the *skian dhu* of the sharp edge hung by his side, and these alone constituted his company. As the hunter sat listening to the howling storm as it whistled by, there entered at the door an apparently poor weather-beaten cat, shivering with cold, and drenched to the skin. On observing her, the hairs of the dogs became erected bristles, and they immediately rose to attack the pitiable cat, which stood trembling at the door. " Great hunter of the hills," exclaims the poor-looking trembling cat, " I claim your protection. I know your hatred to my craft, and perhaps it is just. Still spare, oh spare a poor jaded wretch, who thus flies to you for protection from the cruelty and oppression of her sisterhood." Moved to compassion by her eloquent address, and disdaining to take advantage of his greatest enemy in such a seemingly forlorn situation, he pacified his infuriated dogs, and desired her to come forward to the fire and warm herself. " Nay," says she, " in the first place, you will please bind with this long hair those two furious hounds of yours, for I am afraid they will tear my poor hams to pieces. I pray you, therefore, my dear sir, that you would have the goodness to bind them together by the necks with this long hair." But the curious nature of the hair induced the hunter to dissemble a little. Instead of having bound his dogs with it, as he pretended, he threw it across a beam of wood which connected the couple of the bothy. The witch then, supposing the dogs securely bound, approached the fire, and squatted herself down as if to dry herself. She had not sitten many minutes, when the hunter could easily discover a striking increase in her size, which he could not forbear remarking in a jocular manner to herself. " A bad death to you, you nasty beast," says the hunter; " you are getting very large." " Ay, ay," replied the cat equally jocosely, " as my hairs imbibe the heat, they naturally expand." These jokes, however, were but a prelude to a more serious conversation. The cat, still continuing her growth, had at length attained a most extraordinary size,—when, in the twinkling of an eye, she transformed herself into her proper likeness of the Goodwife of Laggan, and thus addressed him:—" Hunter of the Hills, your hour of reckoning is arrived. Behold me before you, the avowed champion of my devoted sisterhood, of whom Macgillichallum of Razay and you were always the most relentless enemies. But Razay is no more. His last breath is fled. He lies a lifeless corpse on the bottom of the main; and now, Hunter of the Hills, it is your turn." With these words, assuming a most hideous and terrific appearance, she made a spring at the hunter. The two dogs, which she supposed securely bound by the infernal hair, sprung at her in her turn, and a most furious conflict ensued. The witch, thus unexpectedly attacked by the dogs, now began to repent of her temerity. " *Fasten, hair, fasten*," she perpetually exclaimed, supposing the dogs to have been bound by the hair; and so effectually did the hair *fasten,* according to her order, that it at last snapt the beam in twain. At length, finding herself completely overpowered, she attempted a retreat, but so closely were the hounds fastened in her breasts, that it was with no small difficulty she could get herself disengaged from them. Screaming and shrieking, the Wife of Laggan dragged herself out of the house, trailing after the dogs, which were fastened in her so closely that they never loosed their hold until she demolished every tooth in their heads. Then metamorphosing herself into the likeness of a raven, she fled over the mountains in the direction of her home. The two faithful dogs, bleed ing and exhausted, returned to their master, and, in the act of caressing his hand, both fell down and expired at his feet. Regretting their loss with a sorrow only known to the parent who weeps over the remains of departed children, he buried his devoted dogs, and returned home to his family. His wife was not in the house when he arrived, but she soon made her appearance. " Where have you been, my love ? " inquired the husband. " Indeed," replies she, " I have been seeing the Goodwife of Laggan, who has been just seized with so severe an illness that she is not expected to live for any time." " Ay! ay! " says he, " what is the matter with the worthy woman ? " " She was all day absent in the moss at her peats," replies the wife, " and was seized with a sudden colic, in consequence of getting wet feet; and now all her friends and neighbours are expecting her desmission." " Poor woman," says the husband; " I am sorry for her. Get me some dinner; it will be right that I should go and see her also." Dinner being provided and despatched, the hunter immediately proceeded to the house of Laggan, where he found a great assemblage of neighbours mourning, with great sincerity, the approaching decease of a woman whom they all had hitherto esteemed virtuous. The hunter, walking up to the sick woman's bed in a rage, proportioned to the greatness of its cause, stripped the sick woman of all her coverings. A shriek from the now exposed witch brought all the company around her. " Behold," says he, " the object of your solicitude, who is nothing less than an infernal witch. To-day, she informs me, she was present at the death of the Laird of Razay, and only a few hours have elapsed since she attempted to make me share his fate. This night, however, she shall expiate her crime by the forfeiture of her horrid life." Relating to the company the whole circumstances of her attack upon him, which were too well corroborated by the conclusive marks she bore on her person, the whole company were perfectly convinced of her criminality; and the customary punishment was about to be inflicted on her, when the miserable wretch addressed them as follows:—" My ill-requited friends, spare an old acquaintance, already in the agonies of death, from any further mortal degradation. My crimes and my folly now stare me in the face, in their true colours; while my vile and perfidious seducer, the enemy of your temporal and spiritual interests, only laughs at me in my distress; and, as a reward for my fidelity

15

to his interest, in seducing everything **that was amiable,** and in destroying everything that **was good, he**
is now about to consign my soul to **eternal misery.**
Let my example be a warning to all the **people of the**
earth to shun the fatal rock on which **I have split;**
and as a strong inducement for them to do so **I shall**
atone for my iniquity to the utmost of **my ability by**
detailing to you the awful history of my life." **Here**
the Wife of Laggan detailed at full length **the way**
she was seduced into the service of the **Evil One,—**
all the criminal adventures in which she had **been en-**
gaged, and ended with a particular account **of the**
death of Macgillichallum of Razay, and **her attack**
upon the hunter, and then expired.

Meanwhile a neighbour of the Wife of Laggan **was**
returning home late at night from Strathdearn, **where**
he had been upon some business, and had just **entered**
the dreary forest of Monalea, in Badenoch, **when he**
met a woman dressed in black, who ran **with great**
speed, and inquired of the traveller, with **great agita-**
tion, how far she was distant from the **churchyard of**
Dalarossie, and if she could be there by **twelve o'clock.**
The traveller told her she might, if she **continued to**
go at the same pace that she did then. She **then fled**
alongst the road, uttering the most desponding **lamen-**
tations, and the traveller continued his road to **Bade-**
noch. He had not, however, walked many **miles when**
he met a large black dog, which travelled **past him**
with much velocity, as if upon the scent of a **track or**
footsteps; and soon after he met another **large black**
dog sweeping along in the same manner. **The last dog,**

however, was scarcely past, when he met a stout black man on a fine fleet black courser, prancing along in the same direction after the dogs. "Pray," says the rider to the traveller, "did you meet a woman as you came along the hill?" The traveller replied in the affirmative. "And did you meet a dog soon after?" rejoined the rider. The traveller replied he did. "And," added the rider, "do you think the dog will overtake her ere she can reach the church of Dalarossie?" "He will, at any rate, be very close upon her heels," answered the traveller. Each then took his own way. But before the traveller had got the length of Glenbanchar, the rider overtook him on his return, with the foresaid woman before him across the bow of his saddle, and one of the dogs fixed in her breast, and another in her thigh. "Where did you overtake the woman?" inquired the traveller. "Just as she was entering the churchyard of Dalarossie," was his reply. On the traveller's return home, he heard of the fate of the unfortunate Wife of Laggan, which soon explained the nature of the company he had met on the road. It was, no doubt, the spirit of the Wife of Laggan flying for protection from the infernal spirits (to whom she had sold herself), to the churchyard of Dalarossie, which is so sacred a place that a witch is immediately dissolved from all her ties with Satan on making a pilgrimage to it, either dead or alive. But it seems the unhappy Wife of Laggan was a stage too late.

THE BLACKSMITH'S WIFE OF YARROW-FOOT.[1]

SOME years back, the blacksmith of Yarrowfoot had for apprentices two brothers, both steady lads, and, when bound to him, fine healthy fellows. After a few months, however, the younger of the two began to grow pale and lean, lose his appetite, and show other marks of declining health. His brother, much concerned, often questioned him as to what ailed him, but to no purpose. At last, however, the poor lad burst into an agony of tears, and confessed that he was quite worn-out, and should soon be brought to the grave through the ill-usage of his mistress, who was in truth a witch, though none suspected it. "Every night," he sobbed out, "she comes to my bedside, puts a magic bridle on me, and changes me into a horse. Then, seated on my back, she urges me on for many a mile to the wild moors, where she and I know not what other vile creatures hold their hideous feasts. There she keeps me all night, and at early morning I carry her home. She takes off my bridle, and there I am, but so weary I can ill stand. And thus I pass my nights while you are soundly sleeping."

The elder brother at once declared he would take his chance of a night among the witches, so he put the younger one in his own place next the wall, and lay awake himself till the usual time of the witch-wo-

[1] William Henderson, *Folk-Lore of the Northern Counties.*

man's arrival. She came, bridle in hand, and flinging it over the elder brother's head, up sprang a fine hunting horse. The lady leaped on his back, and started for the trysting-place, which on this occasion, as it chanced, was the cellar of a neighbouring laird.

While she and the rest of the vile crew were regaling themselves with claret and sack, the hunter, who was left in a spare stall of the stable, rubbed and rubbed his head against the wall till he loosened the bridle, and finally got it off, on which he recovered his human form. Holding the bridle firmly in his hand, he concealed himself at the back of the stall till his mistress came within reach, when in an instant he flung the magic bridle over her head, and, behold, a fine grey mare! He mounted her and dashed off, riding through hedge and ditch, till, looking down, he perceived she had lost a shoe from one of her forefeet. He took her to the first smithy that was open, had the shoe replaced, and a new one put on the other forefoot, and then rode her up and down a ploughed field till she was nearly worn out. At last he took her home, and pulled the bridle off just in time for her to creep into bed before her husband awoke, and got up for his day's work.

The honest blacksmith arose, little thinking what had been going on all night; but his wife complained of being very ill, almost dying, and begged him to send for a doctor. He accordingly aroused his apprentices; the elder one went out, and soon returned with one whom he had chanced to meet already abroad. The doctor wished to feel his patient's pulse, but she resolutely hid her hands, and refused to show them. The village Esculapius was perplexed; but the husband, impatient at her obstinacy, pulled off the bed-clothes, and found, to his horror, that horseshoes were tightly nailed to both hands! On further examination, her sides appeared galled with kicks, the same that the apprentice had given her during his ride up and down the ploughed field.

The brothers now came forward, and related all that had passed. On the following day the witch was tried by the magistrates of Selkirk, and condemned to be burned to death on a stone at the Bullsheugh, a sentence which was promptly carried into effect. It is added that the younger apprentice was at last restored to health by eating butter made from the milk of cows fed in kirkyards, a sovereign remedy for consumption brought on through being witch-ridden.

THE MILLER OF HOLDEAN.[1]

WHILE the miller of Holdean, in Berwickshire, was drying a melder[2] of oats, belonging to a neighbouring farmer, tired with the fatigues of the day, he threw himself down upon some straw in the kiln-barn, and soon fell fast asleep. After a time he was awakened by a confused noise, as if the killogee[3] were full of people, all speaking together; on which he pulled

[1] W. Henderson, *Folk-Lore of the Northern Counties.*
[2] Grinding.
[3] The empty space before the fireplace in a kiln.

aside the straw from the banks of the kiln, and, looking down, observed a number of feet and legs pad-
dling among the ashes, as if enjoying the warmth
from the scarcely extinguished fires. As he listened,
he distinctly heard the words, " What think ye o' my
feeties ? "—a second voice answering, " An' what
think ye o' mine ? " Nothing daunted, though much
astonished, the stout-hearted miller took up his " beer
mell," a large wooden hammer, and threw it down
among them, so that the ashes flew about; while he
cried out with a loud voice, " What think ye o' my
meikle mell amang a' thae legs o' yourn ? " A hideous rout at once emerged from the kiln amid yells
and cries, which passed into wild laughter; and finally these words reached the miller's ears, sung in a
mocking tone—

> " Mount and fly for Rhymer's tower,
>   Ha, ha, ha, ha !
> The pawky[1] miller hath beguiled us
> Or we wud hae stown[2] his luck
> For this seven years to come,
> And mickle water wud hae run
>   While the miller slept."

RONALDSON OF BOWDEN.[3]

A MAN named Ronaldson, who lived at the village
of Bowden, is reported to have had frequent encoun-
ters with the witches of that place. Among these we

---

[1] Artful.   [2] Stolen.
[3] W. Henderson, *Folk-Lore of the Northern Counties.*

find the following. One morning at sunrise, while he was tying his garter with one foot against a low dyke, he was startled at feeling something like a rope of straw passed between his legs, and himself borne swiftly away upon it to a small brook at the foot of the southernmost hill of Eildon. Hearing a hoarse smothered laugh, he perceived he was in the power of witches or sprites; and when he came to a ford called the Brig-o'-stanes, feeling his foot touch a large stone, he exclaimed, " I' the name o' the Lord, ye'se get me no farther!" At that moment the rope broke, the air rang as with the laughter of a thousand voices; and as he kept his footing on the stone, he heard a muttered cry, " Ah, we've lost the coof!"[1]

THE FARMER'S WIFE OF DELORAINE.[2]

WITCHCRAFT is not named in the next story, but we can scarcely be wrong in assuming it to be the agent at work in it. We must premise that it was, perhaps still is, customary in the Lowlands of Scotland, as in other secluded districts, for tailors to leave their workshops and go into the farmhouses of the neighbourhood to work by the day. The farmer's wife of Deloraine thus engaged a tailor with his workmen and apprentices for the day, begging them to come in good time in the morning. They did so, and partook of the family breakfast of porridge and milk.

[1] Fool. [2] W. Henderson, *Folk-Lore of the Northern Counties.*

During the meal, one of the apprentices observed that the milk-jug was almost empty, on which the mistress slipt out of the backdoor with a basin in her hand to get a fresh supply. The lad's curiosity was roused, for he had heard there was no more milk in the house; so he crept after her, hid himself behind the door, and saw her turn a pin in the wall, on which a stream of pure milk flowed into the basin. She twirled the pin, and the milk stopped. Coming back, she presented the tailors with the bowl of milk, and they gladly washed down the rest of their porridge with it.

About noon, while our tailors were busily engaged with the gudeman's wardrobe, one of them complained of thirst, and wished for a bowl of milk like the morning's. " Is that a' ? " said the apprentice; " ye'se get that." The mistress was out of the way, so he left his work, found his way to the spot he had marked in the morning, twirled the pin, and quickly filled a basin. But, alas! he could not then stay the stream. Twist the pin as he would, the milk still continued to flow. He called the other lads, and implored them to come and help him; but they could only bring such tubs and buckets as they found in the kitchen, and these were soon filled. When the confusion was at its height, the mistress appeared among them, looking as black as thunder; whilst she called out, in a mocking voice, " A'ye loons! ye hae drawn all the milk fra every coo between the head o' Yarrow an' the foot o't. This day ne'er a coo will gie her maister a drop o' milk, though he war gawing to starve." The tailors slunk away abashed, and from that day forward the wives of Deloraine have fed their tailors on nothing but chappit 'taties and kale.

LAIRD HARRY GILLES.[1]

THE Laird Harry Gilles of Littledean was extremely fond of hunting. One day, as his dogs were chasing a hare, they suddenly stopped, and gave up the pursuit, which enraged him so much that he swore the animal they had been hunting must be one of the witches of Maxton. No sooner had he uttered the word than hares appeared all round him, so close that they even sprang over the saddle before his eyes, but still none of his hounds would give them chase. In a fit of anger he jumped off his horse and killed the dogs on the spot, all but one black hound, who at that moment turned to pursue the largest hare. Remounting his horse, he followed the chase, and saw the black hound turn the hare and drive it directly towards him. The hare made a spring as if to clear his horse's neck, but the laird dexterously caught hold of one of her fore-paws, drew out his hunting-knife, and cut it off; after which the hares, which had been so numerous, all disappeared. Next morning Laird Harry heard that a woman of Maxton had lost her arm in some unaccountable manner; so he went straight to her house, pulled out the hare's foot (which

[1] W. Henderson, *Folk-Lore of the Northern Counties.*

had changed in his pocket to a woman's hand and arm), and applied it to the stump. It fitted exactly. She confessed her crime, and was drowned for witchcraft the same day in the well, by the young men of Maxton.

THE MISSING WEB.[1]

" Some time since, when calling at the house of one of my oldest parishioners, who had been a handloom weaver, he fell to speak of other days; and, amongst other things, he told me of the disappearance, some years back, on a fine summer's evening, of a web of linen which had been laid to bleach by the riverside at the foot of the glebe. The fishermen, it seems, were ' burning the water '[2] in the Skerry, and the man who had charge of the web went off to see the salmon ' leistered,' and on his return the web was gone. Of course there was a sensation. The story was soon in everybody's mouth, with abundant suspicions of as many persons as there were yards in the web of linen.

" The web belonged to a very important personage, no less than the howdie, or old village midwife, who was not disposed to sit down quietly under her loss. So she called in the aid of a wise man from Leitholm,

---

[1] W. Henderson, *Folk-Lore of the Northern Counties* (from the narrative of the Rev. R. O. Bromfield, of Sprouston).

[2] Spearing, or " leistering," salmon by torch-light.

and next day told her friend the weaver, my inform-
ant, that she had found the thief, for the wise man
had turned the key. The weaver being anxious to
see something of diablerie, the howdie brought the
wise man to his house; and the door being locked on
all within (four in number), the magician proceeded
as follows. He took a small key, and attached it to
a string, which he tied into the family Bible at a particular place, leaving the key hanging out. Next he
read two chapters from the Bible, one of which was
the history of Saul and the witch of Endor; he then
directed the howdie and another person to support
the key between them, on the tips of their forefingers,
and in that attitude the former was told to repeat the
names of all the suspected parties.

"Many persons were named, but the key still hung
between the fingers, when the wise man cried out,
'Why don't you say Jock Wilson?' This was accordingly done, and immediately the key dropped, *i.e.,*
turned off the finger-ends. So the news spread far
and wide that the thief was discovered, for the key
had been turned and Jock Wilson was the man! He
proved, however, not to be the man to stand such im-
putations, and being without doubt an honest fellow,
he declared 'he wudna be made a thief by the deevil.'
So he went to consult a lawyer, but after many long
discussions the matter died away; and my authority,
the weaver, says it was believed the lawyer was
bribed; 'for he aye likit a dram.'"

THE WITCHES OF DELNABO.[1]

In the time of my grandmother, the farm of Delnabo was proportionally divided between three tenants. At first equally comfortable in their circumstances, it was in the course of some time remarked by all, and by none more forcibly than by one of the said three portioners, that, although superior in point of industry and talent to his two fellow-portioners, one of the tenants was daily lapsing into poverty, while his two neighbours were daily improving in estate. Amazed and grieved at the adverse fortune which thus attended his family, compared to the prosperous condition of his neighbours, the wife of the poor man was in the habit of expressing her astonishment at the circumstance, not only to her own particular friends, but likewise to the wives of her neighbours themselves.

On one of these occasions, the other two wives asked her what would she do to ameliorate her condition, if it were in her power? She answered them she would do anything whatever. (Here the other wives thought they had got a gudgeon that would snap at any bait, and immediately resolved to make her their confidante.) "Well, then," says one of the other two wives, "if you agree to keep our communications strictly secret, and implicitly obey our instructions, neither poverty nor want shall ever assail you more."

[1] W. Grant Stewart, *Highland Superstitions.*

This speech of the other wife immediately impressed the poor man's wife with a strong suspicion of their real character. Dissembling all surprise at the circumstance, she promised to agree to all their conditions. She was then directed, when she went to bed that night, to carry along with her the floor broom, well known for its magical properties, which she was to leave by her husband's side in the course of the night, and which would represent her so exactly that the husband could not distinguish the difference in the morning. They at the same time enjoined her to discard all fears of detection, as their own husbands had been satisfied with those lovely substitutes (the brooms) for a great number of years. Matters being thus arranged, she was desired to join them at the hour of midnight, in order to accompany them to that scene which was to realise her future happiness.

Promising to attend to their instructions, the poor man's wife took leave of her neighbours, full of those sensations of horror which the discovery of such depravity was calculated to produce in a virtuous mind. Hastening home to her husband, she thought it no crime to break her promise to her wicked neighbours, and, like a dutiful and prudent wife, to reveal to the husband of her bosom the whole particulars of their interview. The husband greatly commended his wife's fidelity, and immediately entered into a collusion with her, which displays no ordinary degree of ingenuity. It was agreed that the husband should exchange apparel with the wife, and that he should, in this disguise, accompany the wives to the place appointed, to see what cantrips they intended to perform.

He accordingly arrayed himself in his wife's habiliments, and, at the hour of midnight, joined the party at the place appointed. The "bride," as they called him, was most cordially received by the two Ladies of the Broom, who warmly congratulated the "bride" upon *her* good fortune, and the speedy consummation of *her* happiness. He was then presented with a fir torch, a broom, and a riddle, articles with which they themselves were furnished. They directed their course along the banks of the rolling Avon, until they reached Craic-pol-nain, or the Craig of the Birdspool. Here, in consequence of the steepness of the craig, they found it convenient to pass to the other side of the river. This passage they effected without the use of the navy, the river being fordable at the place. They then came in sight of Pol-nain, and lo! what human eye ever witnessed such a scene before! The pool appeared as if actually enveloped in a flame of fire. A hundred torches blazed aloft, reflecting their beams on the towering woods of Loynchork. And what ear ever heard such shrieks and yells as proceeded from the horrid crew engaged at their hellish orgies on Pol-nain? Those cries were, however, sweet music to the two wives of Delnabo. Every yell produced from them a burst of unrestrained pleasure, and away they frisked, leaving the amiable *bride* a considerable way behind. For the fact is, that he was in no hurry to reach the scene, and when he did reach it, it was with a determination to be only a spectator, and not a participator in the night's performance. On reaching the pool's side he saw what was going on, —he saw abundance of hags steering themselves to and fro in their riddles, by means of their oars (the brooms), hallooing and skirling[1] worse than the bogles, and each holding in her left hand a torch of fir,—whilst at other times they would swirl themselves into a row, and make profound obeisance to a large black ugly tyke,[2] perched on a lofty rock, and who was no doubt the " muckle thief " himself, and who was pleased to acknowledge most graciously those expressions of their loyalty and devotion, by bowing, grinning, and clapping his paws. Having administered to the *bride* some preliminary instructions, the impatient wives desired him to remain by the pool's side until they should commune with his Satanic Highness on the subject of *her* inauguration, directing *her,* as they proceeded on their voyage across the pool, to speed them in their master's name. To this order of the black pair the *bride* was resolved to pay particular attention. As soon as they were embarked in their riddles, and had wriggled themselves, by means of their brooms, into a proper depth of water, " Go," says he, " in the name of the Best." A horrid yell from the witches announced their instant fate— the magic spell was now dissolved—crash went the riddles, and down sank the two witches, never more to rise, amidst the shrieks and lamentations of the Old Thief and all his infernal crew, whose combined power and policy could not save them from a watery

[1] Shrieking.　　　　　　[2] Dog.

end. All the torches were extinguished in an instant, and the affrighted company fled in different directions, in such forms and similitudes as they thought most convenient for them to adopt; and the *wily bride* returned home at his leisure, enjoying himself vastly at the clever manner in which he had executed the instructions of his deceased friends. On arriving at his house, he dressed himself in his own clothes, and, without immediately satisfying his wife's curiosity at the result of his excursion, he yoked his cattle, and commenced his morning labours with as little concern as usual. His two neighbours, who were not even conscious of the absence of their wives (so ably substituted were they by the brooms), did the same. Towards breakfast-time, however, the two neighbours were not a little astonished that they observed no signs of their wives having risen from bed—notwithstanding their customary earliness—and this surprise they expressed to the *late bride,* their neighbour. The latter archly remarked that he had great suspicions, in his own mind, of their *rising* even that day. " What mean you by that ? " replied they. " We left our wives apparently in good health when we ourselves arose." " Find them now," was the reply—the *bride* setting up as merry a whistle as before. Running each to his bed, what was the astonishment of the husbands, when, instead of his wife, he only found an old broom ? Their neighbour then told them that, if they chose to examine Pol-nain well, they would find both their dear doxies there. The grieving husbands accordingly proceeded thither, and with the

necessary instruments dragged their late worthy part-
ners to dry land, and afterwards privately interred
them. The shattered vessels and oars of those unfortunate navigators, whirling about the pool, satisfied their lords of the manner by which they came to
their ends; and their names were no longer mentioned
by their kindred in the land. It need scarcely be
added that the poor man gradually recovered his former opulence; and that, in the course of a short time,
he was comparatively as rich as he was formerly poor.

THE BRAZEN BROGUES.

OR, TOO MANY TO MARRY.

THERE was a strange party assembled at the young farmer Gille Macdonald's that late spring evening, the night of the tryst at Inveraray, from attending which all and sundry were making their way home to the southwards.

Though a fine dry evening, it was a bit chilly; there was still a touch of winter in the season, and so no one was too proud or too robust to join the circle round the ingle, and warm themselves by the cheerful blaze.

243

There was a fisherman from **Strathlachlan, a** drover from Kilmun, two farmers from **away south** about Bute, a merchant from Rothesay, **and a pedlar** from anywhere you please, for he was **always on the** road from there to somewhere else.

Each had much to say for himself about **his luck or** otherwise at the tryst, and they were good **company;** but far and away the best of them all for **conversation** and news was the little pedlar, who sat on **the three-**legged stool in the centre, and had an **answer ready** for each and advice for all.

The conversation turned, as likely it would (for you see they had all been bargaining and selling), **on** how fortunes were made or lost, and one said **this,** and the other said that, each one seeming to **have his** own view of the matter, and deeming his own **way** the best; but what the little pedlar remarked **just** before they broke up for the evening was the **only** thing that Gille Macdonald remembered or **thought** worth listening to.

For the pedlar had said in answer to how **would he** set to work to make his fortune, that, if he was **a bit** bigger, and was a younger and stronger man, he **knew** a place where a fortune could be got for **the digging,** only it needed a stouter heart and a more **adventurous** spirit than he possessed to attempt the search. **So he** for one would still stick to his pack.

After the cup had passed round for the last **time,** and all were moving off to the beds provided **for them,** Gille Macdonald gently touched the sleeve **of the** pedlar, and asked him if he would kindly **wait a**

Gille Macdonald drew the little pedlar towards the ingle, and filling
his glass once more begged him to be seated.—Page 245.

Scottish Fairy Tales.

moment after the others had gone, as he wanted to ask him privately a certain question.

The pedlar was delighted to oblige so kind a host as Gille Macdonald, and said he certainly would.

So when the kitchen was clear of company, Gille Macdonald drew the little pedlar towards the ingle, and filling his glass once more, begged him to be seated, and if it so pleased him, to say what he meant by the place where a fortune was to be had for the digging, if only a brave heart and a stout spirit were there to attempt the deed.

" Oh ! " replied the little pedlar, " that is it, is it ? Well, the place I mean is over on the west side of Kintyre, a day's journey from here on horseback. Across the loch and by the road over the ridge from Tarbert, there is the castle of Taychronan, inhabited by an evil old gentleman who is reputed to be eminently rich ; and that that is not a mere rumour I myself know, for he has a treasure buried in the well in the garden. With these two eyes I saw him shovelling in ducats and gold pieces just as if they were potatoes, only a month ago. I would have liked much to have secured some of them, but you know what a fragile little fellow I am, and I was too much afraid of the old gentleman to do anything of the kind.

" Now, don't let me induce you to go after the treasure ; you are comfortably off, and can want nothing more than what you have got already. I should be sorry if you fell into the old gentleman's clutches, for evil things are spoken of him, and he is said to be not only a selfish old miser, but a powerful magician, and a cruel as well. Now, good night," and the ped-lar walked off to his couch.

In the morning the whole party of the night before left the farm, thanking their host, and going their several ways. As to the pedlar, he had started at cock-crow, to be early on the road, so Gille Macdonald had no further chance to question him about the castle and the treasure, of which he had dreamed all night, waking up in the morning quite determined to investigate, and, if possible, secure it.

So he occupied himself that day in putting his farm in order, and gave instructions to his head ser-vant that this and that should be done in his absence, and this and that should be done if he never came back at all; and this preparation finished, the very next morning he saddled his grey mare and took the road that led to the nearest ferry on Loch Fyne side.

The crossing was accomplished successfully, for it was fine weather for the time of the year, while a light breeze and sunny sky put him in good spirits for his adventure.

A fair was being held at Tarbert when he arrived there; booths were erected up and down the streets, and music and dancing were going on by the shore. There also many people were gathered together from the surrounding country, with mountebanks and singers and such like turning an honest penny among the crowd.

One little chap in especial Gille Macdonald could not help observing with interest, for he would throw three or four somersaults on the hard pavement without stopping—yes, and could throw them backwards and forwards at pleasure for what trifle the spectators might fling him in his upturned hat after each performance.

Amongst others the mannikin pproached Gille

WOULD THROW THREE OR FOUR SOMERSAULTS.

Amongst others the mannikin approached Gille as well.

"Well, then, a copper you must be satisfied with, small friend," said Gille Macdonald; "I can't give you more, for we are both seeking a fortune, I see, in our different ways."

"How so, friend?" said the mannikin. "Where and how do you seek a fortune?"

"With a strong arm and a stout heart," said Gille Macdonald. "I hope to get a fortune by digging;" and he passed up the street.

"Stay," said the mannikin, running after him; "where did you say a fortune was to be got for the digging?"

Well, Gille Macdonald did not like to be interrogated further, and in fact he was angry with himself for having been led to speak of his adventure at all; but he did not wish to seem rude to a poor little mite, so he said, "Oh, not far away; over the hills to the west. Good night."

"Good night," said the dwarf; and Gille Macdonald thought there was a queer tone in the way it was muttered, and somehow he did not like it at all; but everything was soon forgotten in the enjoyment of good company at the inn, where, the host being an old friend of his, he put up for the night.

Early next morning he was astir, and saddled his mare, giving her a good feed, for she had a long journey before her, and he wished to reach Castle Taychronan before nightfall, so that he might be able to have a look round unknown to the old man, and to find out where the well was situated.

As he journeyed on his thoughts naturally turned to the adventure before him, and in a brown study he let the mare jog along as she chose, taking no heed of anything till, with a start, he was aroused by a squeaky little voice beside him, which struck him as strangely familiar. Looking down, he was aware of a little man walking by his side, with a face exactly like the mannikin's he had seen at the fair the day before.

Yet it could not be the same, for that one was so very small and humpbacked, while this, though a wee bit creature, was not anything out of the run of little men. Yet he had the same hunch on his back, the same long pointed red nose and queer squint as had his acquaintance of the fair—yes, and his very voice too, only louder and stronger.

" Well met," quoth the little man.

" Well met," said Gille Macdonald.

" We are fellow-travellers, I see," said the wee man.

" For the present, yes," said Gille Macdonald, and he urged his mare on along the road.

" We'll meet again, maybe, before long," cried the wee man after him.

Now it made Gille Macdonald laugh to think such a crippled creature would ever catch him up again; but something about the dwarf he did not like, and he was not comfortable till he had galloped on a mile, and had lost sight of him.

It was about noon, and Gille Macdonald was giving his mare a quiet walk down that part of the high-road which, having kept to the upper moorland for some miles, here makes a rapid descent towards the sea again at Ronachan Bay. What was his astonishment to hear again the now familiar voice calling to him from the other side of the dyke, and before he regained his composure he saw the old, ugly face peering at him from behind a stunted willow, whose twisted roots crept in and out like snakes among the stonework.

" Well met," quoth the creature; and this time that which accosted him was a full-grown man just about his own size, and Gille Macdonald was not a small man by any means.

A LITTLE MAN WALKING BY HIS SIDE.

Gille Macdonald could not believe his eyes. There was the long red nose, and the squinting eyes, and the round humpy back, but six foot the creature was if an inch. It could not be the same; but that it had some uncanny connections with the mannikin he met at Tarbert, and again already that morning, he felt certain.

You may be sure he liked the meeting less than ever; even his docile old mare shied on one side as the thing now stepped into the middle of the road. But Gille Macdonald thought civility could do no harm, so he gave him good-day as before.

"We are fellow-travellers, I see," said the thing, and he squinted horribly with his ugly eyes.

"For the present, yes," said Gille Macdonald; "but I must be jogging on," and he struck spurs into the mare.

"We'll meet again, maybe, before long," said the man.

It did not need much to make the mare go along the road at a good rate, and not for a while did Gille Macdonald feel the eerie thrill leave him; but young spirits are not easily upset for long, so before an hour had passed he was singing as blithely as before.

It's a long, straight bit of road from Ballochroy to Tayinloan, as every one knows who has made the journey, and at evening, just as Gille Macdonald chanced to be entering upon it, the sun was at his back, and he could see a long way down before him, with everything standing out very clearly.

"What a funy thing," said he, "for people to have planted a tree there right in the middle of the road!" for a little bit ahead there was what seemed to him a young fir-tree sticking up straight before him. "They do odd things in this part of the country, surely." But you may imagine what his astonishment was when he saw the thing move along in the direction in which he was going. He rubbed his eyes, and thought it must be some trick of light and shade. It couldn't be a human being!—yes, it was! and then the strange things he had seen that day flashed upon his mind, and he felt sure this was again another of the same nasty crew he had so wished to avoid.

" I shall most decidedly turn back," said he, and he was giving the rein a pull to one side when the gaunt figure in front turned round, and, stepping to one side, took off its hat with a low bow, and with the same voice as he had heard before said—

" Well met."

" Well met," said Gille Macdonald, shivering all over.

" Pray pass on," said the tall man; " we are fellow-travellers, I see "; and he rolled his squint eyes and shook his long red nose in a fearsome manner.

" For the present, yes," faltered Gille Macdonald. " But, excuse me; I must be pressing on," and he urged his steed past the creature, for now it was just as bad to go backward as forward.

" We'll meet again, maybe," cried the tall man after him, as Gille Macdonald sped along the straight road; for both man and beast were thoroughly frightened by this time, and they wanted to put as much country between themselves and that ugsome thing as they could.

Gille Macdonald did not forget the apparition this time, or his saying they would maybe meet again. At every turn he expected something terrible to appear; under every rock he thought he saw some horrid shape lurking, and ready to pounce. The evening

"Well met," said from somewhere above him, the voice Gille Macdonald knew too well.—Page 253.   *Scottish Fairy Tales.*

also became dark and lowering, which added to his fears. The sun had set, and a fitful moonlight, now bright, now dark, made everything look larger and grimmer than it would appear by day. The trees by the roadside took fantastic shapes, and seemed to stretch out their arms fiercely over the path, with eager claws ready to seize him; in every sigh of the wind he heard again the croaky, familiar voice; in every echo of his mare's hoofs a weird footfall rang behind him.

Suddenly he came to a spot where the road seemingly had no outlet—rocks on this side, rocks on that. "Yet there must be some way through," thought he, "or the road would not lead this way," and he urged his horse forward into the darkness. A plunge! His faithful steed reared high in air, and, throwing his master, coursed back down the road, screaming with fear.

"Well met," said from somewhere above him the voice Gille Macdonald knew too well; and as he lay bruised on the road, he saw in the moonlight a gigantic figure blocking up the whole pass between the two steep rocks through which the road stretched beyond.

"Well met," again said the voice. "But you don't seem to have a civil answer for me as before;" for Gille Macdonald was so terrified his tongue stuck in his jaws, and he could not reply. "I said maybe we would meet again, and, by my troth, the pleasure seems to be all on my side."

"With your permission," said Gille Macdonald,

gasping for breath, " I will now go and see if I can find my horse."

" With my permission you shall do nothing of the sort," replied the figure. " You have come a long way to see my castle, and within it you shall rest this night. Ay, and for many a night to come, for the matter of that."

" Your castle?" said Gille Macdonald. " What do you mean by that?"

" Where gold can be got for the digging: is it not so?" said the voice. " Come, you thief, you hypocrite, you wretched slave! know I am the magician, and Castle Taychronan is my home. There you shall have the digging you looked for, as my slave during your lifetime, with the digging of your own grave at the end of it."

Poor Gille Macdonald had not a word to say, so the giant—for he was a giant indeed of twenty feet by this time—took him up from the road and carried him by his waistbelt to the castle, which was a couple of miles off. Yet the journey only occupied but little time, for the giant's strides were long, and he was in a hurry to get home.

When they arrived at the castle gate he set Gille Macdonald down on the ground, and, putting his head down, he said a queer word below the lintel, and immediately, from being a giant over twenty feet high, he dwindled to the size of a man of seven feet or thereabouts, after which transformation he turned round and drove Gille Macdonald into the castle before him with a cudgel.

They entered now a large and lofty hall, roofed with black oak, dark and grim with smoke and age. There was spread some supper on an oaken board, huge and vast, fit for a giant; while on an open hearth blazed a great fire of pine logs, which lit the hall with a fitful gleam. In its ruddy light Gille Macdonald observed that the only furniture, besides the table and a huge couch in the corner, was five oaken presses set along the wall, all with panels carved in quaint devices, and hinges and locks of burnished brass.

" Serve my dinner," said the giant; " and be quick about it."

Gille Macdonald did so without any demur. He was getting his wits together as best he could, so he did his best to please in the meantime, meditating the while on his unfortunate fate, and wondering whether there was any chance of escape. An idea soon came into his head, and while handing a beaker of wine to the giant, he got up in a chair behind him, and held it for some moments right over his head.

" What are you doing? what are you up to? " said the giant. " What the mischief makes you hold it up there in that way? "

" Oh, I beg your pardon, I'm sure," explained Gille Macdonald; " you see I'm so accustomed———"

" Accustomed to what? " asked the giant sharply.

" To hand the cup to my master at home in this way; he likes me to hold it as near his mouth as he can."

" But that's ridiculously high," said the giant.

"Not a bit of it," explained Gille Macdonald; "you are not the only giant in the kingdom."

"Oh, ah!" said the giant, a bit taken by surprise. Then, recovering himself, he said, "He must be a

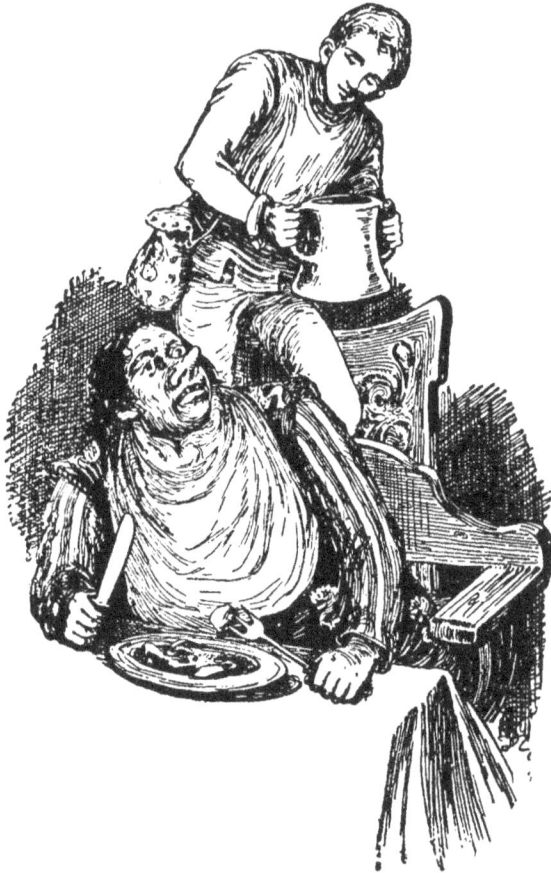

"WHAT ARE YOU DOING?" SAID THE GIANT.

queer creature; but see you, I won't have any of your silly tricks here; so behave."

"You won't be troubled with them very long," said Gille.

" What d'ye mean by that ? " said the giant.

" Only that my master will soon be here to take me away."

" Take you away when you are in my house! I'd like to see any one do that," remarked the giant with a snort.

" So should I," said Gille Macdonald; " and he will, too."

The giant got up with a bounce and went to the fire, where for a space he stood buried in thought. Meanwhile Gille Macdonald did not see any reason why he should not have a bit of the pasty and a sup of the wine; but he did not get long to do it, for the giant, turning round, said, as if to relieve his mind, " Well, he can't find you here, for he don't know where to look for you."

" Your attention, sir, for a moment," said Gille Macdonald. " Do you see these brogues of mine ? well, look at the heels; they are shod with brass. All my master's servants, men, women, and cattle, are shod with shoes of this description, so wherever they go, there he can trace them to the world's end."

" What sort of person do you say your master is ? " said the giant, feigning composure.

" Oh! I can't be bothered to explain," said Gille Macdonald, plucking up his spirits as he saw the giant was losing his. " You'll see for yourself presently; he'll be here before to-morrow evening, most likely, and not in the best humour, either."

At this the giant got still more subdued, and said, " Oh! it does not matter, of course, to me whether

17

your master comes or not; but just tell me, is he as big a man as I was when we met in the pass? I'm not curious, but I only want to know."

" Is that the very biggest you can make yourself?" said Gille Macdonald, not to be taken off his guard.

" Yes," said the giant, " it is, and bigger than what you've been accustomed to."

At this Gille Macdonald burst out laughing. " You'll excuse me," said he, " but you'll be like a baby beside him, if that's all you can do."

At this the giant, in a great state of trepidation, again strode to the fireplace, and kicked the blazing logs about from one side of the hearth to the other in a most vicious manner, just to hide the fright he was now in.

" I think you had better be off at once," said he. " I wish I had never seen your ugly face."

" That's not very civil," said Gille Macdonald, " especially as you were so very anxious for my acquaintance on the road here."

" Get out of the place this minute!" roared the giant. " Here's a piece to drink my health with, if you will only be quiet, and go."

Gille Macdonald took the piece and made for the door; but he was only pretending, for he saw now the giant was completely cowed, and he had no intention of leaving the castle without some treasure after all his troubles; so he turned round, just as he was leaving the hall, and said, " It is really very good of you to give me this piece, and to send me home; it is more than I would have expected, so I think it is only civil to tell you that whether I go or stay my master will come here after me, as once on the trail of the brazen brogues he never leaves it, so you had better be prepared. Hush! there, don't you hear that?" as a gust of wind swept round the tower;

"YOU'LL BE LIKE A BABY BESIDE HIM."

"there he is blowing his nose! Oh! don't alarm yourself; he is miles and miles off still."

"Come in and sit down," said the giant, "and I will make it worth your while to tell me how I can escape the notice of your master; for he seems to be an irascible kind of fellow, and I should not like a quarrel to take place with any friend of yours in my own house."

" Well," said Gille Macdonald, " just you hide till he has come and gone. But stay, I don't see how you are to do that; you're so very big."

" I'll get into that corner by the door," said the giant.

" Get into that corner ? " cried Gille Macdonald. " How can you with your size, indeed ? "

" How can I ? " roared the giant. " I'd have you to know there is no can or cannot in this house for me ; " and he went behind the door and said a very queer word, and there the giant was about five feet high instantly, just the right size for the hiding-place.

" Oh," said Gille Macdonald, " that won't do at all; my master will be poking about all over the place. That's the worst of him, he is so curious, and will be certain to find you out."

" Rot his curiosity ! " said the giant. " Then under the table will do," and he put his head under the table and said a very, very queer word, and in an instant there he was, just small enough to stand under the table.

" That's better," said Gille Macdonald, and he walked to the end of the hall. " But no; I can see you easily from here, and my master has such plaguy sharp eyes."

" Plaguy sharp eyes ! Plague take them and you too ! I won't diminish another inch to please any-body."

"Hush, hush!" said Gille Macdonald, as a louder gust of wind whirled round the castle; "there he is, still a good mile off; but coming fast, and oh! what a cold he's got in his nose! Just make the best of it. But don't blame me if he wrings your neck."

Then the giant rushed out from under the table and said a very, very, very queer word under the footstool, and there he was, sure enough, six inches high, a tiny mannikin squinting at Gille Macdonald from between its two legs.

"I really think he cannot see you there," said Gille Macdonald, "though he is most inquisitive, and does kick things about; so let's see, to make quite sure," and saying this, he gave the footstool a kick with his foot. "No, it won't do; I saw you then quite clearly when the stool moved. Can't you get under something smaller?"

"No, not for you or for your vile master," squeaked the mannikin. "I won't, I won't, I won't!"

"Then take the consequences! There he is at the door," as a fierce gust of wind roared down the chimney. "His nose will be as red as yours if he goes on blowing it at that rate."

Without a word the mannikin crawled out from under the footstool, and scrambling to the hearth, he said a very, very, very, *very* queer word under the hearthstone, and there he was in a moment, as small as a black beetle.

"Where have you got to?" said Gille Macdonald.

"Under the hearthstone," chirruped the mannikin.

" Nonsense; I can see you still under the foot-stool," replied Gille Macdonald.

" You can't," said the mannikin. " I'm under the hearthstone."

" Don't tell me lies! " said Gille Macdonald, " or I'll tell my master."

" Then will this satisfy you? " squeaked the mannikin, and a little, ugly black beetle crawled out from under the hearthstone. " Do you see me now? Are you satisfied now? " said he.

" I'm perfectly satisfied," said Gille Macdonald, and he put his foot on the beetle, and squish, sqrunch! there was nothing but a black patch seen on the floor.

" Well, that's over," and Gille Macdonald sank with a sigh of relief into the giant's chair.

But with a bang all the five doors of the five presses opened, and before he could say with your leave or by your leave, Gille Macdonald found him-self surrounded by five maidens in seagreen-coloured attire, who clasped him round the neck and arms, kissing, tickling, and nearly throttling him, all the time laughing and giggling like wild lunatics.

" Have done! be off! Away with you, saucy wenches! Get off, I say! " choked Gille Macdonald, struggling to be free; but the more he pushed and kicked the closer they hung round about him and embraced him. What would have been the end of it I don't know, if he had not, with a violent effort, got clear, and, flying to the corner of the hall, he stood at bay with the giant's footstool held out before him in defence.

"Have done! be off! Away with you! Get off, I say!" choked Gilie Macdonald, as the maidens hung round about him and embraced him.
Page 262.   *Scottish Fairy Tales.*

"Keep your distance," cried he. "I'll give the first one who comes within a foot of me a nasty smack, I vow I will!" and he whirled the footstool round and round in a circle in front of him.

And there were the five maidens dancing, laughing, kissing their hands to him, and kicking up their legs in a manner he had never seen before.

"Come out of the corner, you coward you!" cried they. "You call yourself a man, and go on in that way? Bah! ugh!" And oh! what faces they made when they said "Ugh!"

"I'll not come out or put the stool down," said Gille Macdonald, "till you promise to behave—that's flat. What is your business? tell me, go about it, and let me go about mine."

"That's just where it is; your business is ours," said they, "and whatever you have to go about, we must go about too. You've got to marry us all, so it is no use fretting about what must be."

"What can't be, you mean," said he. "All of you, did you say? What's the meaning of that? and don't all speak at once," for they began screeching and screaming together in return.

"Well," said the eldest, "look here. Now can we or you help it? We are the King of Loch Lin's daughters, and we have been locked up in those cupboards for three mortal years, because we vowed we would not marry that giant; and we must marry you, because we also vowed that whoever let us out should be our husband. You would not have us forswear ourselves, would you?"

" Well, if that's the case," said Gille Macdonald, " sit down quietly at that table, and we'll talk over the matter seriously; but mind, any misbehaviour, and I will bang each of you over the head."

So they promised to sit quietly at the table if he came out and sat at the end.

So they did, and so he did; but he kept the stool at easy reach of his hand, all the same.

After a great deal of arguing he explained that it was quite impossible for him to marry them all, but that they must choose which of the five should represent the others, and then he would see if anything could be done.

Then it was decided that the green maidens should play for a husband, and whoever won should be his wife. So they took the giant's dambrod from the top of the chimney-piece, and for two hours did they play; but such was the cheating and contriving that none won and none lost. So they said it was evident that he must marry them all.

" No," said Gille Macdonald; " this is ridiculous, and, what is more, it's getting late, and will be next morning very soon. Try each of you a cast of the dice, and we will see if it can be managed that way, perhaps."

So they took the bones and boxes from above the chimney, and threw for a husband; but they all cheated so and contrived so, that none won and none lost. So they said now he *must* marry them all, whatever he said or thought.

" No," said he, " I won't; but do get me some

supper, I'm so famished, and then I'll tell you how we will settle it."

So they got his supper, and sat down, waiting, round the giant's table.

"This is the trial," said Gille Macdonald, when he had finished and collected his thoughts a bit. "To-morrow I will ask you what colour I would my future bride should be dressed in, and whoever names the colour to my taste she shall be my wife. You can't cheat or contrive about that, I fancy."

"Very well," said the green maidens; but the youngest put a draught in Gille Macdonald's cup, when he was not looking, a potion that would make him dream—yes, and speak in his dream too. "Surely now he will tell us the secrets of his mind," said she.

After draining the cup, Gille Macdonald went and lay down before the fire on the giant's couch, and the green maidens made as if they were going upstairs, after giving him good-night; but as soon as he was fast asleep, they crept back into the room, and hid themselves about the room, waiting for what would come to pass.

Sure enough, very soon the draught began to take effect, and he dreamed of his farm and the hillsides of Strachur, speaking out aloud in his dreaming—

"Yellow is the corn in the glen of Ardkinglas;
And yellow is the bracken on the sides of Ben Ima;
Yellow is the hair of my loved one,
And yellow shall be the dye for her kirtle."

Then the green maidens arose, and with a low laugh they left the hall.

The next morning the sun shone through the window and woke Gille Macdonald, but not before the green maidens had come down and prepared the breakfast; for they were so pleased at their liberty, their cheats, and contrivances, that whether the sun

"PUT YOUR QUESTION," THEY SAID.

intended to get up or not, they did, and indeed, I don't think they closed an eye all night.

"Put your question," said the green maidens, when they perceived he was awake.

And Gille Macdonald put the question concerning the colour of his bride's robes to each in turn, and they all answered, "Yellow."

At this Gille Macdonald was so taken aback it was no use his saying they had not guessed right, for his looks said so.

" There now," said they; " you see there is no help for it; you must marry us all."

" Now, really," said Gille Macdonald, " in such a serious business you must give me another chance. But once more I will try you, and if that does not succeed, well, we'll see about it."

So the green maidens said they would have one more trial, and that in all conscience must be the very last; and they laughed together, for they felt quite confident of the result, and as they looked upon Gille Macdonald as a sort of fool to be easily taken in.

" Well, listen," said he; " whoever can tell me what favour it was the cod-fish of Ardminish asked of the widow woman of Gigha, that one I shall marry."

Then they said, " We must go out into the garden and think about the answer for a moment."

" Do so," said Gille Macdonald, " and I will give you five hours for consideration."

So off they went; but, bless you, he knew perfectly well they had gone off to the Loch to see if the cod-fish would tell them for a consideration what favour he asked of the widow woman.

" Now is my chance," quoth Gille Macdonald, and he went without loss of time to the well in the garden, where he found, sure enough, the treasure the old pedlar had told him about. Having filled his wallet, without good-day or with your leave or by your leave to anything or anybody, he went straight out of the door and took the road home.

" Oh, if I could only find my dear old grey mare," he sighed, " how pleased I should be! Ah, then I should feel safe from these bold wenches."

Scarcely were the words out of his mouth, when, turning a corner, he saw his old grey mare grazing by the roadside, and at his call she came whinnying up to him; and I can't say which of the two was the gladder to meet with the other.

On her back he vaulted, and away towards Tarbert they galloped. His heart was as light as his wallet was full; and the mare's head being turned homewards, both were in a hurry, so there was no need for whip or spur. Nor did he wait at Tarbert that evening, but for a large sum (what was money to him now? he got the ferryman to take him across there and then; and by midnight he was at his own hearthside, with his mare in her cosy stable.

Next morning he was out and about with his servants, so eager was he to begin improving his farm with his new wealth, and he worked, and kept his gillies working, till the evening star came and winked at the sun setting over Ben Dearg.

Then it was that, as he rested, leaning over the gate at the end of the field, he thought he heard voices up the road, and looking along there, what should he see about a mile off but five figures in green coming towards him, dancing, gesticulating, and chattering in a most unusual manner! No need, too, for him to ponder what visitors these might be, or what their errand was; so calling to his oldest and ugliest hind, he bade him cover himself with his plaid, and sit down by the hearth with a porridge bowl in his hands, just as if he were supping brose. Then running to the stable, he cut off a foot of his grey mare's tail, which he plaited over the forehead of the hind, letting it fall in grizzly ringlets over his nose.

"Now mind," said he, "to any visitors who chance to come, say you are the goodwife of the house, and ask them their business. As for myself, I will hide behind the peat-stack yonder, and bide the issue."

In less time than I write this, there was a rare tapping at the door, and as the hind bid them enter the five green maidens hurried into the house.

"Is the goodman at home?" said the five green maidens, all at once.

"No; but I'm the goodwife, and may I ask you what is your business?"

At this answer the five green maidens stood for a moment transfixed with rage and wonder, then, shrieking aloud, they gathered up their coats and fled helter-skelter from the house down the road to the loch, and were seen no more.

So Gille Macdonald lived ever afterwards a life of wealth and comfort; and if he is not married yet, he can't say it is for the want of offers, can he?

COMIC TALES.

THE WEE BUNNOCK.[1]

" Some tell about their sweethearts, how they tirled them to
    the winnock,[2]
But I'll tell you a bonny tale about a guid aitmeal bunnock."

THERE lived an auld man and an auld wife at the
side o' a burn. They had twa kye, five hens and a
cock, a cat and twa kittlins. The auld man lookit
after the kye, and the auld wife span on the tow-rock.[3]
The kittlins aft grippit at the auld wife's spindle,
as it tussled owre the hearth-stane. " Sho, sho," she
wad say; " gae wa'," and so it tussled about.

Ae day, after parritch-time, she thought she would
ha'e a bunnock. Sae she bakit twa aitmeal bunnocks, and set them to the fire to harden. After a
while, the auld man came in, and sat down aside the
fire, and takes ane o' the bunnocks, and snappit it
through the middle. When the tither ane sees this,
it rins aff as fast as it could, and the auld wife after't,
wi' the spindle in the tae hand and the tow-rock in

1 Chambers, *Popular Rhymes of Scotland.*
2 Tapped at the window to bring them out.
3 Spinning-wheel.

270

the tither.   But the wee bunnock wan awa', and out
o' sight, and ran till it came to a guid muckle thack
house,[1] and ben[2] it ran boldly to the fireside; and
there were three tailors sitting on a muckle table.
When they saw the wee bunnock come ben, they
jumpit up, and gat in ahint the guidwife, that was
cardin' tow ayont the fire.   " Hout," quo' she, " be
na fleyt;[3] it's but a wee bunnock.   Grip it, and I'll
gie ye a soup milk till't."   Up she gets wi' the tow-
cards, and the tailor wi' the goose, and the twa 'prentices, the ane wi' the muckle shears, and the tither
wi' the lawbrod;[4] but it jinkit[5] them, and ran round
about the fire; and ane o' the 'prentices, thinking to
snap it wi' the shears, fell i' the ase-pit.   The tailor
cuist[6] the goose, and the guidwife the tow-cards; but
a' wadna do.   The bunnock wan awa', and ran till
it came to a wee house at the roadside; and in it rins,
and there was a weaver sittin' on the loom, and the
wife winnin' a clue o' yarn.

   " Tibby," quo' he, " what's tat?"   " Oh," quo'
she, " it's a wee bunnock."   " It's weel come," quo'
he, " for our sowens[7] were but thin the day.   Grip it,
my woman; grip it."   " Ay," quo' she; " what recks!
That's a clever bunnock.   Kep,[8] Willie; kep, man."
" Hout," quo' Willie; " cast the clue at it."   But the
bunnock whipit round about, and but the floor,[9] and
aff it gaed, and owre the knowe,[10] like a new-tarred

[1] Good big thatched house.   [5] Dodged.   [9] **Toward the door.**
[2] In.   [6] Cast.   [10] Knoll.
[3] Frightened.   [7] Pottage.
[4] Ironing-board.   [8] Catch.

sheep or a daft yell cow.[1] And forrit it runs to the neist house, and ben to the fireside. And there was the guidwife kirnin'.[2] "Come awa', wee bunnock," quo' she; " I'se hae ream[3] and bread the day." But the wee bunnock whipit round about the kirn, and the wife after't, and i' the hurry she had near-hand coupit the kirn.[4] And afore she got it set right again, the wee bunnock was aff, and down the brae to the mill. And in it ran.

The miller was siftin' meal i' the trough; but, looking up, " Ay," quo' he, " it's a sign o' plenty when ye're rinnin' about, and naebody to look after ye. But I like a bunnock and cheese. Come your wa's ben, and I'll gie ye a night's quarters." But the bunnock wadna trust itsel' wi' the miller and his cheese. Sae it turned and ran its wa's out; but the miller didna fash his head wi't.[5] So it toddled awa', and ran till it came to the smithy. And in it rins, and up to the studdy.[6] The smith was making horse-nails. Quo' he, " I like a bicker o' guid yill[7] and a weel-toastit bunnock. Come your wa's in by here." But the bunnock was frightened when it heard about the yill, and turned and aff as hard as it could, and the smith after't, and cuist the hammer. But it whirlt awa', and out o' sight in a crack, and ran till it came to a farm-house wi' a guid muckle peat-stack at the end o't. Ben it rins to the fireside. The

[1] A cow that has ceased to give milk.
[2] Churning.
[3] Cream.
[4] Overturned the churn.
[5] Didn't trouble his head about it.
[6] Anvil.
[7] A stoup of good ale.

guidman was clovin' line,[1] and the guidwife hecklin'.[2]
" Oh, Janet," quo' he, " there's a wee bunnock ; I'se
ha'e the hauf o't." " Weel, John, I'se ha'e the tither
hauf. Hit it owre the back wi' the clove." But the
bunnock playt jink-about.[3] " Hout tout," quo' the
wife, and gart the heckle flee at it.[4] But it was owre
clever for her.

And aff and up the burn it ran to the neist house,
and whirlt its wa's ben to the fireside. The guidwife was stirrin' the sowens, and the guidman plettin'
spret-binnings for the kye.[5] " Ho, Jock," quo' the
guidwife, " come here. Thou's aye crying about a
wee bunnock. Here's ane. Come in, haste ye, and
I'll help thee to grip it." " Ay, mither, whaur is't ? "
" See there. Rin owre o' that side." But the bunnock ran in ahint the guidman's chair. Jock fell
among the sprits. The guidman cuist a binning, and
the guidwife the spurtle.[6] But it was owre clever for
Jock and her baith. It was aff and out o' sight in a
crack, and through among the whins,[7] and down the
road to the neist house, and in, and ben to the fireside.
The folk were just sittin' down to their sowens, and
the guidwife scartin' the pat.[8] " Losh," quo' she,
" there's a wee bunnock come in to warm itsel' at our
fireside." " Steek[9] the door," quo' the guidman,
" and we'll try to get a grip o't." When the bun-

[1] Separating lint from the stalk.
[2] Dressing-flax.
[3] " Catch me if you can."
[4] Let fly the comb at it.
[5] Plaiting straw-ropes for the cows.
[6] Stick used for stirring porridge.
[7] Furze.
[8] Scraping the pot.
[9] Fasten.

18

nock heard that, it ran but the house, and they after't wi' their spunes, and the guidman cuist his bunnat.[1] But it whirlt awa', and ran, and better ran, till it came to another house. And when it gaed ben, the folk were just gaun to their beds. The guidman was castin' aff his breeks, and the guidwife rakin' the fire. " What's tat ? " quo' he. " Oh," quo' she, " it's a wee bunnock." Quo' he, " I could eat the hauf o't, for a' the brose I hae suppit." " Grip it," quo' the wife, " and I'll hae a bit too." " Cast your breeks at it—kep—kep ! " The guidman cuist the breeks, and had near-hand smoor't[2] it. But it warsl't[3] out, and ran, and the guidman after't, wanting the breeks. And there was a clean chase owre the craft[4] park, and up the wunyerd, and in amang the whins. And the guidman lost it, and had to come his wa's trottin hame hauf nakit. But now it was grown dark, and the wee bunnock couldna see; but it gaed into the side o' a muckle whin bush, and into a tod's hole.[5] The tod had gotten nae meat for twa days. " Oh, welcome, welcome," quo' the tod, and snappit it in twa i' the middle. And that was the end o' the wee bunnock.

> " Now, be ye lords or commoners,
> Ye needna laugh nor sneer,
> For ye'll be a' i' the tod's hole
> In less than a hunner year."

---

[1] Bonnet, cap.
[2] Smothered.
[3] Struggled.
[4] Croft.
[5] A fox's hole.

THE TALE OF THE SHIFTY LAD, THE WIDOW'S SON.[1]

I.

THERE was at some time or other before now a widow, and she had one son. She gave him good schooling, and she was wishful that he should choose a trade for himself; but he said he would not go to learn any art, but that he would be a thief.

His mother said to him: " If that is the art that thou art going to choose for thine ownself, thine end is to be hanged at the bridge of Baile Cliabh,[2] in Eirinn."

But it was no matter, he would not go to any art, but to be a thief; and his mother was always making a prophecy to him that the end of him would be, hanging at the Bridge of Baile Cliabh, in Eirinn.

On a day of the days, the widow was going to the church to hear the sermon, and was asking the Shifty Lad, her son, to go with her, and that he should give over his bad courses; but he would not go with her; but he said to her: " The first art of which thou hearest mention, after thou hast come out of the sermon, is the art to which I will go afterwards."

She went to the church full of good courage, hoping that she would hear some good thing.

He went away, and he went to a tuft of wood that

[1] Campbell, *Popular Tales of the West Highlands.*
[2] Dublin.

was near to the church; and he went in hiding in a place where he could see his mother when she should come out of the church; and as soon as she came out he shouted, " Thievery! thievery! thievery!" She looked about, but she could not make out whence the voice was coming, and she went home. He ran by the way of the short cut, and he was at the house before her, and he was seated within beside the fire when she came home. He asked her what tale she had got; and she said that she had not got any tale at all, but that "thievery, thievery, thievery, was the first speech she heard when she came out of the church."

He said " That was the art that he would have."

And she said, as she was accustomed to say: " Thine ending is to be hanged at the bridge of Baile Cliabh, in Eirinn."

On the next day, his mother herself thought that, as nothing at all would do for her son but that he should be a thief, she would try to find him a good aid-to-learning; and she went to the black gallows bird of Aachaloinne, a very cunning thief who was in that place; and though they had knowledge that he was given to stealing, they were not finding any way for catching him. The widow asked the Black Rogue if he would take her son to teach him roguery. The Black Rogue said, " If he were a clever lad that he would take him, and if there were a way of making a thief of him that he could do it;" and a covenant was made between the Black Rogue and the Shifty Lad.

When the Shifty Lad, the widow's son, was making ready for going to the Black Rogue, his mother was giving him counsel, and she said to him: " It is against my will that thou are going to thievery; and I was telling thee, that the end of thee is to be hanged at the bridge of Baile Cliabh, Eirinn;" but the Shifty Lad went home to the Black Rogue.

The Black Rogue was giving the Shifty Lad every knowledge he might for doing thievery; he used to tell him about the cunning things that he must do, to get a chance to steal a thing; and when the Black Rogue thought that the Shifty Lad was good enough at learning to be taken out with him, he used to take him out with him to do stealing; and on a day of these days the Black Rogue said to his lad—

" We are long enough thus, we must go and do something. There is a rich tenant near to us, and he has much money in his chest. It was he who bought all that there was of cattle to be sold in the country, and he took them to the fair, and he sold them; he has got the money in his chest, and this is the time to be at him, before the people are paid for their lot of cattle; and unless we go to seek the money at this very hour, when it is gathered together, we shall not get the same chance again."

The Shifty Lad was as willing as himself; they went away to the house, they got in at the coming on of the night, and they went up upon the loft,[1] and they went in hiding up there; and it was the night of

---

[1] The loft meant is the space in the roof of a cottage which is above the rafters, and is used as a kind of store.

SAMHAIN (Halloween); and there assembled many people within to keep the Savain hearty as they used to do. They sat together, and they were singing songs, and at fun burning the nuts, and at merry-making.

The Shifty Lad was wearying that the company was not scattering; he got up and he went down to the byre, and he loosed the bands off the necks of the cattle, and he returned and he went up upon the loft again. The cattle began goring each other in the byre, and roaring. All that were in the room ran to keep the cattle from each other till they could be tied again; and in the time while they were doing this, the Shifty Lad went down to the room and he stole the nuts with him, and he went up upon the loft again, and he lay down at the back of the Black Rogue.

There was a great leathern hide at the back of the Black Rogue, and the Shifty Lad had a needle and thread, and he sewed the skirt of the Black Rogue's coat to the leathern hide that was at his back; and when the people of the house came back to the dwelling-room again, their nuts were away; and they were seeking their nuts; and they thought that it was some one who had come in to play them a trick that had taken away their nuts, and they sat down at the side of the fire quietly and silently.

Said the Shifty Lad to the Black Rogue, " I will crack a nut."

" Thou shalt not crack one," said the Black Rogue; " they will hear thee, and we shall be caught."

Said the Shifty Lad, " I never yet was a Savain night without cracking a nut," and he cracked one.

Those who were seated in the dwelling-room heard him, and they said—

" There is some one up on the loft cracking our nuts; we will go and catch them."

When the Black Rogue heard that, he sprang off the loft and he ran out, and the hide dragging at the tail of his coat. Every one of them shouted that there was the Black Rogue stealing the hide with him.

The Black Rogue fled, and the people of the house after him; and he was a great distance from the house before he got the hide torn from him, and was able to leave them. But in the time that the people of the house were running after the Black Rogue, the Shifty Lad came down off the loft; he went up about the house, he hit upon the chest where the gold and the silver was; he opened the chest, and he took out of it the bags in which the gold and silver was, that was in the chest; and he took with him a load of the bread, and of the butter, and of the cheese, and of everything that was better than another which he found within; and he was gone before the people of the house came back from chasing the Black Rogue.

When the Black Rogue reached his home, and he had nothing, his wife said to him, " How hast thou failed this journey ? "

Then the Black Rogue told his own tale; and he was in great fury at the Shifty Lad, and swearing that he would serve him out when he got a chance at him.

At the end of a little while after that, the Shifty Lad came in with a load upon him.

Said the wife of the Black Rogue, " But I fancy that thou art the better thief! "

The Black Rogue said not a word till the Shifty Lad showed the bags that he had full of gold and silver; then said the Black Rogue, " But it is thou that wert the smart lad! "

They made two halves of the gold and silver, and the Black Rogue got the one half, and the Shifty Lad the other half. When the Black Rogue's wife saw the share that came to them, she said, " Thou thyself art the worthy thief! " and she had more respect for him after that than she had for the Black Rogue himself.

II.

The Black Rogue and the Shifty Lad went on stealing till they had got much money, and they thought that they had better buy a drove of cattle, and go to the fair with it to sell, and that people would think that it was at drovering they had made the money that they had got. The two went, and they bought a great drove of cattle, and they went to a fair that was far on the way from them. They sold the drove, and they got the money for them, and they went away to go home. When they were on the way, they saw a gallows on the top of a hill, and the Shifty Lad said to the Black Rogue, " Come up till we see the gallows; some say that the gallows is the end for the thieves at all events."

They went up where the gallows was, and they were looking all about it. Said the Shifty Lad, "Might we not try what kind of death is in the gallows, that we may know what is before us, if we should be caught at roguery. I will try it myself first."

The Shifty Lad put the cord about his own neck, and he said to the Black Rogue, "Here, draw me up, and when I am tired above I will shake my legs, and then do thou let me down."

The Black Rogue drew the cord, and he raised the Shifty Lad aloft off the earth, and at the end of a little blink the Shifty Lad shook his legs, and the Black Rogue let him down.

The Shifty Lad took the cord off his neck, and he said to the Black Rogue, "Thou thyself hast not ever tried anything that is so funny as hanging. If thou wouldst try once, thou wouldst have no more fear for hanging. I was shaking my legs for delight, and thou wouldst shake thy legs for delight too if thou wert aloft."

Said the Black Rogue, "I will try it too, so that I may know what it is like."

"Do," said the Shifty Lad; "and when thou art tired above, whistle and I will let thee down."

The Black Rogue put the cord about his neck, and the Shifty Lad drew him up aloft; and when the Shifty Lad found that the Black Rogue was aloft against the gallows, he said to him, "Now, when thou wantest to come down, whistle, and if thou art well pleased where thou art, shake thy legs."

When the Black Rogue was a little blink above, he began to shake his legs and to kick; and the Shifty Lad would say, " Oh art thou not funny! art thou not funny! art thou not funny! When it seems to thee that thou art long enough above, whistle."

But the Black Rogue has not whistled yet. The Shifty Lad tied the cord to the lower end of the tree of the gallows till the Black Rogue was dead; then he went where he was, and he took the money out of his pouch, and he said to him, " Now since thou hast no longer any use for this money, I will take care of it for thee." And he went away, and he left the Black Rogue hanging there. Then he went home where was the house of the Black Rogue, and his wife asked where was his master?

The Shifty Lad said, " I left him where he was, upraised above the earth."

The wife of the Black Rogue asked and asked him about her man, till at last he told her; but he said to her, that he would marry her himself. When she heard that, she cried that the Shifty Lad had killed his master, and he was nothing but a thief. When the Shifty Lad heard that he fled. The chase was set after him; but he found means to go in hiding in a cave, and the chase went past him. He was in the cave all night, and the next day he went another way, and he found means to fly to Eirinn.

III.

He reached the house of a wright, and he cried at the door, " Let me in."

" Who art thou ? " said the wright.

" I am a good wright, if thou hast need of such," said the Shifty Lad.

The wright opened the door, and he let in the Shifty Lad, and the Shifty Lad began to work at carpentering along with the wright.

When the Shifty Lad was a day or two in their house, he gave a glance thither and a glance hither about the house, and he said, " O choin ! what a poor house you have, and the king's store-house so near you."

" What of that ? " said the wright.

" It is," said the Shifty Lad, " that you might get plenty from the king's store-house if you yourselves were smart enough."

The wright and his wife would say, " They would put us in prison if we should begin at the like of that."

The Shifty Lad was always saying that they ought to break into the king's store-house, and they would find plenty in it; but the wright would not go with him; but the Shifty Lad took with him some of the tools of the wright, and he went himself and he broke into the king's store-house, and he took with him a load of the butter and of the cheese of the king, and he took it to the house of the wright. The things pleased the wife of the wright well, and she was willing that her own husband should go there the next night. The wright himself went with his lad the next night, and they got into the store-house of the king, and they took with them great loads of each thing that pleased them best of all that was within in the king's store-house.

But the king's people missed the butter and the cheese and the other things that had been taken out of the store-house, and they told the king how it had happened.

The king took the counsel of the Seanagal about the best way of catching the thieves, and the counsel that the Seanagal gave them was that they should set a hogshead of soft pitch under the hole where they were coming in. That was done, and the next night the Shifty Lad and his master went to break into the king's store-house.

The Shifty Lad put his master in before him, and the master went down into the soft pitch to his very middle, and he could not get out again. The Shifty Lad went down, and he put a foot on each of his master's shoulders, and he put out his two loads of the king's butter and of the cheese at the hole; and at the last time when he was coming out, he swept the head off his master, and he took the head with him, and he left the trunk in the hogshead of pitch, and he went home with the butter and with the cheese, and he took home the head, and he buried it in the garden.

When the king's people went into the store-house, they found a body without a head into the hogshead of pitch; but they could not make out who it was. They tried if they could find any one at all that could know him by the clothes, but his clothes were covered with pitch so that they could not make him out. The king asked the counsel of the Seanagal about it; and the counsel that the Seanagal gave was, that they should set the trunk aloft on the points of the spears of the soldiers, to be carried from town to town, to see if they could find any one at all that would take sorrow for it; or to try if they could hear any one that would make a painful cry when they should see it; or if they should not see one that should seem about to make a painful cry when the soldiers should be going past with it. The body was taken out of the hogshead of pitch, and set on the points of the spears; and the soldiers were bearing it aloft on the points of their long wooden spears, and they were going from town to town with it; and when they were going past the house of the wright, the wright's wife made a tortured scream, and swift the Shifty Lad cut himself with the adze; and he kept saying to the wright's wife, " The cut is not as bad as thou thinkest."

The commander-in-chief, and his lot of soldiers, came in and they asked,

" What ailed the housewife ? "

Said the Shifty Lad, " It is that I have just cut my foot with the adze, and she is afraid of blood; " and he would say to the wife of the wright, " Do not be so much afraid; it will heal sooner than thou thinkest."

The soldiers thought that the Shifty Lad was the wright, and that the wife whom they had seen was the wife of the Shifty Lad; and they went out, and they went from town to town; but they found no one besides, but the wife of the wright herself, that made cry or scream when they were coming past her.

They took the body home to the king's house; and the king took another counsel from his Seanagal, and that was to hang the body to a tree in an open place, and soldiers to watch it that none should take it away, and the soldiers to be looking if any should come the way that should take pity or grief for it.

The Shifty Lad came past them, and he saw them; he went and he got a horse, and he put a keg of whisky on each side of the horse in a sack, and he went past the soldiers with it, as though he were hiding from them. The soldiers thought that it was so, or that he had taken something which he ought not to have; and some of them ran after him, and they caught the old horse and the whisky; but the Shifty Lad fled, and he left the horse and the whisky with them. The soldiers took the horse and the kegs of whisky back to where the body was hanging against the mast. They looked what was in the kegs; and when they understood that it was whisky that was in them, they got a drinking cup, and they began drinking until at last every one of them was drunk, and they lay and they slept. When the Shifty Lad say that, that the soldiers were laid down and asleep and drunk, he returned and took the body off the mast. He set it crosswise on the horse's back, and he took it home; then he went and he buried the body in the garden where the head was.

When the soldiers awoke out of their sleep, the body was stolen away; they had nothing for it but to go and tell the king. Then the king took the coun-

sel of the Seanagal; and the Seanagal said to them,
all that were in his presence, that his counsel to them
was, to take out a great black pig that was there, and
that they should go with her from town to town; and
when they should come to any place where the body
was buried, that she would root it up. They went
and they got the black pig, and they were going from
farm to farm with her, trying if they could find out
where the body was buried. They went from house
to house with her, till at last they came to the house
where the Shifty Lad and the wright's widow were
dwelling. When they arrived they let the pig loose
about the grounds. The Shifty Lad said that he
himself was sure that thirst and hunger was on them;
that they had better go into the house, and that they
should get meat and drink; and that they should let
their weariness from off them, in the time when the
pig should be seeking about his place.

They went in, and the Shifty Lad asked the
wright's widow that she should set meat and drink
before the men. The widow of the wright set meat
and drink on the board, and she set it before them;
and in the time while they were eating their meat,
the Shifty Lad went out to see after the pig; and the
pig had just hit upon the body in the garden; and the
Shifty Lad went and he got a great knife and he
cut the head off her, and he buried herself and her
head beside the body of the wright in the garden.

When those who had the care of the pig came out,
the pig was not to be seen. They asked the Shifty
Lad if he had seen her. He said that he had seen her,

that her head was up and she was looking upwards, and going two or three steps now and again; and they went with great haste to the side where the Shifty Lad said the pig had gone.

When the Shifty Lad found that they had gone out of sight, he set everything in such a way that they should not hit upon the pig. They on whom the care of the pig was laid went and they sought her every way that it was likely she might be. Then when they could not find her, they had nothing for it but to go to the king's house and tell how it had happened.

Then the counsel of the Seanagal was taken again; and the counsel that the Seanagal gave them was, that they should set their soldiers out about the country at free quarters; and at whatsoever place they should get pig's flesh, or in whatsoever place they should see pig's flesh, unless those people could show how they had got the pig's flesh that they might have, that those were the people who killed the pig, and that had done every evil that had been done.

The counsel of the Seanagal was taken, and the soldiers sent out to free quarters about the country; and there was a band of them in the house of the wright's widow where the Shifty Lad was. The wright's widow gave their supper to the soldiers, and some of the pig's flesh was made ready for them; and the soldiers were eating the pig's flesh, and praising it exceedingly. The Shifty Lad understood what was the matter, but he did not let on.[1] The soldiers were

[1] Divulge.

set to lie out in the barn; and when they were asleep the Shifty Lad went out and he killed them. Then he went as fast as he could from house to house, where the soldiers were at free quarters, and he set the rumour afloat amongst the people of the houses, that the soldiers had been sent out about the country to rise in the night and kill the people in their beds; and he found means to make the people of the country believe him, so that the people of each house killed all the soldiers that were asleep in their barns; and when the soldiers did not come home at the time they should, some went to see what had happened to them; and when they arrived, it was so that they found the soldiers dead in the barns where they had been asleep; and the people of each house denied that they knew how the soldiers had been put to death, or who had done it.

The people who were at the ransacking for the soldiers went to the king's house, and they told how it had happened; then the king sent word for the Seanagal to get counsel from him; the Seanagal came, and the king told him how it had happened, and the king asked counsel from him. This is the counsel that the Seanagal gave the king, that he should make a feast and a ball, and invite the people of the country; and if the man who did the evil should be there, that he was the man who would be the boldest who would be there, and that he would ask the king's daughter herself to dance with him. The people were asked to the feast and the dance; and amongst the rest the Shifty Lad was asked. The

19

people came to the feast, and amongst the rest came the Shifty Lad. When the feast was past, the dance began; and the Shifty Lad went and he asked the king's daughter to dance with him; and the Seanagal had a vial full of black stuff, and the Seanagal put a black dot of the stuff that was in the vial on the Shifty Lad. But it seemed to the king's daughter that her hair was not well enough in order, and she went to a side chamber to put it right and the Shifty Lad went in with her; and when she looked in the glass, he also looked in it, and he saw the black dot that the Seanagal had put upon him. When they had danced till the tune of music was finished, the Shifty Lad went and he got a chance to steal the vial of the Seanagal from him unknown to him, and he put two black dots on the Seanagal, and one black dot on twenty other men besides, and he put the vial back again where he found it.

Between that and the end of another while, the Shifty Lad came again and he asked the king's daughter to dance. The king's daughter had a vial also, and she put a black dot on the face of the Shifty Lad; but the Shifty Lad got the vial whipped out of her pocket, unknown to her; and since there were two black dots on him, he put two dots on twenty other men in the company, and four black dots on the Seanagal. Then when the dancing was over, some were sent to see who was the man on whom were the two black dots. When they looked amongst the people, they found twenty men on whom there were two black dots, and there were four black dots on the Seanagal; and the Shifty Lad found means to go swiftly where the king's daughter was, and to slip the vial back again into her pocket. The Seanagal looked and he had his black vial; the king's daughter looked and she had her own vial; then the Seanagal and the king took counsel; and the last counsel that they made was that the king should come to the company, and say, that the man who had done every trick that had been done must be exceedingly clever; if he would come forward and give himself up, that he should get the king's daughter to marry, and the one half of the kingdom while the king was alive, and the whole of the kingdom after the king's death. And every one of those who had the two black dots on their faces came and they said that it was they who had done every cleverness that had been done. Then the king and his high counsel went to try how the matter should be settled; and the matter which they settled was, that all the men who had the two black dots on their faces should be put together in a chamber, and they were to get a child, and the king's daughter was to give an apple to the child, and the child was to be put in where the men with the two black dots on their faces were seated, and to whatsoever one the child should give the apple, that was the one who was to get the king's daughter.

That was done, and when the child went into the chamber in which the men were, the Shifty Lad had a shaving and a drone, and the child went and gave him the apple. Then the shaving and the drone were taken from the Shifty Lad, and he was seated in another place, and the apple was given to the child again; and he was taken out of the chamber, and sent in again to see to whom he would give the apple; and since the Shifty Lad had the shaving and the drone before, the child went where he was again, and he gave him the apple. Then the Shifty Lad got the king's daughter to marry.

And shortly after that the king's daughter and the Shifty Lad were taking a walk to Baile Cliabh; and when they were going over the bridge of Baile Cliabh, the Shifty Lad asked the king's daughter what was the name of that place; and the king's daughter told him that it was the bridge of Baile Cliabh, in Eirinn; and the Shifty Lad said—

" Well, then, many is the time that my mother said to me, that my end would be to be hanged at the bridge of Baile Cliabh, in Eirinn; and she made me that prophecy many a time when I might play her a trick."

And the king's daughter said, " Well, then, if thou thyself shouldst choose to hang over the little side wall of the bridge, I will hold thee aloft a little space with my pocket napkin."

And they were at talk and fun about it; but at last it seemed to the Shifty lad that he would do it for sport, and the king's daughter took out her pocket napkin, and the Shifty Lad went over the bridge, and he hung by the pocket napkin of the king's daughter as she let it over the little side wall of the bridge, and they were laughing to each other.

But the king's daughter heard a cry, " The king's

castle is going on fire!" and she started, and she lost her hold of the napkin; and the Shifty Lad fell down, and his head struck against a stone, and the brain went out of him; and there was in the cry but the sport of children; and the king's daughter was obliged to go home a widow.

LOTHIAN TOM.[1]

I.

Tom being grown up to years and age of man, thought himself wiser and slyer than his father; and there were several things about the house which he liked better than to work; so he turned to be a dealer amongst brutes, a cowper of horses and cows, etc., and even wet ware, amongst the brewers and brandy shops, until he cowped himself to the toom halter,[2] and then his parents would supply him no more. He knew his grandmother had plenty of money, but she would give him none; but the old woman had a good black cow of her own, which Tom went to the fields one evening and catches, and takes her to an old waste house which stood at a distance from any other, and there he kept her two or three days, giving her meat and drink at night when it was dark, and made the old woman believe somebody had stolen the cow for their winter's mart, which was grief enough to the

[1] Dougal Graham, *The Comical Tricks of Lothian Tom.*
[2] Empty.

old woman, for the loss of her cow. However, she
employs Tom to go to a fair that was near by, and
buy her another; she gives him three pounds, which
Tom accepts of very thankfully, and promises to buy
her one as like the other as possibly he could get;
then he takes a piece of chalk, and brays it as small
as meal, and steeps it in a little water, and therewith
rubs over the cow's face and back, which made her
baith brucket and rigget.[1] So Tom in the morning
takes the cow to a public-house within a little of the
fair, and left her till the fair was over, and then
drives her home before him; and as soon as they came
home, the cow began to rout as it used to do, which
made the old woman to rejoice, thinking it was her
own cow; but when she saw her white, sighed and
said, " Alas! thou'll never be like the kindly brute my
Black Lady, and ye rout as like her as ony ever I
did hear." But says Tom to himself, " 'Tis a mercy
you know not what she says, or all would be wrong
yet." So in two or three days the old woman put
forth her bra' rigget cow in the morning with the
rest of her neighbours' cattle, but it came on a sore
day of heavy rain, which washed away all the white
from her face and back; so the old woman's
Black Lady came home at night, and her rigget cow
went away with the shower, and was never heard of.
But Tom's father having some suspicion, and looking narrowly into the cow's face, found some of the
chalk not washed away, and then he gave poor Tom

[1] Spotted on body and face.

a hearty beating, and sent him away to seek his fortune with a skin full of sore bones.

II.

Tom being now turned to his own shifts, considered
with himself how to raise a little more money; and so
gets a string as near as he could guess to be the length
of his mother, and to Edinburgh he goes, to a wright
who was acquainted with his father and mother. The
wright asked him how he did; he answered him, very
soberly, he had lost a good dutiful mother last night,
and there's a measure for the coffin. Tom went out
and stayed for some time, and then comes in again,
and tells the wright he did not know what to do, for
his father had ordered him to get money from such
a man, whom he named, and he that day was gone out
of town. . . . The wright asked him how much
he wanted. To which he answered, a guinea and a
half. Then Tom gave him strict orders to be out next
day against eleven o'clock with the coffin, and he
should get his money altogether. So Tom set off to
an ale-house with the money, and lived well while it
lasted. Next morning the wright and his two lads
went out with the coffin; and as they were going into
the house they met Tom's mother, who asked the
master how he did, and where he was going with that
fine coffin? Not knowing well what to say, being
surprised to see her alive, at last he told her that her
son brought in the measure the day before, and had
got a guinea and a half from him, with which he

said he was to buy some necessaries for the funeral.
" Oh, the rogue!" said she, " has he play'd me
that ? " So the wright got his lent money, and so much
for his trouble, and had to take back his coffin with
him again.

III.

Tom being short of money, began to think how he
could raise a fresh supply; so he went to the port
among the shearers,[1] and there he hired about thirty
of them, and agreed to give them a whole week's
shearing at tenpence a-day, which was twopence
higher than any had got that year; this made the
poor shearers think he was a very honest, generous,
and genteel master, as ever they met with ; for he took
them all into an ale-house, and gave them a hearty
breakfast. " Now," says Tom, " when there is so
many of you together, and perhaps from very different parts, and being unacquainted with one another,
I do not know but there may be some of you honest
men and some of you rogues; and as you are all to lie
in one barn together, any of you who has got money,
you will be surest to give it to me, and I'll mark it
down in my book with your names, and what I receive from each of you, and you shall have it all again
on Saturday night, when you receive your wages."
" Oh, very well, goodman, there's mine; take mine,"
said every one faster than another. Some gave him
five, six, seven, and eight shillings—even all that they

[1] Reapers.

had earn'd thro' the harvest, which amounted to near
seven pounds sterling. So Tom, having got all their
money, he goes on with them till about three miles out
of town, and coming to a field of standing corn,
though somewhat green, yet convenient for his purpose, as it lay at some distance from any house—so
he made them begin work there, telling them he was
going to order dinner for them, and send his own servants to join them. Then he sets off with all the
speed he could, but takes another road into the town
lest they should follow and catch him. Now when
the people to whom the corn belonged saw such a band
in their field, they could not understand the meaning of it; so the farmer whose corn it was went off,
crying always as he ran to them to stop; but they
would not, until he began to strike at them, and they
at him, he being in a great passion, as the corn was
not fully ripe. At last, by force of argument, and
other people coming up to them, the poor shearers
were convinced they had got the bite, which caused
them to go away sore lamenting their misfortune.

Two or three days thereafter, as Tom was going
down Canongate in Edinburgh, he meets one of his
shearers, who knew and kept fast by him, demanding
back his money, and also satisfaction for the rest.
" Whisht, whisht," says Tom, " and you'll get yours
and something else beside." So Tom takes him into
the gaol, and calls for a bottle of ale and a dram, then
takes the gaoler aside, as if he had been going to borrow some money from him, and says to the gaoler,
" This man is a great thief. I and other two have been

in search for him these three days, and the other two men have the warrant with them; so if you keep this rogue here till I run and bring them, you shall have a guinea in reward." " Yes," says the gaoler, " go, and I'll secure the rogue for you." So Tom gets off, leaving the poor innocent fellow and the gaoler struggling together, and then sets out for England directly.

IV.

Tom having now left his own native country, went into the county of Northumberland, where he hired himself to an old miser of a farmer, where he continued for several years, performing his duty in his service very well, though sometimes playing tricks on those about him. But his master had a naughty custom, he would allow them no candle at night, to see with when at supper. So Tom one night sets himself next to his master, and as they were all about to fall on, Tom puts his spoon into the heart of the dish, where the crowdy was hottest, and claps a spoonful into his master's mouth. " A pox on you for a rogue," cried his master, " for my mouth is all burnt." " A pox on you for a master," says Tom, " for you keep a house as dark as Purgatory, for I was going to my mouth with the soup and missed the way, it being so dark. Don't think, master, that I am such a big fool as to feed you while I have a mouth of my own." So from that night that Tom burnt his master's mouth with the hot crowdy, they always got a candle to show them light at supper, for his master would feed no more in the dark while Tom was present.

There was a servant girl in the house, who always when she made the beds neglected to make Tom's and would have him do it himself. " Well, then," says Tom, " I have harder work to do, and I shall do that too." So next day when Tom was at the plough, he saw his master coming from the house towards him. He left the horses and the plough standing in the field, and goes away towards his master, who cried, " What is wrong? or is there anything broke with you?" " No, no," said Tom; " but I am going home to make my bed; it has not been made these two weeks, and now it is about the time the maid makes all the rest, so I'll go and make mine too." " No, no," says his master, " go to your plough, and I'll cause it to be made every night." " Then," says Tom, " I'll plough two or three furrows more in the time." So Tom gained his end.

v.

One day a butcher came and brought a fine fat calf from Tom's master, and Tom laid it on the horse's neck, before the butcher. When he was gone, " Now," says Tom, " what will you hold, master, but I'll steal the calf from the butcher before he goes two miles off?" Says his master, " I'll hold a guinea you don't." " Done," says Tom. Into the house he goes, and takes a good shoe of his master's, and runs another way across a field, till he got before the butcher,

near the corner of a hedge, where there was an open
and turning of the way: here Tom places himself
behind the hedge, and throws the shoe into the middle
of the highway; so, when the butcher came up riding,
with his calf before him, " Hey," said he to himself,
" There's a good shoe! If I knew how to get on my
calf again, I would light for it; but what signifies
one shoe without its neighbour?" So on he rides
and lets it lie. Tom then slips out and takes up the
shoe, and runs across the fields until he got before
the butcher, at another open of a hedge, about half-a-
mile distant, and throws out the shoe again on the
middle of the road; then up comes the butcher, and
seeing it, says to himself: " Now I shall have a pair
of good shoes for the lifting; " and down he comes,
lays the calf on the ground, and tying his horse to the
hedge, runs back, thinking to get the other shoe, in
which time Tom whips up the calf and shoe, and
home he comes, demanding his wager, which his master could not refuse, being so fairly won. The poor
butcher not finding the shoe, came back to his horse,
and missing the calf, knew not what to do; but thinking it had broke the rope from about its feet, and
had run into the fields, the butcher spent the day in
search of it amongst the hedges and ditches, and returned to Tom's master at night, intending to go in
search again for it next day, and gave them a tedious relation how he came to lose it by a cursed pair
of shoes, which he believed the devil had dropped in
his way and taken the calf and shoes along with him,
but he was thankful he had left his old horse to carry

him home. Next morning Tom set to work, and makes a fine white face on the calf with chalk and water; then brings it out and sells it to the butcher, which was good diversion to his master and other servants, to see the butcher buy his own calf again. No sooner was he gone with it, but Tom says, " Now, master, what will you hold but I'll steal it from him again ere he goes two miles off?" " No, no," says his master, " I'll hold no more bets with you; but I'll give you a shilling if you do it." " Done," says Tom, " it shall cost you no more;" and away he runs through the fields, until he came before the butcher, hard by the place where he stole the calf from him the day before; and there he lies down behind the hedge, and as the butcher came past, he put his hand on his mouth and cries baw, baw, like a calf. The butcher hearing this, swears to himself that there was the calf he had lost the day before: down he comes, and throws the calf on the ground, gets through the hedge in all haste, thinking he had no more to do but to take it up; but as he came in at one part of the hedge, Tom jumped out at another, and gets the calf on his back; then goes over the hedge on the other side, and through the fields he came safely home, with the calf on his back, while the poor but- cher spent his time and labour in vain, running from hedge to hedge, and hole to hole, seeking the calf. So the butcher returning to his horse again, and finding his other calf gone, he concluded that it was done by some invisible spirit about that spot of ground, and so went home lamenting the loss of his calf. When Tom got home he washed the white face off the stolen calf, and his master sent the butcher word to come and buy another calf, which he accordingly did in a few days after, and Tom sold him the same calf a third time, and then told him the whole affair as it was acted, giving him his money again. So the butcher got fun for his trouble.

THE PLOUGHMAN'S GLORY; OR, TOM'S SONG.

As I was a-walking one morning in the spring,
I heard a young ploughman so sweetly to sing,
And as he was singing these words he did say,
No life is like the ploughman's in the month of May.

The lark in the morning rises from her nest,
And mounts in the air with the dew on her breast,
And with the jolly ploughman she'll whistle and
     she'll sing,
And at night she'll return to her nest back again.

If you walk in the fields any pleasure to find,
You may see what the ploughman enjoys in his mind;
There the corn he sows grows and the flowers do
     spring,
And the ploughman's as happy as a prince or a king.

When his day's work is done that he has to do,
Perhaps to some country walk he will go;

There with a sweet lass he will dance and sing,
And at night return with his lass back again.

Then he rises next morning to follow his team,
Like a jolly ploughman so neat and so trim;
If he kiss a pretty girl he will make her his wife,
And she loves her jolly ploughman as dear as her life.

There's Molly and Dolly, Nelly and Sue;
There's Ralph, John, and Willie, and young Tommy
    too;
Each lad takes his lass to the wake or the fair,
Adzooks! they look rarely I vow and declare.

THE WITTY EXPLOITS OF MR. GEORGE BUCHANAN, THE KING'S FOOL.[1]

I.

MR. GEORGE BUCHANAN was a Scotsman born, and though of mean parentage, made great progress in learning. As for his understanding and ready wit, he excelled all men then alive in the age that ever proposed questions to him. He was servant or teacher to King James the Sixth, and one of his private counsellors, but publicly acted as his fool.

George happened one time to be in company with a bishop, and so they fell to dispute anent education,

[1] *John Cheap the Chapman's Library.* By Dougal Graham (?).

and he blanked the bishop remarkably, and the bishop himself owned he was worsted. Then one of the company addressed himself to him in these words: " Thou, Scot," said he, " should not have left thy country." " For what ? " says he. " Because thou hast carried all the wisdom that is in it hither with thee." " No, no," says he; " the shepherds in Scotland will dispute with any bishop in London, and exceed them very far in education." The bishops then took this as an affront, and several noblemen affirmed it to be as the Scot had said: bets were laid on each side, and three of the bishops were chosen, and sent away to Scotland to dispute it with the shepherds, accompanied with several others, who were to bear witness of what they should hear pass between them. Now George, knowing which way they went, immediately took another road and was in Scotland before them. He then made an acquaintance with a shepherd on the border, whose pasture lay on the wayside where the bishops were to pass; and there he mounted himself in shepherd's dress; and when he saw the bishops appear, he conveyed his flock to the roadside, and fell a-chanting at a Latin ballad. When the bishops came up to George, one of them asked him in French what o'clock it was? To which he answered in Hebrew, " It is directly about the time of day it was yesterday at this time." Another asked him, in Greek, what countryman he was? To which he answered in Flemish, " If ye knew that, you would be as wise as myself." A third asked him, in Dutch, " Where were you educated ? " To which he an-

swered, in Earse, " Herding my sheep between this
and Lochaber." This they desired him to explain
into English, which he immediately did. " Now,"
said they one to another, " we need not proceed any
farther." " What," says George, " are you butchers?
I'll sell you a few sheep." To this they made no
answer, but went away shamefully, and said they
believed the Scots had been through all the nations in
the world for their education, or the devil had taught
them. Now, when George had ended this dispute
with the bishops, he stripped off his shepherd's dress,
and up through England he goes, with all the haste
imaginable, so that he arrived at the place from
whence they set out three days before the judges, and
went every day asking if they were come, so that he
might not be suspected. As soon as they arrived, all
that were concerned in the dispute, and many more,
came crowding in, to hear what news from the Scottish shepherds, and to know what was done. No
sooner had the three gentlemen declared what had
passed between the bishops and the shepherds, whom
they found on the Scots border, but the old bishop
made answer, " And think you," said he, " that a
shepherd could answer these questions? It has been
none else but the devil; for the Scots ministers themselves could not do it; they are but ignorant of such
matters, a parcel of beardless boys." Then George
thought it was time to take speech in hand. " Well,
my lord bishop," says George, " you call them a
parcel of ignorant, beardless boys. You have a great
long beard yourself, my lord bishop, and if grace were

20

measured by beards, you bishops and the goats would have it all, and that would be quite averse to Scripture." "What," says the bishop, " are you a Scot?" "Yes," says George, "I am a Scot." "Well," says the bishop, " and what is the difference between a Scot and a sot?" "Nothing at present," says George, " but the breadth of the table,"—there being a table betwixt the bishop and George. So the bishop went off in a high passion, while the whole multitude were like to split their jaws with laughter.

II.

One night a Highland drover chanced to have a drinking bout with an English captain of a ship, and at last they came to be very hearty over their cups, so that they called in their servants to have a share of their liquor. The drover's servant looked like a wild man, going without breeches, stockings, or shoes, not so much as a bonnet on his head, with a long peeled rung in his hand. The captain asked the drover how long it was since he catched him? He answered, " It is about two years since I hauled him out of the sea with a net, and afterwards ran into the mountains, where I catched him with a pack of hounds." The captain believed it was so. " But," says he, " I have a servant, the best swimmer in the world." "Oh, but," says the drover, " my servant will swim him to death." " No, he will not," says the captain; "I'll lay two hundred crowns on it." " Then," says the drover, " I'll hold it one to one," and staked directly, the day being appointed when trial was to be made. Now the drover, when he came to himself, thinking on what a bargain he had made, did not know what to do, knowing very well that his servant could swim none. He, hearing of George being in town, who was always a good friend to Scotsmen, went unto him and told him the whole story, and that he would be entirely broke, and durst never return home to his own country, for he was sure to lose it. Then George called the drover and his man aside, and instructed them how to behave, so that they should be safe and gain too. So accordingly they met at the place appointed. The captain's man stripped directly and threw himself into the sea, taking a turn until the Highlandman was ready, for the drover took some time to put his servant in order. After he was stripped, his master took his plaid, and rolled a kebbuck of cheese, a big loaf and a bottle of gin in it, and this he bound on his shoulder, giving him directions to tell his wife and children that he was well, and to be sure he returned with an answer against that day se'nnight. As he went into the sea, he looked back to his master, and called out to him for his claymore. " And what waits he for now ? " says the captain's servant. " He wants his sword," says his master. " His sword," says the fellow; " what is he to do with a sword ? " " Why," says his master, " if he meets a whale or a monstrous beast, it is to defend his life; I know he will have to fight his way through the north seas, ere he get to Lochaber." " Then," cried the captain's servant, " I'll swim none with him, if he take

his sword." " Ay, but," says his master, " you shall,
or lose the wager; take you another sword with you."
" No," says the fellow; " I never did swim with a
sword, nor any man else, that ever I saw or heard of.
I know not but that wild man will kill me in the deep
water; I would not for the whole world venture myself with him and a sword." The captain, seeing his
servant afraid to venture, or if he did he would never
see him again alive, therefore desired an agreement
with the drover, who at first seemed unwilling; but
the captain putting it in his will, the drover quit him
for half the sum. This he came to through George's
advice.

III.

George was met one day by three bishops, who paid
him the following compliments:—Says the first,
" Good-morrow, Father Abraham; " says the second,
" Good-morrow, Father Isaac; " says the third,
" Good-morrow, Father Jacob." To which he replied, " I am neither Father Abraham, Father Isaac,
nor Father Jacob; but I am Saul, the son of Kish,
sent out to seek my father's asses, and, lo! I have
found three of them." Which answer fully convinced the bishops that they had mistaken their man.

IV.

A poor Scotchman dined one day at a public-house
in London upon eggs, and not having money to pay,

got credit till he should return. The man, being lucky in trade, acquired vast riches; and after some years, happening to pass that way, called at the house where he was owing the dinner of eggs. Having called for the innkeeper, he asked him what he had to pay for the dinner of eggs he got from him such a time. The landlord, seeing him now rich, gave him a bill of several pounds; telling him, as his reason for so extravagant a charge, that these eggs, had they been hatched, would have been chickens; and these laying more eggs, would have been more chickens; and so on, multiplying the eggs and their product, till such time as their value amounted to the sum charged. The man, refusing to comply with this demand, was charged before a judge. He then made his case known to George, his countryman, who promised to appear in the hour of cause, which he accordingly did, all in a sweat, with a great basket of boiled pease, which appearance surprised the judge, who asked him what he meant by these boiled pease? Says George, " I am going to sow them." " When will they grow? " said the judge. " They will grow," said George, " when sodden eggs grow chickens." Which answer convinced the judge of the extravagance of the innkeeper's demand, and the Scotsman was acquitted for two-pence halfpenny.

v.

George was professor of the College of St. Andrews, and slipped out one day in his gown and slippers, and went on his travels through Italy and sev-

eral other foreign countries, and after seven years returned with the same dress he went off in; and, entering the college, took possession of his seat there,
but the professor in his room quarrelling him for so
doing. " Ay," says George, " it is a very odd thing
that a man cannot take a walk out in his slippers, but
another will take up his seat." And so set the other
professor about his business.

VI.

Two drunken fellows one day fell a-beating one
another on the streets of London, which caused a
great crowd of people to throng together to see what
it was. A tailor being at work up in a garret, about
three or four storeys high, and he hearing the noise
in the street, looked over the window, but could not
well see them. He began to stretch himself, making
a long neck, until he fell down out of the window, and
alighted on an old man who was walking on the
street. The poor tailor was more afraid than hurt,
but the man he fell on died directly. His son caused
the tailor to be apprehended and tried for the murder
of his father. The jury could not bring it in wilful
murder, neither could they altogether free the tailor.
The jury gave it over to the judges, and the judges to
the king. The king asked George's advice on this
hard matter. " Why," says George, " I will give you
my opinion in a minute: you must cause the tailor to
stand in the street where the old gentleman was when
he was killed by the tailor, and then let the old gen-

tleman's son, the tailor's adversary, get up to the window from whence the tailor fell, and jump down, and so kill the tailor as he did his father." The tailor's adversary hearing this sentence passed, would not venture to jump over the window, and so the tailor got clear off.

LITERARY TALES.[1]

THE HAUNTED SHIPS.[2]

" ALEXANDER MACHARG, besides being the laird of three acres of peatmoss, two kale gardens, and the owner of seven good milch cows, a pair of horses, and six pet sheep, was the husband of one of the handsomest women in seven parishes. Many a lad sighed the day he was brided; and a Nithsdale laird and two Annandale moorland farmers drank themselves to their last linen, as well as their last shilling, through sorrow for her loss. But married was the dame; and home she was carried, to bear rule over her home and her husband, as an honest woman should. Now ye maun ken that, though the flesh-and-blood lovers of Alexander's bonnie wife all ceased to love and to sue her after she became another's, there were certain admirers who did not consider their claim at all abated, or their hopes lessened by the kirk's famous obstacle

---

[1] The Editor has adopted this term to denote popular tales, or tales founded upon popular superstition, which have received a literary clothing.

[2] Allan Cunningham, *Traditional Tales of the English and Scottish Peasantry.*

of matrimony. Ye have heard how the devout minister of Tinwald had a fair son carried away, and
bedded against his liking to an unchristened bride,
whom the elves and the fairies provided; ye have
heard how the bonnie bride of the drunken laird of
Soukitup was stolen by the fairies out at the back
window of the bridal chamber, the time the bride-
groom was groping his way to the chamber door; and
ye have heard—but why need I multiply cases? such
things in the ancient days were as common as candle-
light. So ye'll no hinder certain water elves and sea
fairies, who sometimes keep festival and summer
mirth in these old haunted hulks, from falling in
love with the weel-faured wife of Laird Macharg;
and to their plots and contrivances they went, how
they might accomplish to sunder man and wife; and
sundering such a man and such a wife was like sundering the green leaf from the summer, or the fragrance from the flower.

"So it fell on a time that Laird Macharg took his
half-net on his back, and his steel spear in his hand,
and down to Blawhooly Bay gade he, and into the
water he went right between the two haunted hulks,[1]
and, placing his net, awaited the coming of the tide.
The night, ye maun ken, was mirk, and the wind
lowne,[2] and the singing of the increasing waters
among the shells and the peebles was heard for sundry miles. All at once lights began to glance and

[1] Two ancient wrecked vessels, to which the peasantry of
the Solway shore ascribe a sinister character.
[2] Still.

twinkle on board the two Haunted Ships from every hole and seam, and presently the sound as of a hatchet employed in squaring timber echoed far and wide. But if the toil of these unearthly workmen amazed the laird, how much more was his amazement increased when a sharp shrill voice called out, ' Ho! brother, what are you doing now?' A voice still shriller responded from the other haunted ship, ' I'm making a wife to Sandie Macharg!' and a loud quavering laugh, running from ship to ship, and from bank to bank, told the joy they expected from their labour.

" Now the laird, besides being a devout and a God-fearing man, was shrewd and bold; and in plot, and contrivance, and skill in conducting his designs, was fairly an overmatch for any dozen land elves. But the water elves are far more subtle; besides, their haunts and their dwellings being in the great deep, pursuit and detection is hopeless if they succeed in carrying their prey to the waves. But ye shall hear. Home flew the laird,—collected his family around the hearth,—spoke of the signs and the sins of the times, and talked of mortification and prayer for averting calamity; and finally, taking his father's Bible, brass clasps, black print, and covered with calf-skin, from the shelf, he proceeded without let or stint to perform domestic worship. I should have told ye that he bolted and locked the door, shut up all inlet to the house, threw salt into the fire, and proceeded in every way like a man skilful in guarding against the plots of fairies and fiends. His wife looked on all this with wonder; but she saw something in her husband's looks that hindered her from intruding either question or advice, and a wise woman was she.

"Near the mid hour of the night the rush of a horse's feet was heard, and the sound of a rider leaping from its back, and a heavy knock came to the door, accompanied by a voice, saying, ' The cummer drink's[1] hot, and the knave bairn is expected at Laird Laurie's to-night; sae mount, gudewife, and come.'

"'Preserve me!' said the wife of Sandie Macharg; 'that's news indeed; who could have thought it? the laird has been heirless for seventeen years! Now Sandie, my man, fetch me my skirt and hood.'

"But he laid his arm round his wife's neck, and said, 'If all the lairds in Galloway go heirless, over this door threshold shall you not stir to-night; and I have said, and I have sworn it: seek not to know why or wherefore—but, Lord, send us thy blessed morn-light.' The wife looked for a moment in her husband's eyes, and desisted from further entreaty.

"'But let us send a civil message to the gossips, Sandie; and had nae ye better say I am sair laid with a sudden sickness? though its sinful-like to send the poor messenger a mile agate with a lie in his mouth without a glass of brandy.'

"'To such a messenger, and to those who sent him, no apology is needed,' said the austere laird, 'so let him depart.' And the clatter of a horse's hoofs was

---

[1] Gossips' drink.

heard, and the muttered imprecations of its rider on the churlish treatment he had experienced.

" ' Now Sandie, my lad,' said his wife, laying an arm particularly white and round about his neck as she spoke, ' are you not a queer man and a stern ? I have been your wedded wife now these three years; and, beside my dower, have brought you three as bonnie bairns as ever smiled aneath a summer sun.   O man, you a douce man, and fitter to be an elder than even Willie Greer himself,—I have the minister's ain word for't,—to put on these hard-hearted looks, and gang waving your arms that way, as if ye said, " I winna take the counsel of sic a hempie[1] as you." I'm your ain leal wife, and will and maun have an explanation.'

" To all this Sandie Macharg replied, ' It is written—" Wives, obey your husbands; " but we have been stayed in our devotion, so let us pray;' and down he knelt. His wife knelt also, for she was as devout as bonnie; and beside them knelt their household, and all lights were extinguished.

" ' Now this beats a',' muttered his wife to herself; ' however, I shall be obedient for a time; but if I dinna ken what all this is for before the morn by sunket-time,[2] my tongue is nae langer a tongue, nor my hands worth wearing.'

" The voice of her husband in prayer interrupted this mental soliloquy; and ardently did he beseech to be preserved from the wiles of the fiends, and the snares of Satan; ' from witches, ghosts, goblins, elves,

[1] Hussy.   [2] Breakfast-time ; any meal-time.

fairies, spunkies, and water-kelpies; from the spectre
shallop of Solway; from spirits visible and invisible;
from the Haunted Ships and their unearthly tenants;
from maritime spirits that plotted against godly men,
and fell in love with their wives'—

" 'Nay, but His presence be near us!' said his
wife in a low tone of dismay. 'God guide my gudeman's wits; I never heard such a prayer from human
lips before. But Sandie, my man, Lord's sake, rise:
what fearful light is this?—barn, and byre, and
stable, maun be in a blaze; and Hawkie and Hurley,
—Doddie, and Cherrie, and Damson Plum will be
smoored with reek, and scorched with flame.'

" And a flood of light, but not so gross as a common
fire, which ascended to heaven and filled all the court
before the house, amply justified the good wife's suspicions. But, to the terrors of fire, Sandie was as im-
movable as he was to the imaginary groans of the
barren wife of Laird Laurie; and he held his wife,
and threatened the weight of his right hand—and it
was a heavy one—to all who ventured abroad, or even
unbolted the door. The neighing and prancing of
horses, and the bellowing of cows, augmented the hor-
rors of the night; and to any one who only heard the
din, it seemed that the whole onstead was in a blaze,
and horses and cattle perishing in the flame. All
wiles, common or extraordinary, were put in practice
to entice or force the honest farmer and his wife to
open the door; and when the like success attended
every new stratagem, silence for a little while ensued,
and a long, loud, and shrilling laugh wound up the

dramatic efforts of the night. In the morning, when Laird Macharg went to the door, he found standing against one of the pilasters a piece of black ship oak, rudely fashioned into something like human form, and which skilful people declared would have been clothed with seeming flesh and blood, and palmed upon him by elfin adroitness for his wife, had he admitted his visitants. A synod of wise men and women sat upon the woman of timber, and she was finally ordered to be devoured by fire, and that in the open air. A fire was soon made, and into it the elfin sculpture was tossed from the prongs of two pairs of pitchforks. The blaze that arose was awful to behold; and hissings, and burstings, and loud cracklings, and strange noises, were heard in the midst of the flame; and when the whole sank into ashes, a drinking cup of some precious metal was found; and this cup, fashioned no doubt by elfin skill, but rendered harmless by the purification with fire, the sons and daughters of Sandie Macharg and his wife drink out of to this very day. Bless all bold men, say I, and obedient wives!"

———

ELPHIN IRVING.[1]

THE FAIRIES' CUPBEARER.

THE romantic vale of Corriewater, in Annandale, is regarded by the inhabitants, a pastoral and un-

[1] Allan Cunningham, *Traditional Tales of the English and Scottish Peasantry.*

mingled people, as the last Border refuge of those beautiful and capricious beings, the fairies. Many old people yet living imagine they have had intercourse of good words and good deeds with the " good folk "; and continue to tell that in the ancient of days the fairies danced on the hill, and revelled in the glen, and showed themselves, like the mysterious children of the deity of old, among the sons and daughters of men. Their visits to the earth were periods of joy and mirth to mankind, rather than of sorrow and apprehension. They played on musical instruments of wonderful sweetness and variety of note, spread unexpected feasts, the supernatural flavour of which overpowered on many occasions the religious scruples of the Presbyterian shepherds, performed wonderful deeds of horsemanship, and marched in midnight processions, when the sound of their elfin minstrelsy charmed youths and maidens into love for their persons and pursuits; and more than one family of Corriewater have the fame of augmenting the numbers of the elfin chivalry. Faces of friends and relatives, long since doomed to the battle-trench or the deep sea, have been recognised by those who dared to gaze on the fairy march. The maid has seen her lost lover and the mother her stolen child; and the courage to plan and achieve their deliverance has been possessed by at least one Border maiden. In the legends of the people of Corrievale there is a singular mixture of elfin and human adventure, and the traditional story of the Cupbearer to the Queen of the Fairies appeals alike to our domestic feelings and imagination.

In one of the little green loops, or bends, on the banks of Corriewater, mouldered walls, and a few stunted wild plum-trees and vagrant roses, still point out the site of a cottage and garden. A well of pure spring-water leaps out from an old tree-root before the door; and here the shepherds, shading themselves in summer from the influence of the sun, tell to their children the wild tale of Elphin Irving and his sister Phemie; and, singular as the story seems, it has gained full credence among the people where the scene is laid.

When Elphin Irving and his sister Phemie were in their sixteenth year, for tradition says they were twins, their father was drowned in Corriewater, attempting to save his sheep from a sudden swell, to which all mountain streams are liable; and their mother, on the day of her husband's burial, laid down her head on the pillow, from which, on the seventh day, it was lifted to be dressed for the same grave. The inheritance left to the orphans may be briefly described: seventeen acres of plough and pasture land, seven milk cows, and seven pet sheep (many old people take delight in odd numbers); and to this may be added seven bonnet-pieces of Scottish gold, and a broadsword and spear, which their ancestor had wielded with such strength and courage in the battle of Dryfe Sands, that the minstrel who sang of that deed of arms ranked him only second to the Scotts and Johnstones.

The youth and his sister grew in stature and in beauty. The brent bright brow, the clear blue eye, and frank and blithe deportment of the former gave him some influence among the young women of the valley; while the latter was no less the admiration of the young men, and at fair and dance, and at bridal, happy was he who touched but her hand or received the benediction of her eye. Like all other Scottish beauties, she was the theme of many a song; and while tradition is yet busy with the singular history of her brother, song has taken all the care that rustic minstrelsy can of the gentleness of her spirit and the charms of her person.

But minstrel skill and true love tale seemed to want their usual influence when they sought to win her attention; she was only observed to pay most respect to those youths who were most beloved by her brother; and the same hour that brought these twins to the world seemed to have breathed through them a sweetness and an affection of heart and mind, which nothing could divide. If, like the virgin queen of the immortal poet, she walked " in maiden meditation fancy free," her brother Elphin seemed alike untouched with the charms of the fairest virgins in Corrie. He ploughed his field, he reaped his grain, he leaped, he ran, and wrestled, and danced, and sang, with more skill and life and grace than all other youths of the district; but he had no twilight and stolen interviews; when all other young men had their loves by their side, he was single, though not unsought, and his joy seemed never perfect save when his sister was near him. If he loved to share his time with her, she loved to share her time with him alone,

or with the beasts of the field, or the birds of the air.
She watched her little flock late, and she tended it
early; not for the sordid love of the fleece, unless it
was to make mantles for her brother, but with the
look of one who had joy in its company. The very
wild creatures, the deer and the hares, seldom sought
to shun her approach, and the bird forsook not its
nest, nor stinted its song, when she drew nigh; such
is the confidence which maiden innocence and beauty
inspire.

It happened one summer, about three years after
they became orphans, that rain had been for awhile
withheld from the earth, the hillsides began to parch,
the grass in the vales to wither, and the stream of
Corrie was diminished between its banks to the size
of an ordinary rill. The shepherds drove their flocks
to moorlands, and marsh and tarn had their reeds in-
vaded by the scythe to supply the cattle with food.
The sheep of his sister were Elphin's constant care;
he drove them to the moistest pastures during the
day, and he often watched them at midnight, when
flocks, tempted by the sweet dewy grass, are known
to browse eagerly, that he might guard them from the
fox, and lead them to the choicest herbage. In these
nocturnal watchings he sometimes drove his little
flock over the water of Corrie, for the fords were
hardly ankle-deep; or permitted his sheep to cool
themselves in the stream, and taste the grass which
grew along the brink. All this time not a drop of
rain fell, nor did a cloud appear in the sky.

One evening, during her brother's absence with the

flock, Phemie sat at her cottage door, listening to the bleatings of the distant folds and the lessened murmur of the water of Corrie, now scarcely audible beyond its banks. Her eyes, weary with watching along the accustomed line of road for the return of Elphin, were turned on the pool beside her, in which the stars were glimmering fitful and faint. As she looked she imagined the water grew brighter and brighter; a wild illumination presently shone upon the pool, and leaped from bank to bank, and suddenly changing into a human form, ascended the margin, and, passing her, glided swiftly into the cottage. The visionary form was so like her brother in shape and air, that, starting up, she flew into the house, with the hope of finding him in his customary seat. She found him not, and, impressed with the terror which a wraith or apparition seldom fails to inspire, she uttered a shriek so loud and so piercing as to be heard at Johnstone Bank, on the other side of the vale of Corrie.

It is hardly known how long Phemie Irving continued in a state of insensibility. The morning was far advanced, when a neighbouring maiden found her seated in an old chair, as white as monumental marble; her hair, about which she had always been solicitous, loosened from its curls, and hanging disordered over her neck and bosom, her hands and forehead. The maiden touched the one, and kissed the other; they were as cold as snow; and her eyes, wide open, were fixed on her brother's empty chair, with the intensity of gaze of one who had witnessed the appearance of a spirit. She seemed insensible of any one's presence, and sat fixed and still and motionless. The maiden, alarmed at her looks, thus addressed her:— " Phemie, lass, Phemie Irving! Dear me, but this be awful! I have come to tell ye that seven of your pet sheep have escaped drowning in the water; for Corrie, sae quiet and sae gentle yestreen, is rolling and dashing frae bank to bank this morning. Dear me, woman, dinna let the loss of the world's gear bereave ye of your senses. I would rather make ye a present of a dozen mug-ewes of the Tinwald brood myself; and now I think on't, if ye'll send over Elphin, I will help him hame with them in the gloaming myself. So, Phemie woman, be comforted."

At the mention of her brother's name she cried out, " Where is he? Oh, where is he?" gazed wildly round, and, shuddering from head to foot, fell senseless on the floor. Other inhabitants of the valley, alarmed by the sudden swell of the river, which had augmented to a torrent, deep and impassable, now came in to inquire if any loss had been sustained, for numbers of sheep and teds of hay had been observed floating down about the dawn of the morning. They assisted in reclaiming the unhappy maiden from her swoon; but insensibility was joy compared to the sorrow to which she awakened. " They have ta'en him away, they have ta'en him away," she chanted, in a tone of delirious pathos; " him that was whiter and fairer than the lily on Lyddal Lee. They have long sought, and they have long sued, and they had the power to prevail against my prayers at last. They have ta'en him away; the flower is plucked from among the weeds, and the dove is slain amid a flock of ravens. They came with shout, and they came with song, and they spread the charm, and they placed the spell, and the baptised brow has been bowed down to the unbaptised hand. They have ta'en him away, they have ta'en him away; he was too lovely, and too good, and too noble, to bless us with his continuance on earth; for what are the sons of men compared to him?—the light of the moon-beam to the morning sun, the glow-worm to the eastern star. They have ta'en him away, the invisible dwellers of the earth. I saw them come on him with shouting and with singing, and they charmed him where he sat, and away they bore him; and the horse he rode was never shod with iron, nor owned before the mastery of human hand. They have ta'en him away over the water, and over the wood, and over the hill. I got but ae look of his bonnie blue ee, but ae, ae look. But as I have endured what never maiden endured, so will I undertake what never maiden undertook; I will win him from them all. I know the invisible ones of the earth; I have heard their wild and wondrous music in the wild woods, and there shall a christened maiden seek him, and achieve his deliverance." She paused, and glancing around a circle of condoling faces, down which the tears were dropping like rain, said, in a calm and altered but still delirious tone: "Why do you weep, Mary Halliday? and why do you weep, John Graeme? Ye think that Elphin Irving—oh, it's a bonnie, bonnie name, and dear to many a maiden's heart as well as mine—ye think he is drowned in Corrie, and ye will seek in the deep, deep pools for the bonnie, bonnie corse, that ye may weep over it, as it lies in its last linen, and lay it, amid weeping and wailing, in the dowie kirkyard. Ye may seek, but ye shall never find; so leave me to trim up my hair, and prepare my dwelling, and make myself ready to watch for the hour of his return to upper earth." And she resumed her household labours with an alacrity which lessened not the sorrow of her friends.

Meanwhile the rumour flew over the vale that Elphin Irving was drowned in Corriewater. Matron and maid, old man and young, collected suddenly along the banks of the river, which now began to subside to its natural summer limits, and commenced their search; interrupted every now and then by calling from side to side, and from pool to pool, and by exclamations of sorrow for this misfortune. The search was fruitless: five sheep, pertaining to the flock which he conducted to pasture, were found drowned in one of the deep eddies; but the river was still too brown, from the soil of its moorland sources, to enable them to see what its deep shelves, its pools, and its overhanging and hazely banks concealed. They remitted further search till the stream should become pure; and old man taking old man aside, began to whisper about the mystery of the youth's disappearance; old women laid their lips to the ears of their coevals, and talked of Elphin Irving's fairy

parentage, and his having been dropped by an unearthly hand into a Christian cradle. The young
men and maids conversed on other themes; they
grieved for the loss of the friend and the lover, and
while the former thought that a heart so kind and
true was not left in the vale, the latter thought, as
maidens will, on his handsome person, gentle manners, and merry blue eye, and speculated with a sigh
on the time when they might have hoped a return for
their love. They were soon joined by others who had
heard the wild and delirious language of his sister:
the old belief was added to the new assurance, and
both again commented upon by minds full of superstitious feeling, and hearts full of supernatural fears,
till the youths and maidens of Corrievale held no
more love trysts for seven days and nights, lest, like
Elphin Irving, they should be carried away to aug-
ment the ranks of the unchristened chivalry.

It was curious to listen to the speculations of the
peasantry. "For my part," said a youth, "if I were
sure that poor Elphin escaped from that perilous
water, I would not give the fairies a pound of hip-
lock wool for their chance of him. There has not
been a fairy seen in the land since Donald Cargil,
the Cameronian, conjured them into the Solway for
playing on their pipes during one of his nocturnal
preachings on the hip of the Burnswick hill."

"Preserve me, bairn," said an old woman, justly
exasperated at the incredulity of her nephew, "if ye
winna believe what I both heard and saw at the moonlight end of Craigyburnwood on a summer night,

rang after rank of the fairy folk, ye'll at least believe a douce man and a ghostly professor, even the late minister of Tinwaldkirk. His only son—I mind the lad weel, with his long yellow locks and his bonnie blue eyes—when I was but a gilpie of a lassie, *he* was stolen away from off the horse at his father's elbow, as they crossed that false and fearsome water, even Locherbriggflow, on the night of the Midsummer fair of Dumfries. Ay, ay—who can doubt the truth of that? Have not the godly inhabitants of Almsfieldtown and Tinwaldkirk seen the sweet youth riding at midnight, in the midst of the unhallowed troop, to the sound of flute and of dulcimer, and though meikle they prayed, naebody tried to achieve his deliverance?"

" I have heard it said by douce folk and sponsible," interrupted another, " that every seven years the elves and fairies pay kane,[1] or make an offering of one of their children, to the grand enemy of salvation, and that they are permitted to purloin one of the children of men to present to the fiend—a more acceptable offering, I'll warrant, than one of their own infernal brood that are Satan's sib allies, and drink a drop of the deil's blood every May morning. And touching this lost lad, ye all ken his mother was a hawk of an uncannie nest, a second cousin of Kate Kimmer, of Barfloshan, as rank a witch as ever rode on ragwort. Ay, sirs, what's bred in the bone is ill to come out of the flesh."

On these and similar topics, which a peasantry

[1] Tribute paid in kind.

full of ancient tradition and enthusiasm and superstition readily associate with the commonest occur-
rences of life, the people of Corrievale continued to
converse till the fall of evening, when each, seeking
their home, renewed again the wondrous subject, and
illustrated it with all that popular belief and poetic
imagination could so abundantly supply.

The night which followed this melancholy day was
wild with wind and rain; the river came down
broader and deeper than before, and the lightning,
flashing by fits over the green woods of Corrie,
showed the ungovernable and perilous flood sweeping
above its banks. It happened that a farmer, returning from one of the Border fairs, encountered the full
swing of the storm; but mounted on an excellent
horse, and mantled from chin to heel in a good grey
plaid, beneath which he had the further security of
a thick great-coat, he sat dry in his saddle, and proceeded in the anticipated joy of a subsided tempest
and a glowing morning sun. As he entered the long
grove, or rather remains of the old Galwegian forest,
which lines for some space the banks of the Corriewater, the storm began to abate, the wind sighed
milder and milder among the trees; and here and
there a star, twinkling momentarily through the sudden rack of the clouds, showed the river raging from
bank to brae. As he shook the moisture from his
clothes, he was not without a wish that the day would
dawn, and that he might be preserved on a road
which his imagination beset with greater perils than
the raging river; for his superstitious feeling let loose

upon his path elf and goblin, and the current traditions of the district supplied very largely to his apprehension the ready materials of fear.

Just as he emerged from the wood, where a fine
sloping bank, covered with short greensward, skirts
the limit of the forest, his horse made a full pause,
snorted, trembled, and started from side to side,
stooped his head, erected his ears, and seemed to
scrutinise every tree and bush. The rider, too, it
may be imagined, gazed round and round, and peered
warily into every suspicious-looking place. His dread
of a supernatural visitation was not much allayed
when he observed a female shape seated on the ground
at the root of a huge old oak-tree, which stood in the
centre of one of those patches of verdant sward,
known by the name of " fairy-rings," and avoided by
all peasants who wish to prosper. A long thin gleam
of eastern daylight enabled him to examine accurately the being who, in this wild place and unusual
hour, gave additional terror to this haunted spot.
She was dressed in white from the neck to the knees;
her arms, long and round and white, were perfectly
bare; her head, uncovered, allowed her long hair to
descend in ringlet succeeding ringlet, till the half of
her person was nearly concealed in the fleece. Amidst
the whole, her hands were constantly busy in shed-
ding aside the tresses which interposed between her
steady and uninterrupted gaze down a line of old
road which winded among the hills to an ancient
burial-ground.

As the traveller continued to gaze, the figure sud-

denly rose, and, wringing the rain from her long
locks, paced round and round the tree, chanting in
a wild and melancholy manner an equally wild and
delirious song.

THE FAIRY OAK OF CORRIEWATER.

The small bird's head is under its wing,
　　The deer sleeps on the grass ;
The moon comes out, and the stars shine down,
　　The dew gleams like the glass :
There is no sound in the world so wide,
　　Save the sound of the smitten brass,
With the merry cittern and the pipe
　　Of the fairies as they pass.
But oh ! the fire maun burn and burn,
And the hour is gone, and will never return.

The green hill cleaves, and forth, with a bound,
　　Comes elf and elfin steed ;
The moon dives down in a golden cloud,
　　The stars grow dim with dread ;
But a light is running along the earth,
　　So of heaven's they have no need :
O'er moor and moss with a shout they pass,
　　And the word is spur and speed—
But the fire maun burn, and I maun quake,
And the hour is gone that will never come back.

And when they came to Craigyburnwood,
　　The Queen of the Fairies spoke :
"Come, bind your steeds to the rushes so green,
　　And dance by the haunted oak :
I found the acorn on Heshbon Hill,
　　In the nook of a palmer's poke,
A thousand years since ; here it grows !"
　　And they danced till the greenwood shook :

But oh ! the fire, the burning fire,
The longer it burns, it but blazes the higher.

" I have won me a youth," the Elf Queen said,
  " The fairest that earth may see ;
This night 1 have won young Elph Irving
  My cupbearer to be.
His service lasts but for seven sweet years,
  And his wage is a kiss of me."
And merrily, merrily, laughed the wild elves
  Round Corrie's greenwood tree.
But oh ! the fire it glows in my brain,
And the hour is gone, and comes not again.

The Queen she has whispered a secret word,
  " Come hither, my Elphin sweet,
And bring that cup of the charméd wine,
  Thy lips and mine to weet."
But a brown elf shouted a loud, loud shout,
  " Come, leap on your coursers fleet,
For here comes the smell of of some baptised flesh
  And the sound of baptised feet."
But oh ! the fire that burns, and maun burn ;
For the time that is gone will never return.

On a steed as white as the new-milked milk,
  The Elf Queen leaped with a bound,
And young Elphin a steed like December snow
  'Neath him at the word he found.
But a maiden came, and her christened arms
  She linked her brother around,
And called on God, and the steed with a snort
  Sank into the gaping ground.
But the fire maun burn, and I maun quake,
And the time that is gone will no more come back.

And she held her brother, and lo ! he grew
  A wild bull waked in ire ;
And she held her brother, and lo ! he changed
  To a river roaring higher ;

And she held her brother, and he became
  A flood of the raging fire ;
She shrieked and sank, and the wild elves laughed
  Till the mountain rang and mire.
But oh ! the fire yet burns in my brain,
And the hour is gone, and comes not again.

" O maiden, why waxed thy faith so faint,
  Thy spirit so slack and slaw ?
Thy courage kept good till the flame waxed wud,[1]
  Then thy might began to thaw ;
Had ye kissed him with thy christened lip,
  Ye had wan him frae 'mang us a'.
Now bless the fire, the elfin fire,
  That made thee faint and fa' ;
Now bless the fire, the elfin fire,
The longer it burns it blazes the higher."

At the close of this unusual strain the figure sat
down on the grass, and proceeded to bind up her long
and disordered tresses, gazing along the old and un-
frequented road. " Now God be my helper," said the
traveller, who happened to be the laird of Johnstone
Bank, " can this be a trick of the fiend, or can it be
bonnie Phemie Irving who chants this dolorous sang ?
Something sad has befallen, that makes her seek her
seat in this eerie nook amid the darkness and tempest:
through might from aboon I will go on and see."
And the horse, feeling something of the owner's re-
viving spirit in the application of spur-steel, bore
him at once to the foot of the tree. The poor delirious maiden uttered a yell of piercing joy as she
beheld him, and, with the swiftness of a creature
winged, linked her arms round the rider's waist, and

[1] Furious.

shrieked till the woods rang. " Oh, I have ye now, Elphin, I have ye now," and she strained him to her bosom with a convulsive grasp. " What ails ye, my bonnie lass?" said the laird of Johnstone Bank, his fears of the supernatural vanishing when he beheld her sad and bewildered look. She raised her eyes at the sound, and, seeing a strange face, her arms slipped their hold, and she dropped with a groan on the ground.

The morning had now fairly broke: the flocks shook the rain from their sides, the shepherds hastened to inspect their charges, and a thin blue smoke began to stream from the cottages of the valley into the brightening air. The laird carried Phemie Irving in his arms, till he observed two shepherds ascending from one of the loops of Corriewater, bearing the lifeless body of her brother. They had found him whirling round and round in one of the numerous eddies, and his hands, clutched and filled with wool, showed that he had lost his life in attempting to save the flock of his sister. A plaid was laid over the body, which, along with the unhappy maiden in a half-lifeless state, was carried into a cottage, and laid in that apartment distinguished among the peasantry by the name of the chamber. While the peasant's wife was left to take care of Phemie, old man and matron and maid had collected around the drowned youth, and each began to relate the circumstances of his death, when the door suddenly opened, and his sister, advancing to the corpse with a look of delirious serenity, broke out into a wild laugh and said: " Oh, it is wonderful, it's truly wonderful! That bare and death-cold body, dragged from the darkest pool of Corrie, with its hands filled with fine wool, wears the perfect similitude of my own Elphin! I'll tell ye—the spiritual dwellers of the earth, the fairyfolk of our evening tale, have stolen the living body, and fashioned this cold and inanimate clod to mislead your pursuit. In common eyes this seems all that Elphin Irving would be, had he sunk in Corriewater; but so it seems not to me. Ye have sought the living soul, and ye have found only its garment. But oh, if ye had beheld him, as I beheld him to-night, riding among the elfin troop, the fairest of them all; had you clasped him in your arms, and wrestled for him with spirits and terrible shapes from the other world, till your heart quailed and your flesh was subdued, then would ye yield no credit to the semblance which this cold and apparent flesh bears to my brother. But hearken! On Hallowmass Eve, when the spiritual people are let loose on earth for a season, I will take my stand in the burial-ground of Corrie; and when my Elphin and his unchristened troop come past, with the sound of all their minstrelsy, I will leap on him and win him, or perish for ever."

All gazed aghast on the delirious maiden, and many of her auditors gave more credence to her distempered speech than to the visible evidence before them. As she turned to depart, she looked round, and suddenly sunk upon the body, with tears streaming from her eyes, and sobbed out, " My brother! oh, my brother!" She was carried out insensible, and again recovered; but relapsed into her ordinary delirium, in which she continued till the Hallow Eve after her brother's burial. She was found seated in the ancient burial-ground, her back against a broken gravestone, her locks white with frost-rime, watching with intensity of look the road to the kirkyard; but the spirit which gave life to the fairest form of all the maids of Annandale was fled for ever.

Such is the singular story which the peasants know by the name of " Elphin Irving, the Fairies' Cupbearer; " and the title, in its fullest and most supernatural sense, still obtains credence among the industrious and virtuous dames of the romantic vale of Corrie.

COUSIN MATTIE.[1]

At the lone farm of Finagle, there lived for many years an industrious farmer and his family. Several of his children died, and only one daughter and one son remained to him. He had besides these a little orphan niece, who was brought into the family, called Matilda; but all her days she went by the familiar name of Cousin Mattie. At the time this simple narrative commences, Alexander, the farmer's son, was six years of age, Mattie was seven, and Flora, the farmer's only daughter, about twelve.

[1] James Hogg, *The Ettrick Shepherd's Tales.*

How I do love a little girl about that age! There is nothing in nature so fascinating, so lovely, so innocent; and, at the same time, so full of gaiety and playfulness. The tender and delicate affections, to which their natures are moulded, are then beginning unconsciously to form; and everything beautiful or affecting in nature claims from them a deep but momentary interest. They have a tear for the weaned lamb, for the drooping flower, and even for the travelling mendicant, though afraid to come near him. But the child of the poor female vagrant is to them, of all others, an object of the deepest interest. How I have seen them look at the little wretch, and then at their own parents alternately, the feelings of the soul abundantly conspicuous in every muscle of the face and turn of the eye! Their hearts are like softened wax, and the impressions then made on them remain for ever. Such beings approach nigh to the list where angels stand, and are, in fact, the connecting link that joins us with the inhabitants of a better world. How I do love a well-educated little girl of twelve or thirteen years of age!

At such an age was Flora of Finagle, with a heart moulded to every tender impression, and a memory so retentive that whatever affected or interested her was engraven there never to be cancelled.

One morning, after her mother had risen and gone to the byre to look after the cows, Flora, who was lying in a bed by herself, heard the following dialogue between the two children, who were lying prattling together in another bed close beside hers—

22

" Do you ever dream ony, little Sandy ? "

" What is't like, cousin Mattie ? Sandy no ken what it is til dream."

" It is to think ye do things when you are sleeping, when ye dinna do them at a'."

" Oh, Sandy deam a great deal yat way."

" If you will tell me ane o' your dreams, Sandy— I'll tell you ane o' mine that I dreamed last night; and it was about you, Sandy ? "

" Sae was mine, cousin. Sandy deamed that he fightit a gaet Englishman, an' it was Yobin Hood; an' Sandy ding'd him's swold out o' him's hand, an' noll'd him on ye face, an ye back, till him geetit. An' yen thele comed anodel littel despelyate Englishman, an' it was littel John; an' Sandy fightit him till him was dead; an' yen Sandy got on o' ane gyand holse, an' gallompit away."

" But I wish that ye be nae making that dream just e'en now, Sandy ? "

" Sandy 'hought it, atweel."

" But were you sleeping when you thought it ? "

" Na, Sandy wasna' sleepin', but him was winking."

" Oh, but that's not a true dream; I'll tell you one that's a true dream. I thought there was a bonny lady came to me, and she held out two roses, a red one and a pale one, and bade me take my choice. I took the white one; and she bade me keep it, and never part with it, for if I gave it away, I would die. But when I came to you, you asked my rose, and I refused to give you it. You then cried for it, and said I did not love you; so I could not refuse you the flower, but wept too, and you took it.

" Then the bonny lady came back to me, and was very angry, and said, ' Did not I tell you to keep your rose ? Now the boy that you have given it to will be your murderer. He will kill you; and on this day fortnight you will be lying in your coffin, and that pale rose upon your breast.'

" I said, ' I could not help it now.' But when I was told that you were to kill me, I liked you aye better and better, and better and better." And with these words Matilda clasped him to her bosom and wept. Sandy sobbed bitterly too, and said, " She be geat lial, yon lady. Sandy no kill cousin Mattie. When Sandy gows byaw man, an' gets a gyand house, him be vely good till cousin an' feed hel wi' gingebead, an' yeam, an' tyankil, an' take hel in him's bosy yis way." With that the two children fell silent, and sobbed and wept till they fell sound asleep, clasped in each other's arms.

This artless dialogue made a deep impression on Flora's sensitive heart. It was a part of her mother's creed to rely on dreams, so that it had naturally become Flora's too. She was shocked, and absolutely terrified, when she heard her little ingenious cousin say that Sandy was to murder her, and on that day fortnight she should be lying in her coffin; and without informing her mother of what she had overheard, she resolved in her own mind to avert, if possible, the impending evil. It was on a Sabbath morning, and after little Sandy had got on his clothes, and while

Matilda was out, he attempted to tell his mother cousin Mattie's dream, to Flora's great vexation; but he made such a blundering story of it that it proved altogether incoherent, and his mother took no further notice of it than to bid him hold his tongue; " what was that he was speaking about murdering?"

The next week Flora entreated of her mother that she would suffer cousin Mattie and herself to pay a visit to their aunt at Kirkmichael; and, though her mother was unwilling, she urged her suit so earnestly that the worthy dame was fain to consent.

" What's ta'en the gowk[1] lassie the day?" said she; " I think she be gane fey. I never could get her to gang to see her aunt, and now she has ta'en a tirrovy[2] in her head, that she'll no be keepit. I dinna like sic absolute freaks, an' sic langings, to come into the heads o' bairns; they're ower aften afore something uncannie. Gae your ways an' see your auntie, sin' ye will gang; but ye's no get little cousin w'ye, sae never speak o't. Think ye that I can do wantin' ye baith out o' the house till the Sabbath day be ower."

" Oh but, mother, it's sae gousty,[3] an' sae eiry, to lie up in yon loft ane's lane; unless cousin Mattie gang wi' me, I canna' gang ava."

" Then just stay at hame, daughter, an' let us alane o' thae daft nories[4] a' thegither."

Flora now had recourse to that expedient which never fails to conquer the opposition of a fond

[1] Foolish.
[2] Fit of passion.
[3] Ghostly.
[4] Whims.

mother: she pretended to cry bitterly. The good dame was quite overcome, and at once yielded, though not with a very good grace. " Saw ever onybody, sic a fie-gae-to[1] as this? They that will to Cupar maun to Cupar! Gae your ways to Kirkmichael, an' tak the hale town at your tail, gin ye like. What's this that I'm sped wi'."

" Na, na, mother; I's no gang my foot length. Ye sanna hae that to flyre[2] about. Ye keep me working frae the tae year's end to the tither, an' winna gie me a day to mysel'. I's no seek to be away again, as lang as I'm aneath your roof."

" Whisht now, an' haud your tongue, my bonny Flora. Ye hae been ower good a bairn to me, no to get your ain way o' ten times mair nor that. Ye ken laith wad your mother be to contrair you i' ought, if she wist it war for your good. I'm right glad that it has come i' your ain side o' the house, to gang an' see your auntie. Gang your ways, an' stay a day or twa; an', if ye dinna like to sleep your lane, take billy Sandy w'ye, an' leave little cousin wi' me, to help me wi' bits o' turns till ye come back."

This arrangement suiting Flora's intent equally well with the other, it was readily agreed to, and everything soon amicably settled between the mother and daughter. The former demurred a little on Sandy's inability to perform the journey; but Flora, being intent on her purpose, overruled this objection, though she knew it was but too well founded.

Accordingly, the couple set out on their journey

---

[1] Ado.   [2] Complain.

next morning, but before they were half way Sandy began to tire, and a short time after gave fairly in. Flora carried him on her back for a space, but finding that would never do, she tried to cajole him into further exertion. No, Sandy would not set a foot to the ground. He was grown drowsy, and would not move. Flora knew not what to do, but at length fell upon an expedient which an older person would scarcely have thought of. She went to a gate of an enclosure, and, pulling a spoke out of it, she brought that to Sandy, telling him she had now got him a fine horse, and he might ride all the way. Sandy, who was uncommonly fond of horses, swallowed the bait, and, mounting astride on his rung, he took the road at a round pace, and for the last two miles of their journey Flora could hardly keep in view of him.

She had little pleasure in her visit, further than the satisfaction that she was doing what she could to avert a dreadful casualty, which she dreaded to be hanging over the family; and on her return, from the time that she came in view of her father, she looked only for the appearance of Mattie running about the door; but no Mattie being seen, Flora's heart began to tremble, and as she advanced nearer, her knees grew so feeble that they would scarcely support her slender form; for she knew that it was one of the radical principles of a dream to be ambiguous.

"A's unco still about our hame the day, Sandy; I wish ilka ane there may be weel. It's like death."

"Sandy no ken what death *is* like. What *is* it like, Sistel Flola?"

" You will maybe see that ower soon. It is death that kills a' living things, Sandy."

" Aye; aih aye! Sandy saw a wee buldie, it could neilel pick, nol flee, nol dab. It was vely ill done o' death! Sistel Flola, didna God make a' living things?"

" Yes; be assured he did."

" Then, what has death ado to kill them? if Sandy wele God, him wad fight him."

" Whisht, whisht, my dear; ye dinna ken what you're sayin'. Ye maunna speak about these things."

· " Weel, Sandy no speak ony maile about them. But if death should kill cousin Mattie, oh! Sandy wish him might kill him too!"

" Wha do ye like best i' this world, Sandy?"

" Sandy like sistel Flola best."

" You are learning the art of flattery already; for I heard ye telling Mattie the tither morning, that ye likit her better than a' the rest o' the world put thegither."

" But yan Sandy coudna help yat. Cousin Mattie like Sandy, and what could him say?"

Flora could not answer him for anxiety; for they were now drawing quite near to the house, and still all was quiet. At length Mattie opened the door, and, without returning to tell her aunt the joyful tidings, came running like a little fairy to meet them; gave Flora a hasty kiss; and then, clasping little Sandy about the neck, she exclaimed, in an ecstatic tone, " Aih, Sandy man!" and pressed her cheek to his. Sandy produced a small book of pictures, and a pink rose knot that he had brought for his cousin, and was repaid with another embrace, and a sly compliment to his gallantry.

Matilda was far beyond her years in acuteness. Her mother was an accomplished English lady, though only the daughter of a poor curate, and she had bred her only child with every possible attention. She could read, she could sing, and play some airs on the spinnet; and was altogether a most interesting little nymph. Both her parents came to an untimely end, and to the lone cottage of Finagle was she then removed, where she was still very much caressed. She told Flora all the news of her absence in a breath. There was nothing disastrous had happened. But, so strong was Flora's presentiment of evil, that she could not get quit of it, until she had pressed the hands of both her parents. From that day forth, she suspected that little faith was to be put in dreams. The fourteen days was now fairly over, and no evil nor danger had happened to Matilda, either from the hand of Sandy or otherwise. However, she kept the secret of the dream locked up in her heart, and never either mentioned or forgot it.

Shortly after that she endeavoured to reason her mother out of her belief in dreams, for she would still gladly have been persuaded in her own mind that this vision was futile, and of no avail. But she found her mother staunch to her point. She reasoned on the principle that the Almighty had made nothing in vain, and if dreams had been of no import to man they would not have been given to him. And further, she said we read in the Scriptures that dreams were fulfilled in the days of old; but we didna read in the Scriptures that ever the nature of dreaming was changed. On the contrary, she believed that since the days of prophecy had departed, and no more warnings of futurity could be derived by man from that, dreaming was of doubly more avail, and ought to be proportionally more attended to, as the only mystical communication remaining between God and man. To this reasoning Flora was obliged to yield. It is no hard matter to conquer, where belief succeeds argument.

Time flew on, and the two children were never asunder. They read together, prayed together, and toyed and caressed without restraint, seeming but to live for one another. But a heavy misfortune at length befell the family. She who had been a kind mother and guardian angel to all the three was removed by death to a better home. Flora was at that time in her eighteenth year, and the charge of the family then devolved on her. Great was their grief, but their happiness was nothing abated; they lived together in the same kind love and amity as they had done before. The two youngest in particular fondled each other more and more, and this growing fondness, instead of being checked, was constantly encouraged, Flora still having a lurking dread that some deadly animosity might breed between them.

Matilda and she always slept in the same bed, and very regularly told each other their dreams in the morning—dreams pure and innocent as their own stainless bosoms. But one morning Flora was surprised by Matilda addressing her as follows, in a tone of great perplexity and distress—

"Ah! my dear cousin, what a dream I have had last night! I thought I saw my aunt, your late worthy mother, who was kind and affectionate to me, as she always wont to be, and more beautiful than I ever saw her. She took me in her arms, and wept over me; and charged me to go and leave this place instantly, and by all means to avoid her son, otherwise he was destined to be my murderer; and on that day seven-night I should be lying in my coffin. She showed me a sight too that I did not know, and cannot give a name to. But the surgeons came between us, and separated us, so that I saw her no more."

Flora trembled and groaned in spirit; nor could she make any answer to Matilda for a long space, save by repeated moans. "Merciful Heaven!" said she at length, "what can such a dream portend? Do not you remember, dear Mattie, of dreaming a dream of the same nature once long ago?"

Mattie had quite forgot of ever having dreamed such a dream; but Flora remembered it well; and thinking that she might formerly have been the mean, under Heaven, of counterworking destiny, she determined to make a further effort; and, ere ever she arose, advised Matilda to leave the house, and avoid her brother, until the seven days had elapsed. "It can do nae ill, Mattie," said she; "an' mankind hae whiles muckle i' their ain hands to do or no to do;

to bring about, or to keep back." Mattie consented, solely to please the amiable Flora; for she was no more afraid of Sandy than she was of one of the flowers of the field. She went to Kirkmichael, stayed till the week was expired, came home in safety, and they both laughed at their superstitious fears. Matilda thought of the dream no more, but Flora treasured it up in her memory, though all the coincidence that she could discover between the two dreams was that they had both happened on a Saturday, and both precisely at the same season of the year, which she well remembered.

At the age of two and twenty, Flora was married to a young farmer, who lived in a distant corner of the same extensive parish, and of course left the charge of her father's household to cousin Mattie, who, with the old farmer, his son, and one maid-servant, managed and did all the work of the farm. Still, as their number was diminished, their affections seemed to be drawn the closer; but Flora scarce-y saw them any more, having the concerns of a family to mind at home.

One day, when her husband went to church, he perceived the old beadle standing bent over his staff at the churchyard gate, distributing burial letters to a few as they entered. He held out one to the husband of Flora, and, at the same time, touched the front of his bonnet with the other hand; and without regarding how the letter affected him who received it, began instantly to look about for others to whom he had letters directed.

The farmer opened the letter, and had almost sunk down on the earth, when he read as follows :—

" Sir,—The favour of your company, at twelve o'clock, on Tuesday next, to attend the funeral of Matilda A———n, my niece, from this, to the place of interment, in the churchyard of C———r, will much oblige, Sir, your humble servant,

"JAMES A———N.

" Finagle, April 12th."

Think of Flora's amazement and distress, when her husband told her what had happened, and showed her this letter. She took to her bed on the instant, and wept herself into a fever for the friend and companion of her youth. Her husband became considerably alarmed on her account, she being in that state in which violent excitement often proves dangerous. Her sickness was, however, only temporary; but she burned with impatience to learn some particulars of her cousin's death. Her husband could tell her nothing; only, that he heard one say *she died on Saturday.*

This set Flora a calculating, and going over in her mind reminiscences of their youth; and she soon discovered, to her utter astonishment and even horror, that her cousin Matilda had died precisely on *that day fourteen years* that she first dreamed the ominous dream, and that day seven years that she dreamed it again!

Here was indeed matter of wonder! But her blood ran cold to her heart when she thought what might have been the manner of her death. She dreaded, nay, she almost calculated upon it as certain, that her brother had poisoned, or otherwise made away privately with the deceased, as she was sure such an extraordinary coincidence behoved to be fulfilled in all its parts. She durst no more make any inquiries concerning the circumstances of her cousin's death; but she became moping and unsettled, and her husband feared for her reason.

He went to the funeral; but dreading to leave Flora long by herself, he only met the procession a small space from the churchyard; for his father-in-law's house was distant fourteen miles from his own. On his return, he could still give Flora very little additional information. He said he had asked his father-in-law what had been the nature of the complaint of which she died; but he had given him an equivocal answer, and seemed to avoid entering into any explanation; and that he had then made inquiry at others, who all testified their ignorance of the matter. Flora at length, after long hesitation, ventured to ask *if her brother was at the funeral?* and was told that he was not. This was a death-blow to her lingering hopes, and all but confirmed the hideous catastrophe that she dreaded; and for the remainder of that week she continued in a state of mental agony.

On the Sunday following, she manifested a strong desire to go to church to visit her cousin's grave. Her husband opposed it at first, but at last consenting, in hopes she might be benefited by an overflow of tenderness, he mounted her on a pad, and accom-

panied her to the churchyard gate, leaving her there
to give vent to her feelings.

As she approached the new grave, which was by
the side of her mother's, she perceived two aged people whom she knew sitting beside it busily engaged
in conversation about the inhabitant below. Flora
drew her hood over her face, and came with a saun-
tering step towards them, to lull all suspicion that
she had any interest or concern in what they were
saying; and finally she leaned herself down on a flat
grave-stone close beside them, and made as if she were
busied in deciphering the inscription. There she
heard the following dialogue, one may conceive with
what sort of feelings.

" An' then she was aye say kind, an' sae lively, an'
sae affable to poor an' rich, an' then sae bonny an'
sae young. Oh, but my heart's sair for her! When
I saw the mortclaith drawn off the coffin, an' saw the
silver letters kythe, AGED 21, the tears ran down ower
thae auld wizzened cheeks, Janet; an' I said to mysel', ' Wow but that is a bonny flower cut off i' the
bloom! '   But, Janet, my joe, warna ye at the
corpse-kisting ? "[1]

" An' what suppose I was, Matthew ? What's your
concern wi' that ? "

" Because I heard say that there was nane there
but you an' another that ye ken weel. But canna
you tell me, kimmer, what was the corpse like ? Was't
a' fair an' bonny, an' nae blueness nor demmish to
be seen ? "

[1] Ceremony of coffining.

" An' what wad an auld fool body like you be the better, gin ye kend what the corpse was like ?   Thae sights are nae for een like yours to see; an' thae subjects are nae fit for tongues like yours to tattle about.   What's done canna be undone.   The dead will lie still.   But oh, what's to come o' the living ? "

" Ay, but I'm sure she had been a lusty weel plenished corpse, Janet; for she was a heavy ane; an' a deeper coffin I never saw."

" Haud your auld souple untackit tongue.   Gin I hear sic another hint come ower the foul tap o't, it sal be the waur for ye.   But lown be it spoken, an' little be it said.   Weel might the corpse be heavy, an' the coffin deep! ay, weel might the coffin be made deep, Matthew, for there was a stout lad bairn, a poor little pale flower, that hardly ever saw the light o' heaven, was streekit[1] on her breast at the same time wi' hersel'."

*   *   *   *   *   *   *

RAT HALL.[2]

" RATS leaving their usual haunts in your houses, barns, and stackyards, and going to the fields, is an unfortunate omen for the person whose abode they leave."   So wrote one Wilkie, author of a manuscript collection of old Border customs and superstitions, compiled, in the commencement of the present cen-

---

[1] Laid out.   [2] The Editor, *The New Border Tales.*

tury, for the use of Sir Walter Scott. The following incident illustrating the belief is related as having occurred upon the estate of the present writer. In the early years of the present century, the farm of Maisondieu was tenanted by a family named Fortune, who had been for several generations in occupation, and were reputed to have held land in the neighbourhood for above two hundred years. The name Maisondieu, it may be stated i passing, was derived from a religious house, or hospital, "for the reception of pilgrims, the diseased, and the indigent," which had formerly stood upon the present farm lands.

At last a crisis in the history of the Fortune family arrived. The old farmer died, leaving a son of some three or four and twenty years of age to succeed him. Robert Fortune, the younger, was a fine young man, who lacked not spirit or ability so much as principle and steadiness. Left to his own devices, with money in his pocket, and without guide, monitor, or controller, he seemed to have set himself to dissipate alike the reputation and the fortune which had been acquired through the prudence and good conduct of his forbears. He had enrolled himself a member of a local corps of Yeomanry Cavalry, which had been raised in the expectation of a French Invasion; and he was bent upon cutting a dash. He prided himself upon the horses he rode; and many were the scenes of midnight carousal, and of hare-brained prank and horse-play, enacted by himself and his hot-blooded, would-be fire-eating companions in the old farm-house at this period. For a brief time things went as merrily as the marriage bell of the proverb; but then a change set in. Peace was proclaimed, and farmers' prices, which the war had kept high, fell. A succession of bad seasons followed; and, instead of meeting them by retrenchment, young Fortune turned for consolation in the troubles which they brought him to a still more reckless extravagance. His elders shook their heads, and people began to say, when his back was turned, that he was going to the dogs. In time, the pinch of poverty began to be felt at Maisondieu. The Yeomanry had been disbanded, and Robert now sat alone by his black hearth. To drive out the cold, and raise his spirits to the pitch which they had known in happy bygone days, he resorted to the bottle. This, of course, made matters worse. He neglected his business, his accounts were not kept, and his affairs became disordered. The house fell into a state of disrepair, which, being allowed to continue, grew rapidly worse; and the servants, observing their master's weakness, ceased to respect him, and at last, being gained upon by a feeling that he was a man who was going fast down the hill, took to scamping their work or shirking it.

But, if he found himself deserted by his boon companions—friends of a summer day—a new set of associates began to gather in force about poor Bob. If, instead of describing him as going " to the dogs," people had said to the " rats," it would have been more literally correct. Only it was the rats who came to

23

him. They had long infested the farmyard; and
now, in the general relaxing of former strictness,
they had succeeded in effecting an entrance into the
house. And, having once entered, they held the advantage they had gained. At first their presence was
only made known at night, after the lights had been
put out, and the inmates of the house had withdrawn
to bed. Then, indeed, they held high revels in the
kitchen—as a continual sound of skurrying feet, the
occasional whisking of a tail upon the wainscot, the
overturning with a clatter or a crash of some vessel
of tin or earthenware, or the bold bounding of some
more than commonly intrepid adventurer, allowed
all men to be aware. So long, they were heard, and
their devastations were felt; but the devastators were
not seen. But, in course of time, finding themselves
masters of the situation, they grew bolder, and ventured abroad by daylight too. Then it came to be no
uncommon sight to see a rat cross the passage in front
of you; or, on entering the kitchen, to catch sight of
one suspended by his fore-feet, his tail depending behind him, sampling the contents of some butter-jar, or
dripping pot, which had been left unlidded on the
table. When he saw himself detected, the rat would
beat a leisurely retreat; and there was insolence in
his carriage and in the sweep of his tail, as though he
knew his adversary's weakness. It was observed
at this time that though the farmer, his man, and
maid, grew lean, the rats on the farm grew fat. At
last, with high living and impunity, their boldness
grew beyond all bounds, and from the kitchen they

extended their playground so as to comprise the whole house. Then it became a common occurrence for a rat to run across you whilst you lay in bed; or, if your toes peeped out at the foot of a short coverlet, for you to feel one nibbling at them. Or a rat might even hang feeding on the draught-blown, guttering candle at the farmer's very elbow, whilst he himself sat late into the night, plunged in a heavy reverie, the result, in equal parts, of his troubles and his potations. So it is with a certain class of humanity, who feed and flourish amid the misfortune and the decline of their betters. The depredations committed were enormous; for when they could not spoil or devour food or other property, the rats would carry it away. No contrivance was of the smallest use against them, for they soon understood the nature of the most ingenious trap, whilst poison failed to tempt them. Thus, whilst increasing in size, they increased so amazingly in numbers that—its owner being by this time so down in the world as to appear a safe butt for insolence—the old and formerly much respected house of Maisondieu now received from the profane the nickname of "Rat Hall."

It was about this time that the remarkable incident with which my story is concerned was witnessed by an old shepherd in Fortune's service. The family of Hall, a race of shepherds, had been long associated with that of Fortune upon the farm of Maisondieu; and old Bauldy, its present representative, was now, in his own phrase, "the fourth generation serving the fourth generation." Greatly older and by nature more thoughtful than his master, he, of course, viewed the state of matters on the farm with a heavy heart, and looked forward with the gloomiest forebodings to the time when, as it seemed, he must inevitably be separated from that master, whom, in spite of faults, he loved, and from the spot where he had spent a long and happy life-time. Well, one night in spring-time, he was sadly returning to the onstead after a visit to his lambs. A brilliant moon rode in a clear sky, and as he skirted an old hedge which separates the farm premises from a field, at that time in grass, he saw before him a single rat.

" Bad luck to you! " he murmured, under his breath, " for ye have brought bad luck on us."

The rat, which had come out of a rat-hole in the bank (which was perfectly riddled with them), now seemed to look about him. The shepherd watched it. Returning to the hole, it re-appeared, accompanied by a second rat. They in turn looked about them, and perhaps compared notes as to what they saw, for this time one only retired to the hole. It was absent during some moments, and then returned, bringing with it a very large old rat, which it piloted with care. The hair upon the face of the old rat was white with age; and the shepherd observed that it was blind. His interest was by this time thoroughly aroused, and grasping his tall crook with both hands, he rested his cheek against his arms and watched, intently and in silence, from the black shadow of the hedge. And now he witnessed what amazed him. From each of the innumerable rat-holes in the hedge-row, as if by magic, as if from a child's toy, there had started forth a rat, which crouched, motionless and listening, before the entrance to its cave. Their number, and the uniformity of their action, gave to the effect presented the dignity of impressiveness. It was quite clear that they were acting, not by chance, but in the prosecution of some well-thought-out plan, upon some preconcerted signal.

As he watched them, Old Bauldy scarce drew his breath. The night was still; and when they had apparently satisfied themselves that the coast was clear, the rats advanced a little way. And, as, in doing so, they brought their tails and hind-quarters clear of the mouths of the rat-holes, they disclosed the nozzles and bright bead-like eyes of other rats behind them. If it had been curiosity which had at first kept the shepherd motionless, it was the instinct of self-preservation which did so now. An army of rats such as he now beheld might well inspire uneasiness, nay, terror, in a braver man; and, as he gazed, its numbers were being every moment reinforced. For now, above the living silence of a country landscape contemplated by night, a low, but ever gathering and growing rumour was gradually making itself heard. It came from underground; and it was produced by the beating of many thousands of little feet upon the trodden earth of the runs. And, at last, whilst the sound increased in volume, by a hundred mouths the earth began to disgorge its living burthen. Rats! They were of the Norway breed, and first in order came the great males. These are used to live alone; if hunger presses them, they will prey on their own brood; they justly inspire terror. The less formidable females followed, each accompanied by her young. And ever as they swarmed in momentarily increasing numbers, as in the remote historical or mythical Migration of the Nations, the rear rank pushed the front rank before it, till the rats spread far afield, and the very ground seemed alive and moving with their multitudes. Transfixed in the attitude which he had at first assumed, the shepherd watched the spectacle—standing like a man who has been turned to stone, whom no earthly power could have induced to stir a finger. To say that never in his life before had he seen so many rats would be to utter idlest words. In no agonised vision of the night, lying stretched upon his pallet of chaff, whilst his breath froze, and his enemies disported themselves triumphantly, insultingly, upon the bare boards of the loft, peeped in on by a mischievous moon, had he ever *dreamed* of so many!

As has been said, during all this time it had been amply apparent that the rats were not acting without some plan of their own. Instead of following each one his own bent, they moved with the regularity and the discipline of trained forces manœuvring in order. Nothing could have less resembled the blind infatuation of their fellows and predecessors, who had frisked at the heels of the Pied Piper through the streets of Hamelin to their doom. They had far more in common with the grim determination of the instruments of vengeance against Bishop Hatto. But their demeanour, if a little stern, was calm as well as resolute, as, inspired by a single purpose, controlled by a single will, they advanced, marching shoulder to shoulder. There were few stragglers, few weak places in their ranks. Their *morale* was very nearly perfect.

And now, when they had wheeled into the field, a touching incident occurred. The old hoary-faced rat had undoubtedly in his youth been marked by nature for a leader. But times were changed; he was old and blind, and for a moment he stood helpless before his people. For a moment, but no longer. Grasping the position of affairs, the rat who had been the first to appear, stepped forward to the rescue, and saved the situation. In his mouth he was observed to hold, by one of its ends, a straw—the other end of which he now dexterously inserted betwixt the jaws of the Patriarch, so as to form a sort of leading-string. And, thus coupled, the two rats moved off, and were followed by their thousands,—the old rat, through the graceful intervention of the young one, still preserving every tittle of his dignity as a king and father of his people in this momentous crisis of his reign.

The shepherd watched the moving mass, as it passed across the moonlit surface of the field, like the shadow of a cloud, until at last it was lost to sight beyond a rising ground.

Then, and not till then, did he stir. Pulling himself hastily together, he made for the farm-house, and with the freedom which is allowed to an old servant, burst into his master's room. Fortune was seated at the table, his face buried in his hands. A sheet of printed paper lay before him.

" Bob! Bob! " cried the old man, " we are pre-sairved—the rats are gone! "

But Bob only lifted a heavy head and pointed, without speaking, to the paper which lay before him. It was an announcement that, a " displenishing sale " would shortly be held at Maisondieu.

" Lord! and has it come to this? "

" It has, indeed! I had not the heart to break it to you before, Bauldy." And then he added with bitterness, " We must have the usual jollification, I suppose. Well, there will be meat for many to provide that day; but I doubt 'twill be the poison of one."

And so, sure enough, ere the Whitsuntide term-day arrived, the furniture and fittings of Maisondieu farm had fallen to the auctioneer's hammer; and Robert Fortune and his old and faithful shepherd had gone forth homeless, and in opposed directions, to face and fight the world.

It only remains to add that this story, wild as it may appear, is, in its main facts, currently related at the present day among the country-people of Rox-burghshire.

THE END.

www.ingramcontent.com/pod-product-compliance
Lightning Source LLC
Chambersburg PA
CBHW021351090426
42742CB00009B/813